Thomas Hamilton

History of the Irish Presbyterian Church

Second Edition

Thomas Hamilton

History of the Irish Presbyterian Church
Second Edition

ISBN/EAN: 9783744731973

Printed in Europe, USA, Canada, Australia, Japan

Cover: Foto ©Lupo / pixelio.de

More available books at **www.hansebooks.com**

Handbooks for Bible Classes and Private Students.

EDITED BY
REV. MARCUS DODS, D.D.,
AND
REV. ALEXANDER WHYTE, D.D.

NOW READY.

THE EPISTLE TO THE GALATIANS. By JAMES MACGREGOR, D.D., late of New College, Edinburgh. *Price 1s. 6d.*

THE POST-EXILIAN PROPHETS. With Introductions and Notes. By Rev. MARCUS DODS, D.D., Glasgow. *Price 2s.*

A LIFE OF CHRIST. By Rev. JAMES STALKER, M.A. *Price 1s. 6d.*

THE SACRAMENTS. By Rev. Professor CANDLISH, D.D. *Price 1s. 6d.*

THE BOOKS OF CHRONICLES. By Rev. Professor MURPHY, LL.D. Belfast. *Price 1s. 6d.*

THE CONFESSION OF FAITH. By Rev. JOHN MACPHERSON, M.A., Findhorn. *Price 2s.*

THE BOOK OF JUDGES. By Rev. Principal DOUGLAS, D.D. *Price 1s. 3d.*

THE BOOK OF JOSHUA. By Rev. Principal DOUGLAS, D.D. *Price 1s. 6d.*

THE EPISTLE TO THE HEBREWS. By Rev. Professor DAVIDSON, D.D., Edinburgh. *Price 2s. 6d.*

SCOTTISH CHURCH HISTORY. By Rev. N. L. WALKER. *Price 1s. 6d.*

THE CHURCH. By Rev. Prof. BINNIE, D.D. *Price 1s. 6d.*

THE REFORMATION. By Rev. Professor LINDSAY, D.D. *Price 2s.*

THE BOOK OF GENESIS. By Rev. MARCUS DODS, D.D. *Price 2s.*

THE EPISTLE TO THE ROMANS. By Rev. Principal BROWN, D.D., Aberdeen. *Price 2s.*

PRESBYTERIANISM. By Rev. JOHN MACPHERSON, M.A. *Price 1s. 6d.*

LESSONS ON THE LIFE OF CHRIST. By Rev. WM. SCRYMGEOUR, Glasgow. *Price 2s. 6d.*

THE SHORTER CATECHISM. By Rev. ALEXANDER WHYTE, D.D. Edinburgh. *Price 2s. 6d.*

THE GOSPEL ACCORDING TO ST. MARK. By Rev. Professor LINDSAY, D.D., Glasgow. *Price 2s. 6d.*

[Continued on next page.

HANDBOOKS FOR BIBLE CLASSES.

A SHORT HISTORY OF CHRISTIAN MISSIONS. By George Smith, LL.D., F.R.G.S. *Price* 2s. 6d.

A LIFE OF ST. PAUL. By Rev. James Stalker, M.A. *Price* 1s. 6d.

PALESTINE. With Maps. By Rev. Arch. Henderson, M.A., Crieff. *Price* 2s. 6d.

THE BOOK OF ACTS. By Rev. Professor Lindsay, D.D. Part I., Chaps. i. to xii. *Price* 1s. 6d. — Part II., Chaps. xiii. to end. *Price* 1s. 6d.

THE WORK OF THE HOLY SPIRIT. By Rev. Professor Candlish, D.D. *Price* 1s. 6d.

THE SUM OF SAVING KNOWLEDGE. By Rev. John Macpherson, M.A., Findhorn. *Price* 1s. 6d.

HISTORY OF THE IRISH PRESBYTERIAN CHURCH. By Rev. Thomas Hamilton, M.A., Belfast. Price 2s.

THE GOSPEL ACCORDING TO ST. LUKE, Part I., Chaps. i. to xii. By Rev. Professor Lindsay, D.D. Price 2s.

IN PREPARATION.

THE SABBATH. By Rev. Professor Salmond, D.D., Aberdeen.

THE GOSPEL ACCORDING TO ST. JOHN. By Rev. George Reith, M.A., Glasgow. [*Shortly.*]

THE FIRST EPISTLE TO THE CORINTHIANS. By Rev. Marcus Dods, D.D., Glasgow.

THE SECOND EPISTLE TO THE CORINTHIANS. By Rev. Principal David Brown, D.D., Aberdeen.

THE EPISTLE TO THE PHILIPPIANS. By Rev. James Mellis, M.A., Southport.

THE EPISTLE TO THE COLOSSIANS. By Rev. Simeon R. Macphail, M.A., Liverpool.

CHURCH AND STATE. By A. Taylor Innes, Esq., Advocate, Edinburgh.

CHRISTIAN ETHICS. By Rev. Professor Lindsay, D.D., Glasgow.

APOLOGETICS. By Rev. James Iverach, M.A., Aberdeen.

THE BOOK OF EXODUS. By James Macgregor, D.D., late of New College, Edinburgh.

THE DOCTRINE OF SIN. By Rev. Professor Candlish, D.D.

ISAIAH. By Rev. Professor Elmslie, M.A., London.

BUTLER'S THREE SERMONS ON HUMAN NATURE. With Introduction and Notes. By Rev. T. B. Kilpatrick, B.D., Burntisland.

THE NEW TESTAMENT TIMES. By Rev. R. T. Cunningham, M.A., Inch.

HANDBOOKS

FOR

BIBLE CLASSES

AND PRIVATE STUDENTS.

EDITED BY

REV. MARCUS DODS, D.D.,

AND

REV. ALEXANDER WHYTE, D.D.

HISTORY OF THE IRISH PRESBYTERIAN CHURCH.
BY REV. THOMAS HAMILTON, D.D.

Second Edition.

EDINBURGH:
T. & T. CLARK, 38 GEORGE STREET.

PRINTED BY MORRISON AND GIBB,

FOR

T. & T. CLARK, EDINBURGH.

LONDON, ...	HAMILTON, ADAMS, AND CO.
DUBLIN, . . .	GEORGE HERBERT.
NEW YORK, ...	SCRIBNER AND WELFORD.

HISTORY

OF THE

Irish Presbyterian Church.

BY THE

REV. THOMAS HAMILTON, D.D.,

BELFAST.

𝔖𝔢𝔠𝔬𝔫𝔡 𝔈𝔡𝔦𝔱𝔦𝔬𝔫.

EDINBURGH:
T. & T. CLARK, 38 GEORGE STREET.

PREFACE.

―o―

IN writing this handbook I have had two objects in view. First, I wished to do what in me lay to make Irish Presbyterians thoroughly acquainted with their own history. It is neither creditable nor advantageous that so many of us know far more about the past life of other Churches than of our own —are better acquainted with the olden ecclesiastical history of Scotland or England, or even Germany, than of Ireland—and can tell more of Knox and Melville, of Bothwell Brig and the Pentlands, of Latimer and Cranmer, and Luther and Calvin, than of St. Patrick and Edward Brice and Robert Blair, of 'The Eagle Wing' and 'The Black Oath,' of the Sixmilewater Awakening and the persecutions in the days of the Charleses and Anne. Knowledge must prepare the way before loyalty can reign. We cannot be expected to take that interest in, or have that love for, the Church of our fathers which we ought—we cannot clearly comprehend either her position or her rights in this land, unless we know something of her origin, her contendings, her sufferings, her whole past experience. If this book helps in any measure to spread among Irish Presbyterians a knowledge of the history of their Church,—a history of which it is a shame and a loss to be ignorant,—it will have accomplished the first object for which it was penned. I have had another aim in preparing it. Recent political events have called public attention very prominently to Ireland, and largely to the North of Ireland, where Presbyterianism was planted in the beginning of the seventeenth century, and where still its great strength lies. It is well at such a time to see to it that the circumstances and needs of the people are properly understood, that they are read not in the deceptive glare of a passing excitement, but by the calm, clear light of the torch of history. It is especially important, not only to Irish Protestantism but to all Irish interests, that the position and the past of Ulster should be accurately discerned and read. If this handbook helps at all towards the attainment of these desirable, indeed necessary, ends, its second *raison d'être* will have been most gratifyingly vindicated.

Dr. Reid's *History of the Presbyterian Church in Ireland*, with its continuation by Dr. Killen, has no doubt served both purposes to some extent already. We have no more admirable history of any Church. Mr. Froude has well said that it is 'the very best book which has ever been written on these matters.' It is only when one has had occasion, as I have had, to study it minutely, to compare it with the authorities on which it is based, and with other histories which run side by side with it, that the patient research, the arduous toil, the accuracy, the fidelity, the soundness of judgment to which almost every page of that splendid work bears witness, can be fully appreciated or appraised. But evidently this great work is too large and too expensive to be circulated as widely as the history of the Irish Presbyterian Church ought to be. A three-volume book can never be expected to penetrate to the farmhouses and cottages of the country-side, or to the artisans' dwellings in the city, still less to be read by the young generation which is attending Bible Class and Sabbath School. It is not even every wealthy merchant or country gentleman that will study, as it deserves to be studied, a work so large. The existence of a compact and concise handbook on the subject will at all events render ignorance, if not impossible, at least inexcusable, and may have the happy effect of so whetting the appetite of the reader that he will not be satisfied until he has feasted on the rich fare provided by the first and best historians of the Irish Presbyterian Church. Many things also have happened during the nearly twenty years which have passed since the last (and best) edition of this Presbyterian classic was published, not to speak of the more than fifty which have elapsed since the first appearance of its first volume. Valuable State papers have been given to the public, other historians have re-sifted Reid and Killen's materials, re-weighed their conclusions, and thrown fresh light on many transactions with which they deal, while important events have occurred, some of them so lately as this present year, which deserve a more permanent record than they can obtain in the columns of a newspaper. Besides, it will be noticed that the present work carries back our ecclesiastical story further into the past than Dr. Reid has done, so that both at beginning and end it covers a larger ground.

To Reid obligations will be found in many cases acknowledged throughout the work. But much more is due to him than could be acknowledged. Besides other indebtednesses which are owned in the proper place, it is only right also to mention here the large general help derived from President Killen's *Ecclesiastical History of Ireland*, Dr. Witherow's *Derry and Enniskillen*, and *The Boyne and Aghrim*, and valuable hints obtained from the late Dr. Croskery, not only through the medium of various productions of his pen, but in personal intercourse. From the Rev. T. Y. Killen, D.D.,[1] and the Rev. Alexander Gordon of Belfast, the Rev. C. H. Irwin, M.A., Bray, and the Rev. J. Armstrong, Plymouth, not a few helpful kindnesses were also received.

I trust that the handbook may be found to have set in a clear light, and before many eyes, one of the noblest histories which the Church of Christ has to tell, that its perusal may bind Irish Presbyterians in firmer allegiance to their grand old Church, and lead many besides Irish Presbyterians better to understand and appreciate our past history and our present position.

BROOKVALE HOUSE,
BELFAST, *October*, 1886.

[1] While the first edition of this work was passing through the press, Dr. Killen was suddenly cut down on October 21st, 1886. He was born in Ballymena on October 30th, 1826, entered Belfast College in 1842, was licensed by the Presbytery of Carrickfergus in 1848, and laboured successively as a missionary at Camlin, and as pastor of the congregations of 3rd Ramelton, Ballykelly, and Duncairn, Belfast, with great fidelity.

PREFACE TO THE SECOND EDITION.

THE fact that within three months after the first appearance of this little book the preparation of a Second Edition had to be set about, sufficiently demonstrates the need which was felt for some such manual of our Irish Presbyterian Church history. The work has now been carefully revised throughout; typographical and other errors have been corrected; some additions have been made, and an Index has been appended which will facilitate consultation. In this improved form it is hoped that the handbook will be found better fitted than ever to serve the ends for which it was written.

BROOKVALE HOUSE,
BELFAST, *April*, 1887.

CONTENTS.

―o―

CHAPTER I.—(Pp. 1-4.)
INTRODUCTORY.

Early History of Ireland—Who are the real Irish?—Ireland the first Scotland, and the first Scotchmen Irishmen—Introduction of Christianity—The Scoto-Irish Church.

CHAPTER II.—(Pp. 5-14.)
ST. PATRICK.

Difficulty of ascertaining the Facts about him—His Birthplace—Shepherd Life near Ballymena—His Conversion—His Strange Dream—His Theology—The 'Creed of St. Patrick'—Was he the First Primate?—His Church Polity not Prelatic—Where is 'The Church of Ireland' now?—Patrick's Character.

CHAPTER III.—(Pp. 15-22.)
FROM THE BIRTH OF COLUMBA TO THE REFORMATION.

Birth of Columba—The Voyage to Iona—Life in the Monastery—'The Apostle of the Northern Picts'—His Last Sabbath—The Early Irish Monastic System—Bangor Abbey—Columbanus—Gallus—Kilian—Fridolin—Rome gains the upper hand—The Synod of Rathbreasail—The Synod of Kells—Diocesan Episcopacy established—Ireland granted by Pope Adrian IV. to Henry II.—Vices of the Bishops—Deplorable State of the Church.

CHAPTER IV.—(Pp. 23-27.)
FROM THE DAWN OF THE REFORMATION TO THE PLANTATION OF ULSTER.

The Reformation—Causes of its Failure in Ireland—Reign of Edward VI.—Bale, Bishop of Ossory—Romanism re-established by Queen Mary—

Persecutions ordered—Cole's Ludicrous Mishap—Mary's Death—Protestantism re-established—How the Bishops trimmed their Sails—State of Ireland in Elizabeth's Reign—Spenser's Description—Rebellion quelled—Establishment of Trinity College, Dublin.

CHAPTER V.—(Pp. 28-41.)

THE PLANTATION OF ULSTER AND THE PIONEERS OF IRISH PRESBYTERIANISM.

The Flight of the Earls—The Plantation—The New Settlers—Effects of the Plantation—State of Affairs in Scotland—Prelacy reimposed—Laud's Tyranny—Janet Geddes's Stool—The National Covenant—The Second Reformation—The Fathers of the Irish Presbyterian Church—Edward Brice—The Articles of Religion of 1615—The Early Presbyterian Ministers enjoy the Tithes—Hubbard of Carrickfergus—Glendinning—John Ridge of Antrim—Robert Blair of Bangor—James Hamilton of Ballywalter—Robert Cunningham of Holywood—Josias Welsh of Templepatrick—Andrew Stewart of Donegore—George Dunbar of Ballymena and Larne—John Livingstone of Killinchy—Summary.

CHAPTER VI.—(Pp. 42-55.)

BLESSING WITHIN, TROUBLE WITHOUT.

The Sixmilewater Revival—Glendinning—Remarkable Scenes—The Antrim Monthly Meeting—The Beginning of Sorrows—The Friar's Challenge—Sectaries—A Champion of Arminianism—Public Discussion—Persecution of the Ministers—Blair's Sermon before the Primate—Blair and Livingstone suspended by Bishop Echlin—Four of the Ministers deposed—Blair's Journey to London—Wentworth appointed Lord Deputy—Severe Persecutions—The Presbyterians resolve to go to America—Their Plan thwarted—A Lull in the Storm—The Last Communion in Bangor—Ministers silenced—Miserable Death of Echlin—A Remarkable Meeting in Belfast—Five more Ministers silenced—Cunningham's Noble Speech—Death of Brice—'The Eagle Wing'—An Ill-Starred Voyage—The Persecution grows hotter—'The Black Oath'—Terrible Sufferings of the Presbyterians—Case of Mr. Henry Stewart—Proposed Banishment of the Presbyterians from Ulster—Death of Strafford.

CHAPTER VII.—(Pp. 56-63.)

1641 AND ITS ISSUES.

The Rebellion of 1641—Its Designs—Ulster a Sea of Blood—Appalling Sufferings of the Protestants—The Numbers that perished—The Rebellion a Romish Movement—The Massacre at Island Magee—Strange Fictions of Romish Writers—Arrival of Scottish Troops at Carrickfergus—The First Presbytery—Its Members—New Congregations erected.

CHAPTER VIII.—(Pp. 64-73.)
THE TIMES OF THE COMMONWEALTH.

Affairs in England—The Long Parliament—Ussher's Plan of Reconciliation—Prelacy abolished by Parliament—The Westminster Assembly—The Solemn League and Covenant—Governors sent by the Parliament to Ulster—Execution of Charles I.—Views of the Irish Presbyterians—The Belfast 'Representation' and Milton's Reply—Cromwell's Irish Campaign—How Irish Presbyterians fared under Cromwell—Proposal to banish them to Munster—The Tide turns—They are endowed—Growth of the Church—Death of Cromwell.

CHAPTER IX.—(Pp. 74-83.)
UNDER CHARLES II.

Irish Presbyterians help to bring Charles back—Persecution recommences—Jeremy Taylor's Severities—Ejection of 1661—Blood's Plot—More Persecutions by the Bishops—Meetings in Glens and Farmhouses—Presbyterianism mocked in a Dublin Theatre—The *Regium Donum* granted—John Howe at Antrim—Francis Makemie sails to America and organizes the First American Presbytery—The Tennents and 'Log College.'

CHAPTER X.—(Pp. 84-108.)
UNDER JAMES AND WILLIAM.

James II. ascends the Throne—His Efforts to Romanize the Country—The Comber Letter—Shutting of the Gates of Derry—The Apprentice Boys and Bishop Hopkins—Expected Massacre in Ulster—'Lying Dick'—Lundy sent to Derry—The 'Break of Dromore'—The Siege of Derry—Walker not the Governor—Terrible Sufferings in the Maiden City—Rosen's Atrocities—'No Surrender'—Kirke's Squadron—The Relief of Derry—The Defence largely a Presbyterian Exploit—Enniskillen's Gallant Stand—Rev. Robert Kelso—'The Break of Belleek'—Battle of Belturbet—Battle of Lisnaskea—Battle of Newtonbutler—William III.—His Presbyterianism—His Calvinism—His Broad Protestantism—Schomberg lands at Groomsport—His Campaign—King William arrives at Carrickfergus—*Regium Donum* granted at Hillsborough—Battle of the Boyne—Vacillation of the Episcopalians—Renewed Persecution of the Presbyterians—Mr. Ambrose imprisoned—Attempts of the Bishops to have the *Regium Donum* withdrawn—Scandalous State of the Episcopal Church—Case of Rev. John M'Bride of Belfast—Of Rev. William Biggar of Limerick—The Episcopalians seek to deprive Presbyterian Ministers of the Right to solemnize Marriages.

CHAPTER XI.—(Pp. 109-115.)
THE REIGN OF QUEEN ANNE.

The 'Schools of Philosophy'—The Test Act—Its Effects—Determined Efforts to stamp out Presbyterianism—The Belturbet Case—The Nonjuring

Controversy—Establishment of the 'General Fund'—'A Sample of Jet-Black Prelatic Calumny'—Kirkpatrick's 'Presbyterian Loyalty'—Death of Anne—The 'Toleration Act' passed.

CHAPTER XII.—(Pp. 116-122.)

THE 'NEW LIGHT.'

'The Belfast Society'—Rev. John Abernethy's Sermon—The 'Pacific Act'—Case of Rev. Samuel Halliday of Belfast—'Subscribers' and 'Non-Subscribers'—Establishment of Rosemary Street Church—A War of Pamphlets—Case of Rev. Thomas Nevin—The Presbytery of Antrim separated from the Synod of Ulster.

CHAPTER XIII.—(Pp. 123-128.)

THE SECEDERS.

Rise of the Secession in Scotland—Ebenezer Erskine—Establishment of Lylehill Congregation — Ordination of Rev. Isaac Patton — Other early Secession Congregations—The 'Burghers' and 'Antiburghers'—Opposition of the Synod of Ulster—The Ballyrashane Discussion—What the Seceders did for Ireland.

CHAPTER XIV.—(Pp. 129-135.)

A TIME OF DEADNESS.

Character of the 18th Century—Subscription to the Confession of Faith falls into Abeyance in Ireland—Professors Simson and Leechman—Francis Hutcheson—Decadence of the Synod of Ulster—Counteracting Influences—The Seceders—First Irish Associate Presbytery—Rev. Thomas Clark—The Covenanters—Sad State of the Episcopal Church—Large Emigration to America—Its Causes and Effects—Amelioration of the Condition of Irish Presbyterians—Repeal of the Test Act—Validity of Presbyterian Marriages declared—Increase of *Regium Donum*.

CHAPTER XV.—(Pp. 136-145.)

FROM THE RISE OF THE VOLUNTEERS TO THE LEGISLATIVE UNION.

The Volunteers—The Dungannon Meeting—Grattan's Parliament—The Rebellion of 1798—Battle of Antrim—Battle of Ballynahinch—The Insurrection in the South of Ireland—Father Murphy of Boolavogue—Vinegar Hill—Scullabogue Barn—Opposition of the Presbyterians to the Rebellion—The Legislative Union—Another Increase of *Regium Donum*.

CHAPTER XVI.—(Pp. 146-158.)

THE EVANGELICAL REVIVAL.

Signs of returning Life—Visit of the Rev. Dr. Waugh of London—The Belfast Academical Institution—Dr. Cooke—His Early Life—Ministry at Duneane—At Donegore—At Killyleagh—Beginning of the Arian Controversy—The Chase after Smethurst—Ministers called upon to declare themselves—Dr. Stewart—Dr. Montgomery—Debate on the 'Theological Committee'—The 'Remonstrance'—The Lurgan Meeting—Montgomery's Speech—Cooke's Reply—Secession of the Arians—After History of the Two Bodies—Subscription to the Confession of Faith made absolute—Church Extension in Belfast—Dr. Edgar—Dr. Morgan.

CHAPTER XVII.—(Pp. 159-162.)

WORK AND WARFARE.

Rise of the Temperance Movement—Drinking Habits in the Beginning of the Century—Visit to Ireland of Rev. Joseph Penny—Dr. Edgar commences a Temperance Crusade—His Letter in the Belfast *Newsletter*—The First Temperance Society in Europe—The Ulster Temperance Society—Total Abstinence Movement—The National Education Controversy—Dr. Carlile—Dr. Stewart's 'Model Application'—The General Assembly and the Board.

CHAPTER XVIII.—(Pp. 163-173.)

THE UNION OF THE SYNODS, AND AFTER.

Union of the Synod of Ulster and Secession Synod—The Students' Prayer Meeting—Scene at the Union—*Personnel* of the First General Assembly—Establishment of the Foreign Mission—Previous Missionary Enterprises of the Presbyterian Bodies—Establishment of the Jewish Mission—Of the Colonial Mission—Of the Continental Mission—Of the Mission to Soldiers and Sailors—The Bicentenary of Irish Presbyterianism—The College Controversy—Foundation of the Queen's Colleges—Mrs. Magee's Bequests—Assembly's College, Belfast—Magee College, Londonderry—'The Presbyterian Theological Faculty, Ireland.'

CHAPTER XIX.—(Pp. 174-178.)

PRESBYTERIANISM OUTSIDE ULSTER.

In Dublin—Rev. Walter Travers—Trinity College—John Owen and Stephen Charnock—Wood Street Congregation—Cook Street—New Row—Plunket Street—Capel Street—Early Seceding Congregations in Dublin—Boyse—Iredell—Leland—Clonmel and other Southern Congregations—Causes of the Decline of many of them—The Synod of Munster—The Famine—Dr. Edgar's Action—Establishment of the Connaught Schools—Results of the Famine.

CHAPTER XX.—(Pp. 179-187.)
THE LAST THIRTY YEARS.

The Church and Manse Fund—Rev. David Hamilton's Labours—The Revival of 1859—Strange Scenes—Its Results—Foundation of the Sabbath School Society—Of the Presbyterian Orphan Society—Of the Society for the Orphans of Ministers—The 'Irish Church Act'—The Special Assembly of 1870—The Lay Conference—The Commutation and Sustentation Funds—Death of Dr. Cooke—The Instrumental Music Controversy—The Settlement of 1886—Renewal of Intercourse with the Church of Scotland—The General Assembly and Mr. Gladstone's 'Home Rule' Bill.

CHAPTER XXI.—(Pp. 188-192.)
CONCLUSION.

Review of the Church's History—What Presbyterianism has done for Ireland—Ulster changed—Its Agriculture—Manufactures—Prosperity—Kohl's Testimony—Statistics of Pauperism and Crime—Presbyterianism a Moderating Force in the Land—Distinctively Religious Blessings which Ireland owes to it—Present Condition and Future Prospects of the Church.

HISTORY

OF THE

IRISH PRESBYTERIAN CHURCH.

---o---

CHAPTER I.

INTRODUCTORY.

WHEN one begins to inquire into the early history of Ireland, ecclesiastical or civil, it very soon becomes painfully evident that it is only in a glass darkly that we can see it. The native annalists give us indeed plenty of history, but it is such a confused farrago of myth and legend and fable, that it is almost impossible to pierce down through it to any solid rock-bed of fact. They profess to tell us, with the utmost circumstantiality, all about the affairs of the country from the days of Noah. What can one make out of such history? They give us a confused account of successive invasions and colonizations by Fir-Bolgs (who are said to have come over from Greece), and Tuatha de Danaan (whose native country we are told was Scandinavia), and Milesians from Spain. It is not easy to say how far the stories of these incursions are fact and how far fiction, or whether there is substantial substratum of fact in them at all. This much, however, seems clear beyond doubt, that the present inhabitants of all the four provinces of Ireland are the descendants of successive bodies of invaders, who from time to time subjugated or dispossessed the original denizens of the country, so that to speak now of an indigenous population, in any proper sense of the term, is an entire mistake. Those who boast that they are 'the real Irish' are in reality as much strangers and aliens in the land as are the descendants of the Scottish and English colonists. The men of Ulster have just as much, or as little, right to call themselves Irishmen as the men of Munster. If the people of Antrim or Down are not Irish, neither are the people of Tipperary or Galway. It is well to remember this fact in the face of present-day agitations. Whether, however, any solid importance is to be attached to this talk about nationality, in the strict sense of the term, will appear more than doubtful to any one who asks himself what country of the present day is in the hands of its original owners. Certainly not England, on which Saxons, Danes, and Normans swept down, the one after the other, in invading hosts, leaving little or no trace now of the natives who were there before them. And most certainly not Ireland.

The Romans, who subdued the neighbouring island of Britain, and have left so many traces of their presence there, did not cross over to Ireland. Agricola was petitioned by one of the native chiefs to do so, and apparently had some thought of complying with the request, but did not.[1] The Romans knew something of the country, however, calling it Hibernia, or Juverna. It was also known by the name of Scotia, or Scotland. It was not till the tenth century that the present Scotland was called Scotia,[2] being distinguished from Ireland then as Scotia Minor, while the latter was called Scotia Major. Hence the curious fact, which sounds like an Irishism, that Ireland was the first Scotland, and the first Scotchmen were Irishmen. In this fact, and in the frequent intercourse between the two countries,

---

[1] 'That virgin island on which proconsul never set foot.'—Montalembert, *Les Moines d'Occident*, ii. 387.

[2] 'Scotia prior to the tenth century was Ireland, and Ireland alone.'—Skene, *Celtic Scotland*.

not always or usually a friendly intercourse, we have the beginning of those close relations between Ireland and Scotland, which at subsequent periods were so materially to influence the destinies of both countries.

It is more germane to our present purpose, however, to glance at the religious than at the ethnological history of these early periods. At the time when we get our first distinct glimpse of Ireland, Druidism was its prevailing religion — Druidism, with its sacred yew, and rowan, and hawthorn. But the light of Christianity seems to have reached the island at a very early period of the Christian era. Eminent authorities have come to the conclusion that the Scoto-Irish Church is the oldest of all the Protestant Churches represented in modern Christendom. We are accustomed to regard the Waldenses as the most ancient among existing representatives of the faith. But it is asserted by acute and trustworthy investigators that our own Church is much older. It is a common habit to regard Ireland as having been at all times far behind alike in religious and in material progress, and to have owed all she has, that is worth having, to the crumbs which fell from her neighbours' tables. Some of the foremost modern Celtic scholars and investigators,[1] however, assure us that so far from Ireland having been behind other nations in starting on the Christian race, her Christianity is the oldest that is known. Not much certainty can be reached regarding the exact time or mode of its beginning amongst us. In the third century, however, the *Annals of the Four Masters* tell us that Cormac, the chief king of Ireland, provoked the wrath of the Druids by turning from them 'to the adoration of God.'[2] In the fourth century, an Irishman, Cœlestius, the companion of the celebrated Pelagius, was a by no means inconspicuous figure in the controversies of the day; and early in the fifth century we read in a chronicle of the period of 'the Irish believing in Christ.'[3] There was evidently, therefore, at a very early period

[1] M'Lauchlan, *Early Scottish Church.*
[2] *Annals of the Four Masters.*   [3] Prosper's *Chronicon.*

a strong Christian movement in Ireland, resulting in the organization of a Church, and it is the opinion of the learned Ussher that this comparatively pure form of Christianity survived in the country, running as it were underground, like some of our Irish streams, even when Romish corruption was most rampant, until the beginning of the seventeenth century, when the organization of the Presbyterian Church, according to its present model, took place.[1] If this be so, then Irish Presbyterians can trace their ecclesiastical lineage far back indeed, linking themselves on to the simple-minded, uncorrupted believers of an age long before Rome had appeared on the scene to blight our fair isle with her withering influence.

[1] Ussher, *Discourse on the Religion anciently professed by the Irish.*

CHAPTER II.

ST. PATRICK.

ONE figure which stands out prominently in the otherwise obscure early annals of Ireland is that of St. Patrick. His history has been so interlarded with legend and myth that it is no easy task to separate the truth from the fiction. Such absurd stories have been told of him that sober investigators have been tempted to question his very existence, and to set down the accounts of his life as entirely fabulous.[1] There can be no doubt, however, not only of his existence, but of his having exercised a most potent influence over the religious history of the Green Isle. Fortunately we possess two works which he wrote, the authenticity of which is acknowledged by scholars. These are his *Confession* and his *Letter to the Christians*.[2] So long as we keep to these works we are on firm ground: the moment we diverge from them we find ourselves floundering amid a mass of tradition, like some unfortunate traveller who has unwittingly stepped aside from a causeway into the bog which it traverses. From them we gather that his father was a deacon, the son of Potitus, a priest. His family, he says, was a respectable one, a statement which is evidently true, not only from the ecclesiastical position of his father and grandfather, but from the fact that the former, besides being a deacon, was a Roman magistrate (*decurio*). As to the birthplace of Patrick there has been almost as much controversy as about that of

[1] Ledwich, *Antiquities of Ireland*.
[2] *Confessio Sancti Patricii de vita et conversatione sua.* Book of Armagh, 22-25. *Epistola Sancti Patricii ad Christianos Corotici tyranni subditos.*

Homer. Ireland, England, Scotland, Wales, and France all contend for the honour of his nativity. What he says about it himself in his *Confession* is that his father was of a village called Bonavem Taberniæ, and had a farm or small property there, and that it was from this place that he (Patrick) was carried captive. There are two difficulties here. First, he does not tell us where this Bonavem Taberniæ was; and second, he does not expressly tell us that he was born there. His statement is that his father was of that place, and that he himself was carried captive from it. Afterwards, however, in the *Confession*, he speaks of his parents living in Britain, and calls it his 'country.'[1] There seems therefore no reason to doubt that his birthplace was there, and that the patron saint of Ireland was in reality a Scotsman. There is a place called Kil-patrick (*i.e.* the Church of Patrick), situated near Dumbarton, in the Firth of Clyde, which is not unlikely to have been the spot where the great missionary first saw the light.

But if not the land of his birth, Ireland was certainly his adopted country. This came about as follows:—At the age of sixteen he was taken captive by one of the roving bands of freebooters who in those unsettled and lawless times infested the British coasts. In company with other prisoners he was carried across the Channel to the North of Ireland and sold as a slave. Whereabouts on the coast he was landed we do not know, but ultimately he was taken inland, and set to herd cattle close by where the rugged mountain Slemish looks down on the fertile valley of the Braid. Here, where now the well-cultivated fields of one of the most prosperous districts of County Antrim stretch to the river-side, with at intervals a bleach-green or a manufactory preparing the famous Irish linen for the market, with the tall mill chimney-stalks and the church towers of the thriving

---

[1] He says he had been desirous to go 'in Britannias . . . quasi ad patriam et parentes; non id solum, sed etiam usque ad Gallias,'—words which seem to exclude entirely the idea that he was a native of any part of Gaul. Britanniæ is the well-known appellation of Roman Britain.

town of Ballymena rising into the air close by, the young slave lad daily drove his master's cattle and sheep to and from the pasture ground. Wherever he was born, the Ballymena district can undoubtedly claim that the bare feet of the poor slave boy, who was afterwards to win for himself an imperishable renown as one of Ireland's best benefactors, walked through its fields, climbed the steep sides of Slemish, and from its summit doubtless many a time gazed wistfully across the sea to where on the horizon he could dimly descry the hills of his native Scotland.

God often transmutes our afflictions into benefits. He did so with Patrick. His captivity was the means of bringing him the greatest blessing which can come to any man—the conversion of his soul. He had been piously brought up, but like too many had neglected the lessons of his father's house. He says of himself: 'I knew not the true God, and I was carried in captivity into Ireland . . . and there the Lord opened the sense of my unbelief, that even though late I should remember my sins, and be converted with my whole heart unto the Lord my God.'[1] If, then, he was born in Scotland, there can be no doubt he was 'born again' in Ireland. He became very prayerful, often rising in the night to commune with God in the woods and among the hills.

> 'Cold mountains and the midnight airs
> Witnessed the awful fervour of his prayers.

Neither snow, frost, nor rain could keep him back from this loved employment. 'I felt no evil,' he says; 'neither was there any laziness in me, because, as I now see, the Spirit was burning within me.'[2] After six years of slavery he escaped from his master, and, making his way to the coast, procured a passage on board a boat, and after enduring many hardships, was able again to rejoin his parents in Scotland. It must have been a happy day when they clasped to their hearts once more their long lost boy, with the traces of the hardships of his slave

[1] *Confession.* [2] *Ibid.*

life on his weather-beaten face, but with that new light burning there, of which he had known nothing when he was stolen from them, the possession of which more than made amends for the sorrows and privations he had endured at the hands of the Irish slave-drivers.

But he was not to be long in his father's house. He had seen the darkness of Ireland, and he hungered to give it some of his light. A remarkable dream which he had decided him. In the dead of night he saw a man coming to him as if from Ireland, whose name was Victoricius, 'bearing innumerable letters. And he gave me one of them, and I read the beginning of it, which contained the words, "The Voice of the Irish." And while I was repeating the beginning of the letter, I imagined that I heard in my mind the voice of those who were near the wood of Foclut,[1] which is near the Western Sea. And thus they cried—"We entreat thee, holy youth, to come and walk henceforth among us."'[2] Finally, he made up his mind to return as a missionary to Ireland, and the entire remainder of his days seems to have been spent in its service. He appears to have journeyed on evangelistic tours through the whole country. His name is preserved in the nomenclature of many places both in the north and south of Ireland, such as Temple-Patrick, Croagh-Patrick, Sea-Patrick, Down-Patrick, Leck-Patrick, and Inch-Patrick. The beautiful story of his preaching before the King of Meath at Tara, and illustrating the mysterious doctrine of the Trinity by the three-leaved shamrock, is well known, and probably true. There can be no doubt that he was one of the best benefactors of Ireland that she ever saw. 'I am greatly a debtor to God,' he says in the *Confession*, 'who hath vouchsafed me such great grace that many people by my means should be born again to God, and that clergy should be ordained everywhere for them.'[3] But he adds with beautiful humility.— 'I pray those who believe and fear God, whosoever may

---

[1] Supposed to be Tirawley, County Mayo.
[2] *Confession*.   *Ibid.*

condescend to look into or receive this writing, which Patrick the sinner, though unlearned, wrote in Ireland, if I have done or established any little thing according to God's will, that no man ever say that my ignorance did it, but think and let it verily be believed that it was the gift of God.'[1]

The dates of St. Patrick's career are rather uncertain. The best authorities, however, have come to the conclusion that his death took place on the 17th March, now kept as 'Patrick's Day,' either in the year 465 or 493. He is said to have been buried at Downpatrick. His grave is shown there, and is regarded with great veneration by the superstitious.

It is important for many reasons to know what were the exact doctrines which Patrick believed and preached. Various sects claim the authority of his name for their tenets. Roman Catholics constantly speak of him as one of themselves. They call chapels by his name, and place his statue above the entrance doors, attired in full ecclesiastical costume, with a great mitre on the head and a formidable crozier in the hand—articles of dress which the simple, busy missionary in all probability never either saw or wore. At all events, nothing is clearer than that Patrick's theology was as different from Popery as day from night. Romish writers have asserted that he came to Ireland as an emissary of the Pope. It is quite plain, however, that he was nothing of the kind, and that all statements to this effect are to be set down among the many myths, for the propagation of which the Church of Rome has earned a bad pre-eminence. In his *Confession* he tells us with considerable particularity the circumstances under which he came to Ireland; but he has not a word to say about either Rome or the Pope—an omission which would be simply inconceivable if he had been an emissary of the Pontiff. All contemporary documents are equally silent on this pretended Romish mission.[2] Not one of them gives the slightest hint of it.

---

[1] *Confession.*
[2] Cf. *The Life and Doctrine of St. Patrick*, by W. D Killen, D.D., President of Assembly's College, Belfast.

The success of Patrick's labours makes this silence all the more significant. If Rome could have taken credit for what Patrick did, her history plainly tells us that she undoubtedly would. All Christendom would have rung with the praises of the great papal legate, and of the Pope himself for planning his mission. But there is nothing of all this in the history of the time. Many letters of Leo I., who was Pope from 440-461, are still in existence, but not one of them mentions Patrick's enterprise. Moreover, he himself never appeals to any papal commission when his authority is impugned. There cannot be a shadow of a doubt, therefore, that the whole story of the Romish origin of his labours is a pure fiction. Besides, Patrick's teaching was very far removed indeed from Romanism. Romanism glorifies the Virgin Mary. There is no trace of Mariolatry in any of Patrick's writings. The Church of Rome puts our blessed Lord into a very subordinate place. With Patrick, Christ is all in all. The Bible receives but little honour from Rome. Patrick knew it well himself, and looked to it as the supreme standard of truth. In fact, if we make a list of the distinctive tenets of Romanism, and a similar list of the doctrines which Patrick believed and taught, and place the two over against each other, their dissidence will be found simply startling. As to clerical celibacy, his own father and grandfather were ecclesiastics, yet both were married, and we find Patrick himself appointing married men to office in the Church. Auricular confession, a cardinal pillar of Romanism, he never once mentions. We find no trace of his anointing the dying to prepare them for another world, no glorification of the Mass, no mention of Purgatory in his writings. The impudence of any attempt to make out Patrick to have been a Romanist is only equalled by its futility. His whole spirit and teaching and aims were not only not Rome's, but were as different from hers as possible.

One passage from the *Confession* contains such a clear explication of Patrick's theology in his own words that we quote it entire. It will give a better idea not only of his beliefs, but of his spirit, than any words of ours. After speaking of his capture at Bonavem Taberniæ, he says, 'I am not able, nor would it be right, to be silent on such great benefits and such great grace as [God] hath vouchsafed unto me in the land of my captivity, for this is our recompense, that after we have been corrected and brought to know God, we should exalt and confess His wondrous works before every nation which is under the whole heaven: that there is none other God, nor ever was, nor shall be hereafter, except God the Father, unbegotten, without beginning, from whom is all beginning, upholding all things, as we have said: and His Son, Jesus Christ, whom we acknowledge to have been always with the Father before the beginning of the world, spiritually with the Father, in an ineffable manner begotten before all beginning: and by Him were made things visible and invisible; and being made man, and having overcome death, He was received into heaven unto the Father. And the Father hath given unto Him all power, above every name, of things in heaven, and things in earth, and things under the earth, that every tongue should confess that Jesus Christ is Lord and God. Whom we believe and we look for His coming, who is soon about to be the Judge of quick and dead, who will render unto every man according to his works, and hath poured into us abundantly the gift of the Holy Ghost and the pledge of immortality, who maketh the faithful and obedient to become the sons of God the Father and joint heirs with Christ. Whom we confess and worship, one God in the Trinity of the sacred Name. For He Himself hath said by the prophet, "Call upon me in the day of thy tribulation and I will deliver thee, and thou shalt magnify me."'[1]

This simple, Scriptural 'Creed of St. Patrick,' as it has been called, is as remarkable for what it does not contain as for what it does. There is not the faintest Romish tinge about it. It is the devout expression of the beliefs of a soul which draws its inspiration fresh from the well-springs of Holy Scripture. It is undeniably and conspicuously Protestant (if the anachronism of

[1] *Confession. Book of Armagh*, fol. 22.

the term used in such a connection may be pardoned). It is distinctly Trinitarian, and thoroughly evangelical.

Some Episcopalians claim Patrick and the Church of which he was the leading spirit as lending countenance to their system. One of the grounds on which the more exclusive among them claim the title of 'The Church of Ireland' is that they are the representatives and successors of the primitive Irish Church, of which Patrick was the leading figure. But the claim is entirely untenable. For example, they represent Patrick as the first primate, whereas it is well known among scholars that neither in Patrick's day, nor for hundreds of years afterwards, was there any such personage as either an archbishop or bishop of Armagh. Scholarly episcopal writers acknowledge this.[1] To represent the Church of Patrick's day as prelatic in its organization is equally incorrect. Diocesan Episcopacy gives to a few bishops the oversight of a whole country. But Patrick's system seems to have been to give every congregation a bishop of its own. One statement represents him as erecting in Ireland 365 churches and appointing 365 bishops, one bishop for each church. Another increases these numbers, but preserves the same relative proportions, making the number of churches 700, with 700 bishops. In both cases the double principle of a bishop for each church and a church for each bishop is recognised. But this is the polity of Presbyterianism, not of Episcopacy, and, what is more important, is the polity of the New Testament, which recognises no higher ecclesiastical order among the ordinary office-bearers of the Church than that of the teaching elder, who, with the ruling elder, is the only bishop known to it.[2] The Church of Ireland of Patrick's day, and for many a long year afterwards,[3] was certainly, therefore, not a prelatic Church, and for a prelatic Church to claim to be its suc-

---

[1] Cf. King's *Memoir introductory to the Early History of Armagh*, Preface, Armagh 1854; and Todd's *St. Patrick, Apostle of Ireland*, p. 172.

[2] Cf. Acts xx. 17, 28.

[3] 'There seems to have been a bishop in every village.'—Goldwin Smith, *Irish History and Irish Character*, p. 33.

cessor and representative on account of being prelatic is surely to betray a strange ignorance of facts. With the overthrow of this position the claim to be the 'Church of Ireland,' which is built upon it,—a title the use of which wise and moderate Episcopalians themselves deprecate, — must also fall to the ground.

It is surely a little childish to be over-anxious for the shelter of the authority and prestige of Patrick. He was most godly, earnest, and laborious, but he was only, after all, a poor unlettered man, who spent his youth not in study, but in tending cattle on the sides of Slemish, and along the banks of the Braid Water. The age in which he lived was not an enlightened or learned age. He enjoyed none of the advantages or opportunities for arriving at truth which we possess. He himself tells us that he hesitated about writing his *Confession*, because, he says, 'I have not read like others, who have been well imbued with sacred learning.' It is surely, therefore, rather senseless to be over-earnest in the effort to secure the sanction of the authority and example of this humble man for our opinions or our Churches. We have the Bible to guide us, and better means by far of ascertaining its meaning than poor Patrick ever enjoyed. It is the Church which conforms to the pattern laid down there, and not the Church which corresponds most nearly to the Church of St. Patrick, which is the true apostolic Church. The authority or example of a Paul or a Peter is worth ten thousand times more than those of all the saints in the Romish calendar. If, however, any stress is to be laid upon Patrick's teaching, or upon the Church organization which he set up, it is plain that neither Romanism nor Protestant Episcopacy can claim the benefit of either. The simple, scriptural character of the Presbyterian Church, with its absence of either primates or diocesan bishops, with its minister for every congregation and the Holy Scriptures for its supreme law, and with no rites or ceremonies allowed save such as are authorized in the Word of God, approaches far more nearly to the spirit and genius of

Patrick, and of the Church for which he lived and laboured, than either of them, or than any other Church of the present day.

Patrick would have been remarkable in any age, but he was certainly a marvellous man for his times and environments. In reading his life and works one cannot but be impressed by his prayerfulness, his humility, his strong belief in a guiding and overruling Providence, his deep and accurate knowledge of the Bible, his firm grasp of the doctrines of grace, his stedfast faith, his love to Christ, his devotion to His service, and his fine evangelistic spirit. He was by no means free from faults, but he was certainly one of the noblest characters and greatest benefactors not only that Ireland has ever seen, but that all history can produce. 'He was a good man, full of faith and of the Holy Ghost; and much people was added unto the Lord.' When he had served his generation by the will of God, and fallen on sleep, he left Ireland a very different country from what he found it. Druidism had received its death-blow, and in the short space of one lifetime Christianity had been established on a firm basis.

CHAPTER III.

FROM THE BIRTH OF COLUMBA TO THE REFORMATION.

AFTER the death of Patrick various corruptions gradually came into Irish Christianity. Darkness crept over the land. But there arose from time to time lights in the gloom. One of the most celebrated of these was the ever-to-be-remembered Columba, or Columbkille, as he is sometimes called. Columba was a native of the County Donegal, one of whose wildest and most romantic glens is called, after him, Glen-Columbkille. He was born in the year 521 at Gartan,[1] in the shadow of the wild Derryveagh mountains, from behind which Errigal shoots its towering cone to the sky. Entering the Church, he soon rose to a position of conspicuous eminence and influence. Becoming, however, involved in some of the controversies of that turbulent time, he determined to leave Ireland. The hand of Providence, which so often makes the wrath of man to praise Him, was in his departure. As Patrick was brought from Scotland to become 'The Apostle of Ireland,' Columba was to be sent from Ireland to Scotland to become 'The Apostle of the Northern Picts;' and as we in Ireland must ever hold ourselves indebted to the great Scottish missionary for what he did for our country, so Scotsmen can never forget that it is to this illustrious Irishman that unquestionably is due the first evangelization of great part of North Britain. Thus to some extent we repaid the debt which we owed our neighbours across the Channel.

St. Patrick had lain almost a hundred years in his grave

[1] *Life of Columba*, by Adamnan, edited by Reeves, 1875.

when Columba,[1] along with twelve companions, sailed from Ireland across the Channel. We can picture the little company to ourselves, embarking in their skin-boats, and steering forth to seek a place which should be at once a quiet retreat for themselves and a convenient centre of missionary effort. Conspicuous among the exiles is the tall, commanding figure of Columba himself, with his eagle eye and noble bearing. By his orders the boats sail towards Scotland. By and by we see them coasting along its islands. Finally they drop anchor in the pellucidly green waters of a lovely bay of Iona. They land, and soon rude huts of wood and wattles are built to serve as 'cells;' for Columba had devoted himself to the monasticism already becoming prevalent. A plain church of similar materials is raised. Cattle are procured, and turned out to graze on the short clovery grass, sweet with thyme, which the sandy soil of the island still grows.[2] Some of the brethren attend to them, others to the raising of crops of oats and barley on the sheltered slopes of the hills. The Sound, still famous for its flounders,[2] supplies the refectory with fish in abundance. Columba, assisted by the most competent of the brethren, devotes himself to his favourite task of transcribing the Scriptures. Often, too, the sails of the leathern boats are seen hoisted to bear the missionary, Bible in hand, to preach to the inhabitants of some of the neighbouring isles or of the mainland itself; for one of the advantages of Iona was that while an island, and thus affording to the little company a delightful security and seclusion, cut off as it is by a blue ribbon of sea, six miles broad, from the nearest shore, it lay so close to it that it was easy to proceed on periodical evangelistic tours. To the marvellous success of these tours history bears ample testimony. So, between the labours of his cell, where the midnight lamp, fed by oil obtained from the bodies of seals, such as still bask in the sun on the rocks of the island, threw its rays on the pages of the holy volume which he

[1] The date usually given is 563.
[2] Cf. *Iona*, by the Duke of Argyll.

was never weary of transcribing, and the labours of the mission journey among the barbarous inhabitants of the mainland, to whom his commanding figure and persuasive voice soon became familiar and dear, the days passed quickly and quietly away. At length old age overtook him, and the weight of nearly fourscore years bent the form, once so splendidly erect, to the ground. The saint had a presentiment that death was coming, and the story of how it came is one of the most pathetic things in history. A June sun was lighting up the waters of the Sound, and the distant Paps of Jura, and the low, dark island of Staffa nearer at hand, and the hills of Morven, with their brightest colours. It was a Saturday, and as Columba looked out upon the magnificent panorama he said, 'This day is in the sacred volume called the Sabbath, which meaneth rest, and to-day is verily a Sabbath for me, as it is the last with me of this present toilsome life, on which, after my wearisome labours, I come to enjoy my Sabbath.' Staff in hand, he ascended a little knoll, and gave the island and his brethren his blessing. This done, he returned to his cell and resumed his loved work of transcribing the Bible. He had reached the thirty-fourth Psalm, and he wrote on till he came to the tenth verse: 'They that seek the Lord shall not want any good thing.' Then he felt that his work was done. 'Here I must stop,' he said; 'let Baithune write the rest.'[1] He went to the little church for evening service, and then, returning to his cell, lay down on the stone floor, with his head on his stone pillow. Here he reposed till the bell rang for service next morning. Then he rose and proceeded again to the church. But when the others had reached it after him they found the old man lying dead. So on Sabbath morning, the 9th June 597, the venerable Columba entered into the Sabbath of eternity.

The monastic system in Columba's day had not yet degenerated into the loathsome thing which it subsequently became. In those wild times there were many things to induce contem-

[1] Adamnan's *Columba*, by Reeves.

plative men, who desired to devote themselves to study and Christian work, to retire into some secluded place, where, undisturbed by the din of tribal wars, they could pursue their quiet labours together and in peace. The Irish and Scottish monasteries, such as Columba founded, became also schools for the education of the people—the only schools of the time. They were specially colleges for the training of young men for the Church. They developed into centres of missionary activity, and they were the only places where the Scriptures were transcribed, and where copies of them could be obtained. In Bangor, County Down, was a famous example of such a monastery. Comghall, said to have been a native of Magheramorne, near Larne, was its founder, and we are told that he had at one time no fewer than 3000 monks under his jurisdiction.[1] The title, 'Isle of Saints,' by which Ireland was known in the seventh century, was largely given because of the multiplication of these mingled seats of religion and learning over the country. Columba's monastery at Iona was modelled after the Irish pattern. The life led in it was a busy, simple, quiet, useful life. But a system like this, which involves the violation of natural laws and derives no authority from Scripture, has in it elements of corruption which are sure sooner or later to lead to that terrible relaxation of morals which, an eminent Roman Catholic writer says, 'the religious orders, by a mysterious and terrible judgment of God, have never been able to resist.'[2] The monastic cell soon became a very different thing from what it was in Columba's day.

Ireland during these early centuries left its impress upon more countries than Scotland. The gospel which it had received, it freely gave to many lands besides. Missionaries from its shores travelled not only to Britain, but to France, to Germany, to Switzerland, and Italy. Ireland became the missionary nation of the period *par excellence*. Her Christian sons 'saw in incessant visions a world known and unknown to be conquered for

---

[1] Lanigan, *Ecclesiastical History of Ireland*, ii. 63, 67.
[2] Montalembert, *Les Moines d'Occident*, iv. 78.

Christ.'[1] Columbanus, towards the end of the sixth century, settled in France, establishing in Burgundy a monastery similar to that of Iona, which attained great celebrity. Gallus, one of his disciples, became a well-known evangelist in Switzerland, where the canton of St. Gall still perpetuates his name. Kilian, or Killen, laboured in a similar manner in Wurzburg in the seventh century, and 'Fridolin the traveller' in another part of Germany, both with large results. Irishmen have reason to be proud of the labours and successes of these enterprising and eminent fellow-countrymen of theirs.

Meanwhile, however, Romish corruptions had been gradually stealing in. For a long time Irish ecclesiastics boldly opposed the extravagant claims of the Pope, so that for centuries the Christianity of Ireland was purer than that of any other nation in Christendom. But, little by little, the pure stream of her early religion, such as we see it in the time of Patrick, became corrupted, until it was lost in a foul and fœtid quagmire, reeking with filth. One need not dwell on these times of defection. Still, successive Popes had trouble in bringing the Irish Church into entire conformity to the Romish ideal. In 1110 a memorable synod was held, with Gillebert, the Pope's legate, as its president. This assembly is known as the Synod of Rathbreasail, and the whole country was placed by it under the government of twenty-three bishops and two archbishops.[2] But for long this arrangement had little respect paid to it. More than forty years after the synod, its decisions were still not universally carried out. Many 'parochial bishoprics' still existed. Another legate, Cardinal Paparo, was therefore now sent over from Rome. Another synod was summoned and met at Kells in County Meath under his presidency. The island was again divided into dioceses, this time the number being thirty-eight. We find a proof of the continued existence of parochial or village bishoprics, in a resolution of this synod, which enacted that, 'on the death of village bishops

---

[1] Montalembert, *Les Moines d'Occident*, ii. 597.
[2] Lanigan, *Ecclesiastical History of Ireland.*

... there should be chosen to succeed in their stead, arch-presbyters to be appointed by the diocesans, who should superintend the clergy and laity in their respective districts.'[1] The primitive non-prelatic arrangements of the Church evidently died hard. Rome was determined that her iron rule should supersede them; but the task was not an easy one. The Synod of Kells was convened because the decrees of the Synod of Rathbreasail had not been carried out; but its own decrees were very imperfectly obeyed. Rome, however, has many weapons in her armoury. If one fails, she is seldom at a loss for another. She was bent upon the entire subjugation of Ireland to her rule, and she shrank from no means of attaining her end. Adrian IV. became Pope. He was an Englishman, the only Englishman who has ever ruled in the Vatican, his real name being Nicholas Breakspear. He knew that Henry II. of England was anxious to add Ireland to his dominions, and so in 1155 he issued a bull, which is at once the 'stumbling-block and the despair' of Romish historians, telling the king that 'His Holiness held it right that for extending the borders of the Church, restraining the progress of vice, for the correction of manners, the planting of virtue, and the increase of the Christian religion, you enter that island and execute therein whatever shall pertain to the honour of God and the welfare of the land, and that the people of that land receive you honourably, and reverence you as their lord, the rights of their Churches still remaining sacred and inviolate, and,' the prudent Pope, with a keen eye to the monetary profits of the transaction, is careful to add, 'saving to St. Peter the annual pension of one penny' (equal, it is said, to at least two shillings and sixpence of our present money) 'from every house.'[2] In this audacious and high-handed style was Ireland handed bodily over to England. Irish Roman Catholics should bear carefully in mind that it is to the Pope of Rome they owe

---

[1] Wilkins, *Concilia*, i. 547.

[2] For the full text of this famous bull, see *Cambrensis Eversus*, Kelly's edition, ii. 410-414.

their subjugation to Britain, of which they complain so much. Being the infallible Head of an infallible Church, surely he did not err. How strange that it is the Irish Roman Catholics, headed by their own priests and bishops, who, with the sanction of the present Pope, rebel against the action of Pope Adrian IV., and are bent upon taking from England a possession with which the see of Rome gifted her!

It was some time before Henry was able to take possession of the kingdom which had thus been so haughtily handed over to him. But at length, in 1171, he landed at Waterford and proceeded to assume the sovereignty of Ireland, which he was able without much difficulty to do, and thence dates the period of the English connection.

From the English occupation to the Reformation the country was in no very prosperous state. The strict English authority was limited to 'the Pale,' which varied from time to time in extent, and the rest of the land was largely left to its own devices. The people were oppressed rather than governed, and they groaned besides under the exactions and the vices of the Romish bishops and priests, who now, under the fostering wing of England, rode rough-shod over them. The rapacity of these men was only equalled by their licentiousness. It is a shame even to speak of the things which were 'done of them in secret.' The monasteries became dens of the foulest vice. The bishops set an example of open immorality, and the subordinate clergy were not slow to follow their lead. The Bible almost entirely disappeared from the land, and in its place the grossest and most degrading superstition became rampant. Simony prevailed everywhere. The Popes themselves, who successively ruled over the spiritual affairs of the country from Rome, were frequently perfect monsters of iniquity, and it is not surprising if the stream did not rise above the level of its fountain. The sole object of the bishops seems to have been their own enjoyment and aggrandizement. To think of them as ministers of religion is impossible, when we read of one besieging a brother bishop in his own cathedral, loading him with chains, and immuring him in a dungeon from which he barely escaped with his life,—of another who earned for himself the significant nicknames of 'Burn-Bill' and 'Scorch-Villain,' from his having burned all his tenants' title-deeds, of which he had fraudulently got possession, and of a third starving to death six persons whose property he had got into his hands. We can see for ourselves that a sad change had indeed come over Ireland since the days of good St. Patrick. The land, temporally and spiritually alike, was in a state of the most deplorable misery when the era of the Reformation arrived, bringing hope of better things—a hope, however, which was too long of being fully realized, owing to circumstances hereafter to be described.

CHAPTER IV.

FROM THE DAWN OF THE REFORMATION TO THE PLANTATION OF ULSTER.

THE first step towards accepting the Reformation in Ireland was taken in May 1537, when the Irish Parliament threw off the authority of the Pope and declared the King supreme head on earth of the Church of Ireland. But the change was little more than a change of authority. No reformation worthy of the name can be propagated by mere royal proclamations or Acts of Parliament, and it was the misfortune of Ireland, not only at the era of the Reformation, but for centuries after, that no wise efforts were made to win the people over to Protestantism. It came to them weighted by the fact that it was the religion of conquerors, who oppressed them by penal laws, and in many other ways manifested their hatred and contempt for them. A creed so presented was, indeed, heavily handicapped. But, in spite of this disadvantage, had wise measures been adopted for instructing the Irish people in Scripture truth, the religious history of the country would doubtless have soon received a very different tinge. Ireland suffers to this day from the mistakes made at the time of the introduction of the reformed religion. The same Parliament which established Protestantism re-enacted in all their stringency several of the penal laws against the native Irish. Marriage and fosterage with them were forbidden under the severest penalties, and it was ordered that no ecclesiastical preferment was to be conferred on any one who did not speak English, except in case, after repeated proclamations in the nearest market town, no person so qualified could be found.[1] Not a very likely way surely to commend Protestantism to the people! It need not be wondered at,

[1] *Irish Statutes*, 28th of Henry VIII. cap. 15.

therefore, that the Reformation scarcely made any progress in Ireland in Henry's day. The reign of his son and successor, Edward VI., was too short to allow of any great advance. One excellent appointment he made, that of the godly Bale (1495-1563) to the bishopric of Ossory, which, if it had been followed up by the preferment of men of like spirit to the other sees, and the appointment of like-minded clergymen to the various parishes, would have done incalculable good. Mary, however, succeeded Edward VI., and the Christian work which had been begun was stopped. Romanism resumed its ascendancy, and the persecuting spirit both of the queen and her Church are sufficiently indicated by the instructions which she issued to her Irish Lord Deputy and Council—instructions which are worth noting for many reasons. They were required, 'by their example and all good means possible, to advance the honour of God and the Catholic faith, to set forth the honour and dignity of the Pope's Holiness and the See Apostolic of Rome, and from time to time to be ready with their aid and secular force, at the request of all spiritual ministers and ordinaries, to punish and repress all heretics and Lollards, and their damnable sects, opinions, and errors.'[1] There is no uncertain sound about these instructions. An Act of the Irish Parliament, which was passed in June 1556, breathes the same spirit, declaring that 'all persons, preaching or teaching, or evidently suspected of preaching or teaching, against the Catholic Faith' might be arrested by the bishop of the diocese, and, on their refusal to abjure, delivered to the secular arm, and ' burnt for the terror of others.'[2]

A curious story is told of the miscarriage of one of Mary's projects for the persecution of Irish Protestants. In October 1558 she despatched Dr. Cole, Dean of St Paul's, to Dublin, with orders to the Lord Deputy vigorously to put down Protestantism in Ireland. When he had reached Chester on his way, he showed his commission with great exultation to the mayor, and boasted loudly of the end which was about to be put

[1] Richard Cox, *History of Ireland*, 303.   [2] *Irish Statutes*, 9th of Mary.

to the heretics across the Channel. The woman of the house where he stayed hearing of these boasts, and having some Protestant friends in Dublin, in whose safety she was of course interested, determined to baulk the envoy's designs. So, watching her opportunity, she quietly removed the royal commission out of the box in which her guest carried it, and put in its place a pack of cards. Cole, ignorant of the trick which had been played upon him, proceeded on his journey, and in due time arrived in Dublin. A meeting of the Privy Council was convened to receive him. The Lord Deputy presided, and the royal messenger explained at length Her Majesty's wishes, concluding by handing to the Secretary the box in which had been deposited the queen's warrant. What was his astonishment and dismay when, on being opened, there was seen, not the formidable document which was expected, but the pack of cards, with the knave of clubs uppermost! The Lord Deputy, entering into the humour of the incident, exclaimed: 'Let us have a new commission, and we will shuffle the cards in the meantime.' Cole hastened back to London, by no means in an enviable frame of mind, we may be sure. The new commission was obtained; but before her orders could be carried into effect, the bloody queen was called to her account. So narrowly did Irish Protestants at this period escape the horrors of Smithfield.

Queen Elizabeth now ascended the throne, and Protestantism was established once more. It could not, however, but have a very evil influence on the Irish mind to see this religious vacillation on the part of the rulers—first, Romanism overturned and Protestantism established; then Protestantism put down and Romanism restored; and now the tables turned again. But from such indecision Ireland has suffered on more occasions than this. The instructive spectacle which was now witnessed of bishops who had been zealous Romanists under Mary, changing their religion with the change of the times, and becoming as zealous Protestants under Elizabeth, was not calculated to impress the Irish with any very high opinion of the men sent over to be their spiritual instructors. The Irish primate, Curwin, was among those who thus trimmed their sails to suit the prevailing wind. 'In the time of Henry VIII. he ... defended the supremacy of the crown and vindicated Henry's marriage with Anne Boleyn. When the pious Frith was in prison for denying purgatory and transubstantiation, Curwin preached against him in the royal presence, and thus stimulated the king to sign the death-warrant for his martyrdom. The primate now made another evolution ... and superintended the establishment of Protestantism.'[1] Is it not a marvel to find Irish Episcopalians glorying in such a man as one of the precious links of the apostolical succession?

Ireland continued in a wretched state during most of the reign of Elizabeth. Civil war disturbed and desolated the kingdom, one Irish chief after another having risen in rebellion against the English power. This disturbed condition of affairs, joined to the neglect of their duty by the clergy, left the land a prey to misery and ignorance and superstition. The poet Spenser, who in the latter years of Elizabeth's reign was quietly penning his *Faerie Queene* in Kilcolman Castle, undisturbed by the din which raged around him, gives a melancholy account of the state of matters. 'Not one amongst an hundred,' he says, 'knoweth any ground of religion, or any article of his faith;' while of the clergy he adds, 'Ye may find gross simony, greedy covetousness, fleshly incontinence, careless sloth, and generally all disordered life in the common clergyman—they neither read Scriptures, nor preach to the people, nor administer the Communion. But Baptism they do, for they christen, yet after the Popish fashion.' Of the bishops he says: 'In the remoter dioceses they do not at all bestow the benefices which are in their own donation upon any, but keep them in their own hands, and set their own servants and horse boys to take up their tithes and fruits.'[2] No wonder the Reformation did not make much progress under such a regime. It would have been a miracle if it had done so.

[1] Killen, *Ecclesiastical History of Ireland*, i. 373.
[2] Spenser's *State of Ireland*, Dublin, 1763, 129.

Two things, however, were done in Elizabeth's reign which prepared the way for the coming of better times. The first of these was the complete overthrow of rebellion all over the country. While it was disturbed by intestine war, while property was insecure and pillage frequent, not much progress or prosperity could be expected. Before Elizabeth died, in March 1603, the last rebel against her authority had either been destroyed or had given in his submission. The second was the erection of Trinity College, Dublin, which became the seat of the first university ever established in Ireland. It was built on the site of the old monastery of All-Hallows, on a piece of ground called Hoggin Green, then described as 'near Dublin,' though the college is now almost in the heart of the city. The foundation stone was laid on March 13, 1592, and it was noted, as a curious and auspicious circumstance, that during the whole of the time of building not a shower of rain fell by day to interfere with the work. On January 9, 1594, the first students were admitted, one of the earliest enrolled being a youth destined to attain no mean celebrity,—James Ussher, afterwards Archbishop of Armagh. It deserves to be noted that the first regular Provost was a Presbyterian clergyman, the Rev. Walter Travers, and two of the first Fellows, James Fullarton and James Hamilton, were of the same creed. The former was afterwards knighted, and the latter was subsequently raised to the peerage under the title of Lord Claneboy, and became the founder of the noble family of which the Earl of Dufferin is now the representative. Presbyterians thus occupy a very important and distinguished position in the early history of Trinity College,[1] and there is no reason why, under the liberal regime of the present day, they should not do so again.

[1] Of late years the constitution of the university, which had become almost entirely an Episcopal seminary, has been greatly improved. Catechetical lectures are now delivered in the college under the authority of the Board to the Presbyterian students by some of the Presbyterian ministers of Dublin, and these lectures rank as of the same academic value with the Episcopalian catechetical lectures.

CHAPTER V.

THE PLANTATION OF ULSTER AND THE PIONEERS OF IRISH PRESBYTERIANISM.

ONE September day in the year 1607, a small vessel of the old-fashioned type of naval architecture which prevailed two hundred and fifty years ago might have been seen working its way out of the wildly beautiful Lough Swilly, on the north-western coast of Ireland. Sailing cautiously along, with the lofty Slieve Snaght towering to the sky from out the wilds of Innishowen on the right, and the other Donegal mountains frowning down on the left, she at length leaves the calm waters of the picturesque lough behind, and finds herself on the rougher surface of the open sea. On her deck, as she rounds the point, may be discerned the figures of two gentlemen, who ever and anon, as the little vessel leaves Ireland farther and farther behind, cast many a regretful look at the mist-crowned hills and the woods beginning to assume their ruddy autumn tints, and the rolling corn-fields, already yellow for the reaping hook. These were O'Neill, Earl of Tyrone, and O'Donnell, Earl of Tyrconnel. For long they had been the leading spirits of Irish disaffection. Followed by thousands of devoted followers, they had faced the soldiers of Queen Elizabeth on many a battle-field. Now, their power broken, and all their plots disconcerted, they leave Ireland for ever, to seek an asylum on the Continent. From the day of their departure may be said to date a new era of Irish history. Since their downfall all Irish rebellions have been foredoomed to failure from their very inception. As the ship which carried them from our shores disappeared on the horizon, the prospects of independence for Ireland vanished for ever.

The flight of the two fugitive earls, and the overthrow of the other rebel leaders who had long kept the north of Ireland in constant turmoil, placed at the disposal of the Government vast tracts of land, now forfeited to the Crown. The way was thus open for the carrying out on a large scale of a project which had been often contemplated, and sometimes actually attempted, but without success, the project of establishing in Ulster bodies of Scotch and English settlers, who would at once be valuable inhabitants, developing the resources of the country by their industry and enterprise, as the natives had failed to do, and who would, at the same time, faithfully guard 'the back door of the kingdom,' as Ireland was then and might still rightfully be styled. This Plantation of Ulster, as the enterprise was named, marks one of the most important eras in the history of Ulster and Ireland, and especially of the Irish Presbyterian Church.

The project was carried out in the following manner:—The forfeited lands, having been carefully surveyed, were divided into proportions of 1000, 1500, and 2000 acres each, and these tracts of country were granted to approved settlers on certain conditions. 'The occupiers of the largest proportions were bound within four years to build a castle and bawn (*i.e.* a walled enclosure, usually with towers at the angles; within it was placed the house or castle, and it was sufficient to secure the inmates and their cattle from the incursions of the marauding Irish), and to plant on their estates forty-eight able men, eighteen years old and upwards, of English or Scottish descent. Those of the second class were obliged to build within two years a strong stone or brick house and bawn; and those of the third class a bawn; while both were bound to plant a proportionable number of British families on their possessions, and to have their houses furnished with a sufficiency of arms.'[1]

It may interest many in these days of land agitation to know that the yearly rent fixed for the land thus granted was at the

[1] Reid, *History of the Presbyterian Church in Ireland*, i. 81.

rate of 'six shillings and eightpence for every threescore English acres,' or a fraction more than a penny per acre,—less than that, indeed, for a quantity of forest and bog was thrown in, in each case, without charge.[1] As much timber as was required for building was also allowed free of charge.[2]

The chief agent of the Government in the carrying out of this great plan was Sir Arthur Chichester, ancestor of the noble family of Donegal. He was appointed Lord Deputy of Ireland in 1605. Most of the nobility of the north of Ireland date the acquisition of their Irish estates from this Plantation, and the ancestors of very many of the people came over from Scotland or England under their auspices. The corporation of the city of London obtained, among the rest, a grant of nearly the whole of the present county of Londonderry, then called the county of Coleraine, on condition of their building and fortifying the towns of Londonderry and Coleraine, and otherwise expending £20,000 on the property, and complying with various other conditions.

Soon the sound of the axes of many settlers rang through the forests of Ulster, and of their crowbars and hammers in the quarries, as they felled trees and hewed out stone for the erection of homesteads. Castles, houses, and bawns rose quickly all over the country.[3] The fields presented scenes of busy labour such as they had long been strangers to. Cattle browsed peacefully on the rich pasture lands, herds of swine fattened in the woods, while plough and harrow and spade transformed what had been a waste into such fields as the new inhabitants had left behind them across the Channel. They needed to be men of stout heart and watchful eye, as well as skilful and industrious hand. In the long nights of winter the howling of packs of hungry

---

[1] 'Collection of such orders and conditions as are to be observed by the undertakers,' printed in Harris's *Hibernica*, 123-130.

[2] Hill's *Plantation in Ulster*, 82.

[3] Pynnar in his *Survey* of 1615 tells us that at that time there had been erected 107 castles with bawns, 19 castles without bawns, 42 bawns without castles or houses, and 1897 dwelling-houses of stone and timber.

wolves[1] around his dwelling admonished the settler of the need of bawn and well-barred gate, while the saffron-dyed garment of a wood-kerne, gleaming in the distance among the trees, or an arrow flying from his bow of tough native yew, often told the newcomers that they were in an enemy's country. But they bravely held their ground. Clusters of houses, destined to be the germs of important towns, rose quickly under the hands of mason and carpenter, each with its earthen rampart or its stone wall for protection against the enemy. Londonderry grew up on the Foyle, and Coleraine at the mouth of the Bann. A few thatched houses, with a humble Presbyterian Church amongst them, formed themselves into Ballymena in the heart of the County Antrim. Carrickfergus had already crouched for four hundred years behind the shelter of its castle, and a church and castle, with a few fishermen's cabins, also marked the site where Belfast, the town of the Lagan ford, was destined to develop into the chief commercial town of Ireland, with a busy population of nearly a quarter of a million of inhabitants. But both towns received a great accession of strength and influence from the Plantation, while in County Down such places as Newtownards, Bangor, Donaghadee, and Killyleagh owe their existence to the same potent factor.

The Plantation altered the whole history of the north of Ireland. To it may largely be attributed the fact that Ulster, which has fewer natural advantages than either Munster, Leinster, or Connaught, is the most prosperous, the most industrious, the most law-abiding, and the most loyal part of all Ireland. The difference between Scotland and Spain, or between the Protestant and Romish cantons of Switzerland, is not greater or more apparent than that between Ulster and its sister provinces.

---

[1] We find many proofs of how troublesome and numerous wolves were in Ireland in the seventeenth century. In 1662, Sir John Ponsonby reported to the Irish House of Commons from the Committee of Grievances that a bill should be brought in to encourage the killing of wolves and foxes. Wolves were not extinct in the country until the year 1710. The last is said to have been killed at Wolfhill, near Belfast.

With a bleaker climate and a less fertile soil, it is richer and more peaceful by far than they. The traveller from the south can see from the windows of his railway carriage the change as he enters Ulster, and the Government returns show what a vast difference there is in crime and in the cost of maintaining order in the one province as compared with the others. If Ulster is still what Irish writers described it long ago to be, 'the thumb in the hand which is able to grip and to hold against the four fingers,' Leinster, Munster, Connaught, and Meath, she owes it to the influx of the Scotch Presbyterians and English Puritans who settled on her soil at the Plantation. Up to the time of their coming, the northern province was just like the others, as turbulent, as difficult to govern, as unprosperous. They stamped a new character upon it, which it has retained to this day. England would soon know the difference if she had not, helping her to govern Ireland, 'the vertebral column of Ulster, giving it at once its strength and uprightness.'

A very large number of the new settlers were from Scotland. James I. being himself a Scotchman, many of his countrymen naturally obtained from him concessions of land. Besides, the north of Ireland lying so close to the 'Land o' Cakes,' that on a bright summer day the tourist, standing on Fair Head, within view of the Giant's Causeway, might almost fancy that he could throw a stone across to the Mull of Cantyre, which lies opposite,[1] with its snowy farmhouses and green fields gleaming in the sun, it is easy to understand how so many of the settlers came from Ayrshire and Wigtownshire, and the neighbouring Scottish counties.[2] A cheap farm was as great an attraction then as it is now. Adventurous spirits, whose finances had run low, were glad of the opportunity of a chance in a new country, new, yet within sight of the old. Besides, as the early years of the seventeenth century rolled on, the state of affairs in Scotland

---

[1] The distance between the two points is less than 20 miles.

[2] The names which prevail in these counties prevail also to this day in the north of Ireland.

grew more and more uncomfortable for those who wished to enjoy the simple forms, the mingled freedom and order, and the pure doctrines, of Presbyterianism. Many were glad to escape to a land which promised them rest and immunity from persecution. Ulster was for a time what America afterwards became, the refuge of the oppressed. So it came about that in those years so many of the old, clumsy vessels of the period were seen crossing the Channel to the North of Ireland, each with its group of settlers aboard, sometimes individuals, sometimes whole families with all their household 'plenishing' along with them, and, in their pockets, what spare cash could be realized by the sale of unnecessary or unportable property. Those old-fashioned boats carried the fortunes of Ulster.

To understand the after history of this scion from the Scottish tree which was thus transplanted to Ireland, we must know something of the history of the parent stock. Presbyterianism had, after a long struggle with Romanism, and after the shedding of much precious martyr blood, been established under the leadership of the 'man who never feared the face of clay,' the brave John Knox (1505–1572), who, trained for the Romish priesthood, and actually ordained to that office, was brought to see the horrible unscripturalness of Popery, and became its most implacable foe. The foundations of a free and well-ordered Presbyterian Church were laid so broad and deep that Scotland has ever since remained Presbyterian to the core. In 1560 the first General Assembly met. But Knox had not long been dead when James VI. (of Scotland) began to show signs of a wish to reintroduce the Prelacy which had been got rid of along with the other incidents of Romanism. In the early part of his reign, James had indeed expressed a great love for Presbyterianism. At a well-remembered meeting of the General Assembly, he made a speech in which he praised God that 'he was born in such a time as the time of the light of the gospel, and to be king in the sincerest Kirk in the world. The Kirk of Geneva,' said he, 'keepeth Pasch and Yule (*i.e.* Easter and

Christmas). What have they for them? They have no institution (*i.e.* no Scripture warrant). As for our neighbour Kirk in England, it is an ill-said Mass in English, wanting nothing but the liftings (*i.e.* the elevations of the host). I charge you, my good people, ministers, doctors, nobles, gentlemen and barons, to stand to your purity, and I, forsooth, so long as I brook my life and crown, shall maintain the same against all deadly.' A brave speech this! But Scottish Presbyterianism was soon to learn that it must not put its trust in princes—no matter how bravely they speak. James began by and by to interfere in the affairs of the Church. 'But,' said Andrew Melville, 'your Majesty, there are two kings and two kingdoms in Scotland. There is King James, the head of this commonwealth, and there is Christ Jesus, the King of the Church, whose subject James the Sixth is, and of whose kingdom he is not a king, nor a lord, nor a head, but a member. We will yield to you your place, and give you all due obedience. But again, I say you are not the Head of the Church.' It was a noble remonstrance. James felt it keenly, and evidently made up his mind that if he was to get his will, he must have a more manageable and obsequious kind of Church than those stiff-necked Presbyterians. Accordingly, Prelacy was stealthily introduced, his idea being that he could rule the bishops, and the bishops would rule the ministers. In 1603 he succeeded to the English throne by the death of Elizabeth, and the threat which not long after his accession he uttered against the Puritans boded ill for the liberties of the Scottish Church. 'I'll make them conform,' he said, 'or I'll harry them out of the land.' Scotland was deprived of the free right of holding General Assemblies. Andrew Melville, who had spoken so plainly of the respective rights of King James and King Jesus, was committed to the Tower, where he lay four long years, and, in the end, a full-fledged Prelacy was imposed upon Scotland, notwithstanding all the king's fair speeches. The well-known Five Articles of Perth were passed, intended to conform the practice of the Church of Scotland to that of its English sister. So matters went on, till in 1625 James died and Charles I. succeeded him. Under the advice and influence of Archbishop Laud, he determined to push things to a still further extreme. Knox's Liturgy had hitherto been in use, for neither Knox nor Calvin had any objection to a liturgy *per se*. Laud determined to introduce one of his own compilation, which was simply an amended edition of the Romish Missal. The much-enduring people could bear the gradual filching away of their liberties and their religion no longer. When the 'Dean of Edinburgh,' clad in his surplice, began to read the new Service-Book in St. Giles's Church, a poor apple-woman, Janet Geddes by name, lifted the three-legged stool on which she sat, and crying out—'Fause loon! dost thou say Mass at my lug?' flung it at the affrighted man's head. He fled from the church in terror, and a great tumult began. The people were ripe for resistance, and they rose against their oppressors. As sometimes among the Alps a single word has ere now brought, thundering down the mountain side, a tremendous avalanche, which had hung there so delicately poised that the slightest vibration of the air has sufficed to hurl it on the valleys and villages below, so the one act of that poor old apple-woman brought down upon the infatuated oppressors of Scotland the people's terrible vengeance. Quick measures were taken to carry out the work which old Janet had begun. The National Covenant, originally drawn up in 1580, which bound all who subscribed it to adhere to and defend at all hazards the doctrine and discipline of the Church of Scotland, was renewed on 1st March, 1638, all ranks—nobles, ministers, and people—signing it with the greatest enthusiasm. In November of the same year the famous Glasgow Assembly met, with Alexander Henderson in the Moderator's chair. It formally abolished the Episcopal form of Church government, which had been so unwarrantably imposed, removed the bishops from their offices, declared the Five Articles of Perth null and void, and condemned the Service-Book which had been attempted to be introduced, the Moderator ending his closing address with the famous words,—'We have now cast down the walls of Jericho. Let him that rebuildeth them beware of the curse of Hiel the Bethelite,'—words which should evermore ring in the ears of all who would give up, at the bidding of any man, or for any price, dearly bought privileges for which our fathers had to contend so long and suffer so much.

It was during the time that these events were transpiring in Scotland that the Plantation of Ulster was going on, and it can easily be understood how Scotchmen, weary of the strife which then raged in their native land, would gladly turn their eyes across the Channel to the haven of refuge which was thus opened up to them. God has His own strange ways of accomplishing His purposes. It would not be correct to say that Presbyterianism in Ireland dates from the Plantation. As we have already seen, the first regular Provost of Trinity College, Dublin, in the reign of Queen Elizabeth, was a Presbyterian, as were also two of its first Fellows, and, if our investigation of the history of Ireland at a very much earlier date is correct, a Church order, characterized by much of the simplicity and freedom of Presbyterianism, and certainly much more essentially Presbyterian than Popish or Prelatic, existed here in times still earlier. It is from the early years of the seventeenth century, however, that the present organization of the Irish Presbyterian Church dates, and hence a deep interest must always attach to the history of those years, and to the lives and labours of the men who were honoured during them to be the pioneers of the good cause. The first of these in point of time was Edward Brice, who in 1613[1] began to exercise his ministry in Broadisland, a quiet rural district lying between Carrickfergus and Larne. Brice had been for many years minister of Drymen, in Stirlingshire.[2] But having signalized

---

[1] 'Presbyterianism entered Ulster almost as soon as Episcopacy, for though the Irish Reformation dates formally from 1537, it had not touched the northern province till 1605.'—Croskery, *Irish Presbyterianism*, p. 9.

[2] Mr. Brice, or Bryce, as he is called in the Scottish records, was born about the year 1569 at Airth, in Stirlingshire, on the borders of the Firth of Forth. He is said to have been a younger son of Bruce, the laird of Airth,

himself by his opposition to the introduction of Prelacy into the Church in Scotland, he had been obliged to fly the kingdom, and was led by various reasons to cross to Ireland. His coming here was sanctioned by the then Bishop of Down, Echlin, as was that of several others of the early Presbyterian ministers. Echlin appointed him prebendary of Kilroot, and Brice was recognised as minister of the parish, preached in the church, and enjoyed the tithes, though all the while he was a Presbyterian, conducted service according to the Presbyterian fashion, and continued to preach the doctrine which he had taught across the Channel. He had left Scotland for his hatred to even a modified Prelacy, and it was not likely that in Ireland he would accept it in its undiluted form.

The fact is, the Irish Established Church was at this time in a wonderfully comprehensive mood. James Ussher, its Primate, had been taught in his youth by a Presbyterian tutor, and had studied in a college with a Presbyterian

and the names Brice and Bruce seem to be interchangeable, for we find that in this present century the lineal descendant of Edward Brice changed by royal licence his name from Brice to Bruce. Brice entered Edinburgh College about 1589, and, among other professors, studied under Charles Ferme (or Fairholm). He was laureated on 12th August, 1593, and it is stated that he became a regent in the University. In 1595 he entered the Church, becoming minister of the next parish to that in which he was born, Bothkennar, which is said to have this peculiarity, that 'not a stone is to be found in the whole of it of the size of a peppercorn' (*New Statistical Account of Scotland*). Here he officiated for nearly seven years. In 1602 he received translation to a larger sphere, the parish of Drymen, also in Stirlingshire, where he laboured for upwards of eleven years. It was while minister here that, in 1607, he signalized himself by his vigorous opposition to the introduction of a disguised Prelacy in the shape of the appointment of the Archbishop of Glasgow as constant Moderator of Synod. Finally, he was deposed by Spotswood and the Presbytery of Glasgow on 29th December, 1613, on a serious charge. He then fled to Ireland, and commenced his ministry in Broadisland, or 'Braidenisland,' as it is called in the old records, preaching alternately, it is said, at Templecorran and Ballykeel in Island Magee. Pennies are still in existence bearing the name of his eldest son Robert, who amassed a considerable fortune at Castle Chester, then a place of some importance as a mail packet station. *Vide* Scott's *Fasti Eccl. Scot.* and *The Dictionary of National Biography*, 1886.

Provost at its head. He was a godly man, with little or no sectarian bigotry about him. As its standard, the Church adopted in 1615 the 'Articles of Religion, agreed upon by the Archbishops and Bishops, and the rest of the Clergy.'[1] These reveal to us its temper and character. They are thoroughly evangelical, very moderate, and their theology distinctly Calvinistic. It is especially to be noted that they make no mention of the three orders of bishops, priests, and deacons which are so dear to Episcopalians. They ignore also the necessity for episcopal ordination, and by implication concede the validity of ordination by presbyters. They disclaim the observance of Lent as a religious fast, and they claim no authority for decreeing rites and ceremonies.[2] On this comprehensive foundation the Irish Church was then formally settled. Its terms of communion were limited only in respect of doctrine, a subject on which there existed almost universal conformity all through the three kingdoms.[3] The Irish Episcopal Church has changed since those days—changed not for the better. But it can easily be understood how Brice and the other Presbyterian ministers who came over at this time to Ulster occupied the parish churches of such a body, received the tithes, and were recognised by the bishops of the dioceses in which they respectively laboured as the parochial clergy, all the time that they were not prelatically ordained, conducted service after the simple scriptural fashion to which they had been accustomed in their own country, preached a thoroughly Calvinistic theology, and were, as they had been before, Presbyterian ministers. They could do and be all this with a perfectly good conscience

---

[1] *Vide* Killen's *Ecclesiastical History of Ireland*, i. 525.

[2] It is an interesting fact that the Westminster Confession of Faith is largely based upon these Irish Articles of 1615, and owes much to them. Cf. Mitchell's *Westminster Assembly*, p. 372, and Schaff's *Creeds of Christendom*, i. p. 761. The Irish Presbyterian ministers of the beginning of the seventeenth century had thus substantially the same doctrinal standard as their successors at the close of the nineteenth.

[3] Reid, *History of the Presbyterian Church in Ireland*, i. 95.

in a Church whose standards were the 'Articles of Religion' of 1615.

Brice's ministry at Broadisland was a very zealous one. ' In all his preaching he insisted most on the life of Christ in the heart, and the light of His Word and Spirit on the mind, that being his own continual exercise.'[1]

Another of the early ministers was Mr. Hubbard, who became minister of Carrickfergus about 1621. He was an Englishman, having been minister of a nonconforming congregation at Southwark, London. Persecution, however, drove him to Ireland; and it says much for the acceptance with which he had ministered to his people, and for their attachment both to him and to principle, that they resolved to accompany him *en masse* in his exile. The men of those days were ready to submit to inconveniences and sacrifices for the sake of religion, with which, alas! these modern times are not so familiar. Hubbard is described by Blair as 'an able, gracious man.' He was not spared long to the infant Church, having died in the beginning of 1623; and when he was taken from them, his congregation quietly went back again to London. Shortly after his death we find James Glendinning ministering in Carrickfergus, and at the same time occupying the position of incumbent of the parish of Carnmoney. He was a man of considerable pulpit power, but eccentric, as will hereafter appear. In 1619, John Ridge became minister of Antrim. He, like Hubbard, was an Englishman who had been obliged to flee from his native country on account of Episcopal intolerance. Blair describes him as 'the judicious and gracious minister of Antrim.'

Robert Blair was, however, probably the ablest of this goodly band of early Presbyterian ministers. He had been a professor in Glasgow College, but his opposition to the Prelacy which was then being foisted alike on the Church and the universities,

---

[1] Livingstone's *Life*, p. 78. Edinburgh 1854. It is an interesting fact that the Rev. W. D. Killen, D.D., President and Professor of Ecclesiastical History in Assembly's College, Belfast, is a lineal descendant of Brice.

obliged him, too, to leave the kingdom. He came to Ireland in 1623, and became minister of Bangor, after carefully and candidly explaining beforehand that 'he could not submit to the use of the English liturgy nor Episcopal government.'[1] Blair was a man of eminent piety and scholarship, and a preacher of rare ability. He was particularly noted for his prayerfulness, often spending whole nights on his knees. James Hamilton, a nephew of Lord Claneboy, was another of these pioneers of Ulster Presbyterianism. In 1625 he became minister of Ballywalter, where he laboured with great assiduity. In 1615, Robert Cunningham was settled in Holywood. 'To my discerning,' says Livingstone, 'he was the one man who most resembled the meekness of Jesus Christ in all his carriage that ever I saw.'[2]

Josias Welsh, son of the celebrated John Welsh of Ayr, and grandson of John Knox, was settled first at Oldstone, and afterwards at Templepatrick. The country peopled called him 'The Cock of the Conscience,' from the extraordinary searching and awakening character of his preaching. Andrew Stewart, whom Livingstone describes as 'very straight in the cause of God,' settled in Donegore in 1627. George Dunbar, who had been minister of Ayr, and had been twice ejected for his resolute attachment to Presbyterianism, and was for a long time imprisoned at Blackness, officiated successively at Carrickfergus (after the removal of Glendinning), at Ballymena, and at Larne. Last to be mentioned, but far from least, was John Livingstone, who had been silenced in Scotland for his opposition to Prelacy. In 1630 he received a unanimous call from the parish of Killinchy, which he accepted, and here he proved himself one of the most faithful and notable of those early ministers.

These men may be called the fathers of the Irish Presbyterian Church, and they are fathers of whom any children may well

---

[1] Blair's *Life*. The celebrated Dr. Hugh Blair of Edinburgh, the author of the well-known *Lectures on Rhetoric*, was the great-grandson of Robert Blair.

[2] Livingstone's *Life*. Blair was born at Irvine in 1593.

be proud. They were all men of deep-seated principle. They had suffered and were ready to suffer again, rather than countenance a form of Church government of which in conscience they could not approve. They were men well fitted to have their names standing at the head of the clergy-roll of a Church which has always insisted on an educated ministry, being almost all graduates of one of the universities of the day, and more than one professors. Several of them had noble blood flowing in their veins, James Hamilton being a nephew of Lord Claneboy, Livingstone a great-grandson of Lord Livingstone, and Josias Welsh great-grandson of Lord Ochiltree. Above all, they were men of intense earnestness, burning with a love of souls, and largely baptized with the Holy Spirit. It is not remarkable that the labours of such pastors were so signally blessed.

CHAPTER VI.

BLESSING WITHIN, TROUBLE WITHOUT.

THROUGH a rich valley of the County Antrim runs the river Sixmilewater. Taking its rise in the mountains above the town of Larne, it flows through green meadows and fertile corn-fields, past Ballynure, and Ballyclare, and Templepatrick, finally falling into Lough Neagh at Antrim. This stream will long be associated in the ecclesiastical history of the North of Ireland with a remarkable religious awakening which took place in the country adjoining, shortly after the settlement of the early Presbyterian ministers. The history of this movement is not a little curious. Among the names which we have mentioned occurs that of the Rev. James Glendinning, minister at Carrickfergus. He was a good man, but evidently not possessed of very superior gifts, for Blair, who used sometimes to cross the Lough from Bangor, and thus became acquainted with him, advised him to leave Carrickfergus, then the leading town of the North of Ireland, and retire into a country charge, as better suited to his capacities. He took the advice and went to Oldstone, not far from Antrim. 'He was,' says a narrative of the period, 'a man who would never have been chosen by a wise assembly of ministers, nor sent to begin a reformation in this land, for he was little better than distracted, yea, afterwards, did actually distract. Yet this was the Lord's choice to begin the admirable work of God, which I mention on purpose, that all men may see how the glory is only the Lord's in making a holy nation in this profane land, and that it was "not by might, nor by power, nor by man's wisdom, but by my Spirit, says the Lord." . . . At Oldstone, God made use of him to awaken the consciences of a lewd and secure people thereabouts. . . . Seeing the great lewdness and ungodly sinfulness of the people, he preached to them nothing but law, wrath, and the terrors of God for sin. And in very deed for this only was he fitted, for hardly could he preach any other thing. But, behold the success! For the hearers, finding themselves condemned by the mouth of God speaking in His Word, fell into such anxiety and terror of conscience that they looked on themselves as altogether lost and damned, as those of old, who said, "Men and brethren, what shall we do to be saved?" And this work appeared not in one single person or two, but multitudes were brought to understand their way, and to cry out, "What shall we do?" I have seen them myself stricken and swoon with the Word; yea, a dozen in one day carried out of doors as dead, so marvellous was the power of God smiting their hearts for sin, condemning and killing. . . . And this spread through the country to admiration, so that, in a manner, as many as came to hear the Word of God went away slain with the words of His mouth. . . . For a short time this work lasted as a sort of disease for which there was no cure, the poor people lying under the spirit of bondage, and the poor man who was the instrument of it, not being sent, it seems, to preach gospel so much as law, they lay for a time in the most deplorable condition, slain for their sin, and knew of no remedy.'[1]

The neighbouring ministers, hearing of this movement, came to Mr. Glendinning's help. Some of them were as well fitted to heal as he was to wound. One method which they adopted for the needed instruction of the people and the carrying on of the work which had begun, was the establishment of what soon became a famous and much blessed institution, the Antrim Monthly Meeting. This was held on the first Friday in each month, and no doubt, to some extent, served in those times, before there was

[1] Stewart's *History of the Church of Ireland after the Scots were naturalized*. Killen's edition. Belfast 1866. Many readers will notice the curious correspondence of this movement in certain features with the Ulster revival of 1859.

any regular Presbytery, the purposes of a consultative Church court, as well as of a religious service. The ministers seem all to have attended. Glendinning himself came, until 'he was smitten with a number of erroneous and enthusiastic opinions, and embracing one error after another,' ended by setting out 'on a visit to the Seven Churches of Asia.' Ridge, the minister of Antrim, would be always present. Welsh, of Templepatrick, was also close at hand, and could conveniently attend. Dunbar came over from Larne, where a good work similar to that at Oldstone broke out and issued in much blessing. Blair crossed the Lough from Bangor, and Cunningham, Livingstone, and Hamilton came also over from County Down. Sir Hugh Clotworthy, the godly Presbyterian ancestor of the Massareene family, entertained all most hospitably in Antrim Castle. In summer they had four sermons, and in winter three, each day of meeting, and such was the general thirst for the Word, that crowds flocked to hear from all quarters. The movement was thus not only fostered, but spread, and resulted in the conversion of many, and in a general elevation of the standard of religion all over the country. It was, indeed, what a contemporary writer quaintly calls it,—'a bright and hot sun-blink of the gospel.'[1]

The sky was soon to be overcast, however. As is usually the case at any such time, sectaries, more anxious to bring grist to their own denominational mill than to promote the salvation of souls, gathered about the Sixmilewater. First came the Romanists. Two friars challenged the ministers to maintain their doctrines in a public discussion. There was no hesitation about accepting the invitation. Blair and Welsh stepped forward to take up the glove. But when the two champions of Presbyterianism appeared on the appointed day, lo! no friars were to be found, and though they waited long for them, still they came not. The preliminary conferences had shown their reverences what manner of men they had to deal with, and they thought it better to fly than to face a conflict in which they felt they would be defeated.

[1] Fleming's *Fulfilling of the Scripture*, i. 400.

They were doubtless right. Next came a body of 'Separatists' from London, who would not join in the meetings conducted by the ministers, but held little gatherings of their own and tried to draw away the people after them. It is curious how history repeats itself. The very same tactics, which were thus tried two hundred and fifty years ago, have often since perplexed Irish Presbyterian ministers working for the Master during times of awakening. The efforts of these men, however, were as unsuccessful as those of the friars. After them a propagator of Arminianism appeared on the scene, one Mr. Freeman. With great self-confidence he undertook to confute the whole body of the ministers on the tenets of Calvinism. Blair met him, however, in a public discussion with such effect that on the second day he fled in confusion, so evidently discomfited that the gentleman who had patronized him publicly renounced his fellowship in presence of the Meeting, after which, we learn, he was 'deserted of the people who formerly admired him, turned very solitary, and at last fell into mischievous practices.'[1]

But there was one form of opposition with which these faithful servants of God could not so easily cope. They were well able to defend the truth against all gainsayers. But against the strong arm of persecution they had no defence save God. The northern bishops now began to endeavour to put them down. They seem to have discovered that their Presbyterianism was too staunch and too deeply rooted to be easily won over to Episcopacy, as they had perhaps hoped at one time it might be. Echlin, bishop of Down, was the first to lay snares for them. He directed Blair to preach at one of the Primate's triennial Visitations, hoping to entangle him. He obeyed, and one cannot but admire the courage and the fidelity to principle which the brave minister displayed in the sermon which he prepared and preached on the occasion before assembled bishops and clergy. It was a strong Presbyterian discourse, which left it in no one's power to say that he taught in private what he was ashamed

[1] Adair's *Narrative*, p. 31.

publicly to avow or defend. Taking as his text 2 Cor. iv. 1, he showed that 'Christ our Lord had instituted no bishops but presbyters or ministers, and proved this first from the Holy Scriptures, next from the testimonies of the more pure among the ancient fathers and divines, and lastly, from the testimonies of the more moderate divines, both over sea and in England, not forgetting to rank the learned Dr. Ussher, their Primate, among the chief.'[1] It speaks well for the moderation of Ussher that no harm came to the brave preacher for this sermon. This and other plans for entangling the ministers having failed, Echlin determined to proceed to extremities in another way, and accordingly, in September 1631, he formally suspended Blair and Livingstone from the ministry. Ussher, however, on being appealed to, interposed, and Echlin was obliged to remove the suspension. Disappointed at this, the enemies of Presbyterianism carried the matter to London, where the intolerant Laud was now supreme in matters ecclesiastical, and through his influence orders were issued to Echlin by the Irish Government directing him to bring Blair, Livingstone, Welsh, and Dunbar to trial. Accordingly he summoned them before him, and on their refusal to give up their Presbyterianism and conform to Episcopacy, he deposed them all from the office of the ministry in 1632. Ussher was powerless in this case, the order for trial having come from the King. To the King, therefore, Blair determined to appeal. A journey from Bangor to London was a serious undertaking in those days, but he made up his mind to face it, rather than give up his beloved work of preaching Christ. So he set out, his people agreeing to spend two nights every week in united prayer for him during his absence. His appeal was so far successful that the King issued an order to Wentworth, then Lord Deputy of Ireland, to have the matter tried over again.

---

[1] Blair's *Life*. The reader will scarcely require to be reminded that modern Church of England divines, like Lightfoot and Hatch, have themselves abandoned as hopeless the attempt to found Prelacy on a Scriptural basis.

Encouraged by this, Blair returned to Bangor, and all four ministers recommenced their preaching; 'only,' says Blair, 'for form's sake I did not go up to the pulpit, but stood beside the precentor.' Wentworth did not come over to undertake the government of Ireland till July, 1633. No one who knows anything of the character of this haughty and bigoted man would expect that he would do much for the restoration of the deposed ministers. Blair waited on him in Dublin, but Wentworth said he knew the King's mind on the matter as well as Blair, and 'reviled the Church of Scotland, and upbraided me,' says Blair, 'bidding me come to my right wits, and then I should be regarded.' The outlook for the Presbyterians of Ulster was now dark in the extreme. With Charles I. in London and Laud at his ear, and the crafty and cruel Wentworth in Dublin Castle, there seemed little hope of their being able to enjoy their religion any longer in peace. So much was this felt, that they began to turn their eyes wistfully across the Atlantic in search of an asylum from their persecutors, where they could, without molestation,

'Worship God in simple form,
As Presbyterians do.'

Livingstone and another gentleman were accordingly commissioned to sail to America and select a place for a settlement. On this errand they proceeded to London, and thence to Plymouth. But one circumstance after another deterred them from fulfilling their mission, and they came back. It would have been a sad calamity, not only for Ulster, but for the whole kingdom, if Presbyterianism had been rooted out of Ireland in this way, and the bishops left in supreme power. God had 'some better thing' in store for us. The ministers and their people must brave the tempest. They must 'through much tribulation' enter the kingdom.

A slight lull in the storm now came. Wentworth had designs in the interest of his royal master for which he required the support of the entire kingdom, and therefore when, in May, 1634, Lord Castlestuart, an Irish Presbyterian nobleman, interceded for the restoration of the four deposed ministers, he yielded so far as to instruct Echlin to remove his sentence for six months. Echlin promptly obeyed the Viceroy's order, and reponed the four ministers for the stipulated period. The joy of their congregations was intense, and, as Blair tells us, 'the people made more progress in the ways of God than ever before.'[1] But their rejoicing was shortlived. Bramhall, bishop of Derry, remonstrated with Wentworth on the impropriety of his allowing Presbyterian ministers to preach in the kingdom, and in November their six months' freedom was taken from them, and so, writes Blair, 'all hopes of further liberty being cut off, we closed with celebrating the sacrament of the Lord's Supper, and solemnly delivered up our people to the great Bishop of Souls, from whom we had received our charge.'[2] The scene in Bangor at that last Communion must have been most affecting. Pastor and people were about to be severed, perhaps for ever. A tyrannical hand had closed the preacher's mouth. Welsh of Templepatrick, and Stewart of Donegore, were, happily for them, called away at this period from their troubles to their reward, the latter, on his deathbed, foreseeing the sorrows which were fast coming on the Church and his own loved parish, saying—'Woe to thee, Donegore, for the nettles and the long grass shall be in greater plenty in thee than ever were people to hear the Word of God!' Echlin, the weak but bigoted instrument in this suppression of the truth, soon after died also. His deathbed was miserable. When the doctor asked him what ailed him, 'he was long silent, and with great difficulty uttered the words—" It is my conscience, man;" to which the doctor answered, "I have no cure for that."'[3] It is not to be wondered at that it should have been said in the country that 'God did smite the bishop for suppressing of Christ's ministers.'

Echlin died in 1634, and was succeeded in the following year

[1] Blair's *Life*, p. 82.   [2] *Ibid.* p. 82.   [3] *Ibid.* p. 84.

by another Scotchman, Henry Leslie, who was scarcely consecrated till he too took up the role of persecutor. He first laid hands on Livingstone and deposed him from the ministry, so that all that he and Blair and the other brethren could do, was to go among their people by stealth to encourage them to hold fast. The 'bright and hot sun-blink of the gospel' was gone, and in its stead a dark, dreary night now settled down upon Ulster.

On Thursday, 11th August, 1636, a remarkable gathering was held in the old parish church of Belfast, which stood, surrounded by a graveyard, at the foot of High Street, on the site of the present St. George's. The building was filled with a large and deeply interested assemblage, comprising many of the nobility, gentry, and clergy of the town and neighbourhood. At two o'clock the Bishop of Down came in. He had preached a violent sermon the day before in support of Episcopacy, and now he had summoned five Presbyterian ministers before him to answer for their refusal to accept it. The scene, as described to us by histories of the period, reminds one of similar episodes in the life of Luther, when he was called before diets and other imposing assemblies for his Protestantism, or of the still earlier times, when apostles themselves were brought before councils and governors to answer for teaching and preaching in the name of Jesus. The five godly men, the venerable Brice, the pious Ridge, the Christ-like Cunningham, the prayerful Calvert, and the noble and learned Hamilton, are called forward to give an account of themselves. There is a lengthened conference, Hamilton at the request of his brethren acting as spokesman, and explaining respectfully but firmly why they cannot accept Episcopacy. The conference is too long in the opinion of the Bishop of Derry, who is present to assist his brother prelate in his godly work, and who at length persuades him to cut the proceedings short. The meeting is abruptly adjourned, to assemble again on the following day. At nine on that summer morning, as the sunlight streams into the old church, the bishops are once more in their seats, and once more the five brave, downtrodden servants of Christ are brought before them. All eyes look on with the deepest interest as, after more appeals on the part of Leslie, he calls upon them to hear their sentence—one of 'perpetual silence within this diocese.' As Cunningham heard it, he uttered the following memorable words in his own meek, gentle style : ' I have now lived these twenty years amongst you in this kingdom, serving the Lord in His holy ministry, and thought so to have spent the rest of my days, which cannot be very long, for my body is very crazed, in the same employment. My doctrine and life for that time are known to most who are here present. I appeal to all their consciences if they can say anything against me in either of them. Yea, I ever kept me close to the commission of my Lord. But now I am required to receive impositions upon my ministry which are against my conscience. I rather lay down my ministry at the feet of my Lord and Saviour Christ, of whom I did receive it, than to live with an evil conscience in the free liberty of it.' It is no wonder that as these brave and solemn words were uttered, the sounds of weeping and sobbing were heard all over the church. It was a scene at which angels might have wept. But the bishop would hear no more. Abruptly rising, he took his departure, and the five godly servants of Jesus passed out into the High Street of Belfast, grieving that they were to be permitted to preach no more the Gospel which they loved, but, who can doubt, also rejoicing that they were accounted worthy to suffer persecution for the name of their Lord ? The Presbyterian Church of Ireland has good reason to be proud of those men, and of the story of that day. One of the five did not long survive the sad scene. The venerable Brice went back to his congregation heartbroken that he was to be allowed no more to break among them the bread of life, and before the year was out he was dead.

The scene now shifts to the shore of Belfast Lough, beside where the little village of Groomsport, with its rock-bound harbour, and its beach of firm, yellow sand, looks across at the grim old castle of Carrickfergus. Here there might have been seen building in 1636 a small vessel, though larger than any required for the ordinary occupations of the inhabitants. The continued persecutions to which the Presbyterians were being subjected had forced upon their attention again the project of leaving Ireland altogether, and seeking in the New World a refuge from their oppressors, as Miles Standish and his companions had sought and found it some fifteen or sixteen years before. Accordingly, they set about constructing a ship of about 150 tons burden, to carry them across the Atlantic. It was a perilous venture. But what else could they do? A hundred and forty of them therefore made up their minds to face the dangers of the deep in this small craft, and all the dangers and uncertainties of a new and as yet unsettled land, rather than live any longer in a country which denied them peace. In hope of a speedy passage, they named the ship the *Eagle Wing*. At length she was completed and provisioned, and, when all was ready, on 9th September, 1636, the little company got on board, and, watched by many anxious and tearful eyes, the *Eagle Wing* weighed her anchor, rounded the Gobbins, and bore out for the open sea. Contrary winds ere long drove her into Loch Ryan; but at length she set sail once more, and by and by these new pilgrim fathers found themselves clear of Ireland, and steering due west for New England. A fair wind carried them a thousand or twelve hundred miles on their way. But then came fearful weather, which made sad havoc of the little *Eagle Wing*. Their rudder broke; their sails were torn by the furious gales; heavy seas came sweeping in over the round-house, and poured down into the cabin below. A leak was sprung which took hard work at the pumps to deal with, and at length the captain declared that it was impossible to face the storm any longer. The ship was put about. In miserable plight they headed back again for Ireland, and by the 3rd November, 1636, they were at anchor again in Carrickfergus Bay, gathering that it was not the Lord's will that they should go to America. For the failure of this second attempt at escape from their troubles, as of the previous project in the same direction, Ireland has reason to be profoundly thankful to Him who maketh the winds His messengers, and ruleth the raging of the sea. It would have been worse for the whole country, but especially for Ulster, had our fathers succeeded in their enterprise.

Blair, Livingstone, and several others of the silenced ministers, disappointed in their hope of reaching America, now sought refuge in Scotland; and having to their great joy got rid of the pastors, Wentworth and the bishops turned their persecutions upon the people. A commission was issued by the Lord Deputy, authorizing the Bishop of Down summarily to arrest and to imprison during pleasure the Presbyterians in his diocese. This nefarious document was not allowed to remain a dead letter. Numbers of peaceable people were committed to jail, like common felons, for the sole offence of being Presbyterians, and numbers more were forced to fly to Scotland. A Court of High Commission was set up in Dublin, which inflicted cruel hardships on the poor people. No sex, no rank, was spared. Mrs. Pont, a minister's wife, was thrown into prison at the instance of the Bishop of Raphoe, and kept there for almost three years. Lady Clotworthy was ordered to appear before the Court to answer for her Presbyterianism. Bramhall, bishop of Derry, committed a minister in his diocese to jail 'for his lewd praying for the success of Scotland in the maintenance of religion.' Sir Robert Adair, a zealous Presbyterian, ancestor of the well-known family on whose property Ballymena stands, was indicted for treason, his property confiscated, and he himself obliged to fly to Scotland. Certainly, if Presbyterianism was not entirely stamped out in Ulster at this period, it was not for want of the most strenuous and cruel efforts that the Episcopalians could make. Had our brave forefathers not been so wedded by conscience and affection to their pure, Scriptural faith, and firmly determined to hold by it at all costs, not a vestige of it would have been left in the land.

In their fury the dominant party now resolved upon the adoption of a new weapon, more illegal and more terrible than any which had yet been tried. This was an oath, popularly called the Black Oath, which all Presbyterians were to be obliged to take, or suffer 'the uttermost and most severe punishments which may be inflicted.' According to this oath they were required not only to swear allegiance to King Charles, but to swear also that they would never at any time oppose anything he might be pleased to command, and further, that they would renounce and abjure all covenants, such as the National Covenant, which had been the means of saving Presbyterianism in Scotland. All above the age of sixteen were to swear this 'upon the Holy Evangelists;' and that none might escape, the Episcopal ministers and churchwardens were required to make a return of all the Presbyterians resident in each parish, that every individual among them might be made amenable.

Great numbers of the people refused to take such an oath. They were quite prepared to swear allegiance to the King, notwithstanding all that they had suffered under him. But to promise that, no matter what he might command, they would never oppose him, and to renounce the covenants which had proved such safeguards and helps to the maintenance of true religion, they felt they dared not, and they determined to refuse, and abide the consequences. Those consequences Wentworth and his ready tools, the bishops, were not slow to visit on them to the very utmost. The details of the cruelties which they inflicted are not merely harrowing—they are sickening. One's blood begins to boil as one reads of them, and thinks that they were inflicted on our fathers for the sole crime of being Presbyterians. Respectable men were, on their refusal to perjure themselves by taking the Black Oath, bound together with chains and thrown into dismal dungeons. Pursuivants from Dublin travelled up and down Ulster, arresting and imprisoning. The most exorbitant penalties were inflicted. Mr. Henry Stewart, a gentleman of large property, his wife and two daughters, and a servant named James Gray, on refusing to take the oath, were arrested by a sergeant-at-arms, carried up to Dublin, and committed to jail. On 10th September, 1639, they were brought before the Star Chamber, 'a court in which the substance as well as the forms of law and justice were equally despised,'[1] and in which several of the bishops sat. They were all pronounced guilty of high treason. Mr. Stewart explained that he had no objection whatever to swear allegiance to the King, but as he conceived the latter part of the oath bound all who took it to yield him ecclesiastical obedience in regard to whatever he would be pleased to enjoin, he dared not in conscience enter into such an engagement. Wentworth assured him that he was perfectly right in his interpretation of the oath, that it *was* intended to bind the Presbyterians to conform to every doctrine and rite which were either then enjoined or might thereafter be enjoined, by royal authority, and that he would prosecute all who refused to take it 'to the blood,' and drive them 'root and branch' out of the kingdom. The sentence of the Court was then pronounced. Mr. Stewart was fined in £5000, Mrs. Stewart in £5000 more, their two daughters in £2000 each, and Gray, the servant, also in £2000, making £16,000 altogether. To crown all, they were to lie in jail in Dublin until the last farthing of these monstrous impositions should be paid!

But bad as all this was, it is as nothing when compared with other atrocities which were indulged in, to compel submission to this monstrous oath. Respectable women, far advanced in pregnancy, were forced to travel long distances to appear before the Commissioners. If they hesitated to attend, or refused to swear, they were treated in the most cruel manner, notwithstanding their condition. The woods in some parts of the country were thronged with crowds of defenceless females who had fled thither to escape the persecutors who had no mercy on either sex or age. In other places they sought refuge in mountain caves, while numbers fled from the country altogether, leaving their houses and farms to go to ruin. In his determination to extirpate Presbyterianism 'root and branch' out of the land, Wentworth even meditated a more daring measure

[1] Reid, i. 259.

than any yet adopted — no less than the banishment of every Presbyterian from Ulster. He actually drew up a plan for this purpose. Ships were to be provided at the public expense to carry the hated Presbyterians away, and, under severe penalties, every one of them was to be obliged to depart within a prescribed period. That such a villanous project should ever have been entertained may well astonish us. The fact that it was planned, and arrangements made for carrrying it out, shows the hatred with which the Lord Deputy and the bishops regarded the faith of our forefathers. Fortunately, not only for Presbyterianism but for Ireland, Wentworth's sun was now about to set. The eyes of the nation were opened to the folly of the course he had been too long allowed to pursue. The famous Long Parliament met. Wentworth, who had been created Earl of Strafford by Charles I., was impeached for his misdeeds. He was tried, found guilty, and beheaded on Tower Hill on the 12th of May, 1641, and so ignominiously ended the areer of this clever but unscrupulous and cruel man. It is no wonder that his memory holds among Irish Presbyterians that bad pre-eminence which Claverhouse and Dalzell gained for themselves in Scotland. It says much for the truth and vitality of Presbyterianism, that all the combined efforts of himself and his myrmidons could not destroy it out of the land, and it says much too for the fidelity and conscientiousness of Ulster-men, that his utmost cruelties could not make them swerve from their allegiance to their creed. The three arch-persecutors of the period, Charles I., Wentworth, and Laud, all lost their heads by the axe. Laud died by the hand of the public executioner in January, 1645, and Charles in January, 1649.

CHAPTER VII.

1641 AND ITS ISSUES.

SCARCELY had Ulster been delivered from the tyranny of Strafford when another fiery trial swept over her—the terrible rebellion of 1641. The objects of this outbreak were the extinction of British power in Ireland, the restoration of the forfeited estates to the descendants of their former owners, the utter extirpation of Protestantism, and the establishment of Romanism in its place. The rebellion broke out with all the suddenness and fury of a tornado on Saturday, 23rd October, 1641. Part of the programme was the seizure of Dublin Castle; but fortunately it was saved through the vigilance and energy of a Presbyterian elder, Captain Owen O'Connolly, who obtained private information of the intended attempt, and communicated it to the Lords Justices, in time to save the Castle and capital. The force of the insurrection spent itself on Ulster, and here the havoc which it wrought was appalling. No one was prepared for it, and the Protestants, being almost defenceless, were in many cases butchered like sheep. Led on by Sir Phelim O'Neill, the insurgents seized upon castle after castle, and town after town, frequently ruthlessly massacreing all the inhabitants. Dungannon, Newry, Monaghan, Dromore, and many other places were thus seized. Fortunately Enniskillen was secured by Sir William Cole, who also supplied information which saved Derry and Newton-limavady. Coleraine too received timely warning, and was not only saved, but proved a welcome haven of refuge to many terror-stricken Protestants. Carrickfergus, Lisburn, and

SICKENING ATROCITIES.

Belfast also remained untaken. But outside these places, Ulster became a veritable field of blood. Far and wide over the country the eye beheld towns and villages, the dwelling of the Protestant clergyman and the farmhouse of the Protestant husbandman, all in flames. Behind hedges and ditches droves of Protestants, stripped absolutely naked, crouched for shelter, the husband trying in vain to shield his trembling wife, and the mother her wretched children, from the fury of pitiless assassins, and the biting cold of one of the severest winters that could be remembered. The river Blackwater in Tyrone is said to have run red with the blood of murdered Protestants.

These atrocities do not depend upon hearsay. Thirty-two volumes of sworn depositions still exist in the library of Trinity College, Dublin, to attest the reality of the horrors of the awful time. It is sickening to read them, and the worst cannot be set down in print. We can tell of the infants whose brains were dashed out against walls before their helpless and horrified mothers' faces; of others who were flung into boiling pots, or tossed into ditches to the pigs; of poor Protestants whose eyes were gouged out of their heads, their hands cut off, or their ears, in fiendish savagery; of many who were actually buried alive; of women, first stripped naked, then ripped up with knives; of men from whose bodies the rebels cut slices of flesh, and then roasted their victims alive; of 300 Protestants, men, women, and children, at Loughgall, stripped naked and driven into the church, the doors locked, and fierce men, liker wolves or tigers than human beings, let loose upon them daily, to kill and outrage as they pleased; of women broiled on hot gridirons, and men 'hanged twice or thrice till half dead,' then let down and butchered; of 196 Protestants drowned at Portadown Bridge in one day, and 1000 said to have been killed there altogether in the same manner; of the special cruelties reserved for the Protestant ministers, to whom ordinary deaths were in many cases denied as too good; of some hanged, then dismembered and their heads cut off, and pieces of their own bodies thrust into their mouths in mockery; of thirty of them massacred in one district, of one hanged at his own church door, another thrown into Lough Neagh and drowned, and a third, the Rev. Thomas Murray of Killyleagh, who was actually crucified, in blasphemous mockery of the awful tragedy of Calvary, between two other Protestant gentlemen, his two sons killed, and actually cut to pieces before their mother's eyes, then her own body frightfully mutilated, and her tongue cut half out. One can tell these things, though it is a sickening tale. But worse remains, over which a veil must be thrown; things for which a parallel can only be found in the foul deeds which made Cawnpore and Lucknow infamous in the days of the Indian mutiny.[1] In addition to those actually killed, multitudes perished of cold and hunger in the fields, and of sickness brought on by the privations to which they were exposed. The numbers of dead bodies which lay unburied tainted the air. A pestilential fever broke out, of which multitudes died. In Coleraine 6000 persons are said to have fallen victims to it, so that the living, unable to give the dead proper burial, 'laid the carcases in great ranks, into vast and wide holes, laying them so close and thick as if they had packed up herrings together.'[2] Carrickfergus, Belfast, and Lisburn also suffered awfully from this plague. The estimates of the total numbers that perished, either directly by the hands of the rebels or by the diseases which followed, vary considerably, as we might expect. Some of the highest authorities assert that several hundreds of thousands lost their lives by the swords of the Romanists alone. It is certain that the carnage was appalling. What it would have been had that patriotic Presbyterian elder not saved Dublin Castle we can only guess. As it was, the country received a blow from which it took long to recover.

[1] Cf. *Ireland in the Seventeenth Century, or the Irish Massacres of 1641, their Causes and Results, Illustrated by Extracts from the Unpublished State Papers.* By M. Hickson. 2 vols. London 1884. Every effort has been made by Romish writers to disprove the terrible and most damaging revelations made in these volumes, but utterly in vain.

[2] Temple, *History of the Irish Rebellion*, p. 138.

The abominable and infamous cruelties of this rebellion lie as a terrible blot on the Romish Church. From the beginning it was a Romish rebellion. Sir Phelim O'Neill declared that 'he would never leave off the work he had begun till Mass should be sung or said in every church in Ireland, and that a Protestant should not live in Ireland, be he of what nation he would.'[1] The priests joined in planning it, and were among the foremost in urging it to the utmost extreme. 'At a meeting in the Abbey of Multifarnham, in Westmeath, held about a fortnight before the commencement of hostilities, some of the clergy present recommended a general massacre as the safest and most effectual method of putting down Protestant ascendancy. . . . Evor M'Mahon, Roman Catholic bishop of Down and Connor, prompted Sir Phelim O'Neill to the commission of some of his most revolting atrocities. The Roman Catholic clergy of all grades appear ever and anon upon the stage during the worst scenes of this dismal tragedy.'[2] A Romish bishop was the brain of the whole enterprise. The priests commonly anointed the rebels before sending them to their murderous work, assuring them that if they chanced to be killed they would escape purgatory and go immediately to heaven.[3] They told their people that 'the Protestants were worse than dogs, they were devils, and served the devil, and the killing of them was a meritorious act.'[4] The massacre of 1641 was really an Irish St. Bartholomew, only more terrible and inhuman, and it is no wonder that, though more than 200 years have passed since the scenes we have described, their memory has left behind in Ulster a dread, amounting almost to terror, of being ever again placed in the power of Rome.

It is not to be wondered at that the cold-blooded massacre of

---

[1] Lodge, v. 114.
[2] Killen, *Ecclesiastical History of Ireland*, ii. 40, 41.
[3] *A True and Credible Relation of the Massacre of the English Protestants in Ireland.* London, 1642.
[4] Froude, *The English in Ireland*, i. 108.

so many Protestants should have deeply incensed their co-religionists. They would not have been men if they had not been moved by the awful tales of fiendish cruelty perpetrated on their unoffending fellow-subjects, many of them women and children, which were flying through the country. On one occasion their natural resentment led some of them into a terrible reprisal. In January, 1642, Allister M'Donnell, with a band of blood-thirsty followers, had committed a series of outrages in the North. They had murdered a number of Protestants in their beds at Kilrea. They had waylaid and massacred seventy or eighty old men, women, and children on the public road near Ballintoy. It is not remarkable that the news of these butcheries aroused extreme anger, and that a number of men determined on showing the Romanists that they were engaged in a game at which two could play. On Sabbath, 9th January, 1642, they met in the little village of Ballycarry, and, being joined by some soldiers from the neighbouring garrison of Carrickfergus, proceeded to the peninsula of Island Magee close by and put to death some thirty or so of the Roman Catholic inhabitants. 'The island' has since been inhabited entirely by Protestants.[1]

Scotland, which had so often befriended Ireland, again came opportunely to her assistance at this hour of need. Ten thousand men were voted by her Parliament for the relief of the country. In February, 1642, Major-General Monro was sent over to Carrickfergus with the first contingent of these,—an event which proved of even greater importance in the ecclesiastical than it did in the civil history of the country. Carrickfergus was during all

[1] As an illustration of the strange shifts to which Romish writers have been driven in order to extenuate the atrocities perpetrated by their co-religionists, it is worthy of remark that some of them actually allege this outrage, committed in January, 1642, as the cause of the insurrection which broke out, as we have seen, in October, 1641! No one, however, who is familiar with Romish ways or Romish literature will be astonished at such delightful fidelity to historical accuracy. The story that 3000 Roman Catholics were driven by the Protestants over the cliffs at the Gobbins is another illustration of their talent for invention. It is a pure fabrication.

the spring of that year the scene of unwonted bustle. Ships were continually arriving in the harbour and disembarking regiment after regiment of Scottish soldiers, who made the streets alive as they marched to the old Castle to take up their quarters. Along with most of the regiments might be seen their chaplains, grave and godly Presbyterian ministers, sent with the men to look after their spiritual concerns, and it is to a number of these that we owe the first proper organization of the Presbyterian Church in Ireland.

When the army had made some progress in the pacification of the country, and had settled down in Carrickfergus, after effectually breaking the power of the rebels, these chaplains set about establishing a proper ecclesiastical discipline among the troops. First of all, they erected a Session in each regiment, composed of such officers as were most distinguished for piety. When four such Sessions had been constituted, they found themselves in a position to hold a meeting of the court next in order, and accordingly, on 10th June, 1642—a memorable day—the first regular Presbytery ever held in Ireland met. It was composed of five ministers and four ruling elders. The names of the ministers are worth preserving. They were the Rev. Hugh Cunningham, who remained in this country after the departure of his regiment, and settled at Ray, County Donegal; Rev. Thomas Peebles, who also stayed behind and became minister of the united parishes of Dundonald and Holywood; Rev. John Baird, who was subsequently installed in Dervock; Rev. John Scott and Rev. John Aird, both of whom seem to have afterwards returned to Scotland. All of these were regimental chaplains. Two others, the Rev. James Simpson and the celebrated Rev. John Livingstone, were absent on duty elsewhere. Mr. Baird preached on the occasion from Ps. li. 18,—'Do good in Thy good pleasure unto Zion; build Thou the walls of Jerusalem.' A moderator and clerk were appointed according to the customary presbyterial order, and various arrangements made for the further establishment of the Presbyterian cause. The

Presbytery resolved to meet, for a time at all events, weekly, each meeting to be opened with a sermon. Those nine men probably had little thought of what were to be the ultimate and far-reaching issues of their meeting on that June day. The grain of seed which they sowed has, indeed, grown into a great tree.

The Presbytery soon found ample work to do. Applications for ministers came in from the neighbouring parishes (for the recent rebellion had almost swept religion clean out of the land), 'upon which the Presbytery moved that there should be elderships erected with the consent of the congregations, and that by their help a present supply might be procured, and in due time ministers settled among them.'[1] This was accordingly soon after reported to have been done in Ballymena, Antrim, Cairncastle, Templepatrick, Carrickfergus, Larne, and Belfast,[2] in County Antrim, and in Ballywalter, Portaferry, Newtownards, Donaghadee, Killyleagh, Comber, Holywood, and Bangor, in Down. Petitions were sent to the General Assembly of the Church of Scotland asking for more ministers. There was no superabundance of pastors, however, in Scotland, and all that the Assembly therefore could do, was to commission six of its best ministers to go over temporarily to Ireland. Blair and Hamilton were the first of these brethren to arrive, and their counsel and labours did no little to encourage and build up the Church on a firm foundation. At several subsequent Assemblies, this course of sending over several ministers to preach in Ireland for three months each was followed. In this way and others the Church of Scotland proved herself a nursing mother to the infant organization. Several years of busy, quiet work followed. The havoc wrought by the rebellion had left the land almost desolate. But in a remarkably short time prosperity seemed to return to both Church and country. The people who had fled returned to their farms. The parish churches were soon filled

---

[1] Adair's *Narrative*.
[2] The date of the erection of the first Session in Belfast is July, 1644.

on Sabbaths with hearty and earnest congregations, who sang their psalms and offered their prayers in the simple Presbyterian fashion, and to whom godly Presbyterian ministers preached sermons full of Christ. 'So the Church . . . had peace, being edified, and walking in the fear of the Lord and in the comfort of the Holy Ghost was multiplied.'[1]

[1] Acts ix. 31, R.V.

CHAPTER VIII.

THE TIMES OF THE COMMONWEALTH.

WHILE the events of which we have spoken in the previous chapter were transpiring, affairs in England had taken a strange turn. Charles I. had come to an open rupture with the Parliament, and hostilities had broken out, which, before they ended, were to stain English soil with some of the best English blood. One of the first things which the Long Parliament, as it afterwards came to be called, determined to do, was to overthrow the power of the bishops and to establish some more Scriptural and popular form of Church government. One plan for effecting this end deserves to be noticed here, both on account of its own historic interest, and because its author was that distinguished Irishman whom we have already on several occasions had occasion to mention, the godly and learned Archbishop Ussher. He proposed to unite Presbyterians and Episcopalians on the basis of the following four propositions:—
1. The incumbent with the churchwardens and sidesmen to exercise discipline in each parish, to present refractory offenders to the next Monthly Synod, and in the meantime to debar them from the Lord's Table. 2. Monthly Synods to be held of all the incumbents within certain districts corresponding to the rural deaneries; in these a suffragan or rural dean to preside; the majority to decide and to be empowered to censure errors of doctrine appearing within their districts, with liberty to appeal to the Diocesan Synod. 3. Diocesan Synods to be held once or twice in the year, consisting of all the suffragans in the diocese, with a select number of the incumbents out of each rural

deanery, the bishop or superintendent, 'call him whether you will,' to be moderator, and the majority to decide. 4. The Provincial Synod to consist of all the bishops and suffragans, with representatives chosen by the clergy of each diocese within the province, the primate to be moderator, and both the primates and Provincial Synods to constitute a National Council to meet every third year, wherein all appeals from inferior synods might be received, all their acts examined, and all ecclesiastical constitutions which concern the state of the Church of the whole nation established.[1] Different minds will take different views of this attempt at union. But none can fail to admire and appreciate the motives which suggested its conception, or to wish that some feasible plan could have been formulated long since for the union of the *disjecta membra* of British Protestantism. The Parliament, however, was not just then in the mood for compromises. It had had enough of Prelacy. First, the bishops were deprived of their seats in the Legislature; next, a manifesto, agreed to by both Lords and Commons, declared that Church government by archbishops, bishops, etc., 'is evil, and justly offensive, and burdensome to the kingdom, a great impediment to reformation, and very prejudicial to the civil government, and that we are resolved the same shall be taken away.' Making good their words by deeds, both Houses next passed a bill 'for the utter abolishing and taking away of Prelacy.' This was in January, 1643. In June of the same year they issued an ordinance summoning the celebrated 'Westminster Assembly of Divines' to consult as to the 'settling such a government in the Church as may be agreeable to God's Holy Word, and to bring it into nearer agreement with the Church of Scotland and other reformed Churches abroad.' Of this Assembly this is not the place to speak at length. It is worthy of notice, however, that it was the most really Catholic council which the world ever saw. Episcopalians,[2] Presbyterians, and Independents

---

[1] Abridged by Reid, i. 400.

[2] 'The Assembly was designed to include among its members adherents of

sat side by side in that Jerusalem Chamber at Westminster Abbey, which has been the scene of so many memorable meetings. England, Scotland, and Ireland were all represented in it. It had both clerical members and lay assessors, among them some of the most learned men of the day,—men whose names have become famous in history. The Presbyterian Churches, therefore, which hold by the Westminster Confession of Faith and the Shorter and Larger Catechisms, enjoy the singular distinction of having as their standards symbols formulated not by a Presbyterian Assembly, but by divines of all the Protestant Churches.[1] The Directory of Public Worship, drawn up by this body, was established in England in 1645, and the use of the Book of Common Prayer abolished throughout the country, Church government by Sessions, Presbyteries, and General Assemblies being ordained.

Another important event in the history of this period was the passing of the celebrated 'Solemn League and Covenant,' which was agreed upon between England and Scotland in 1643. This covenant pledged all who signed it to six heads. 1. 'The preservation of the Reformed religion in the Church of Scotland;' 'the reformation of religion in the kingdoms of England and Ireland, in doctrine, worship, discipline, and government, according to the Word of God and the example of the best Reformed Churches;' and the bringing of the three kingdoms to 'the nearest conjunction and uniformity in religion, Confession of Faith, form of church government, Directory for Worship, and catechizing.' 2. 'The extirpation of Popery, Prelacy,' and 'whatsoever shall be found to be contrary to sound doctrine and the power of godliness.' 3. The preservation of 'the rights and privileges of the Parliaments, and the liberties of the

all the chief parties among English Protestants, with the exception of that of Archbishop Laud. . . . Almost all the clerical members named upon it were in Episcopalian orders.'—Mitchell's *Westminster Assembly*, 116.

[1] No wonder Her Excellency, the Countess of Aberdeen, said in distributing prizes to the Sabbath-school scholars of the Dublin Presbytery on a recent occasion—' We are all proud of our Catechism.'

kingdoms,' and the preservation and defence of 'the King's Majesty's person and authority, and the preservation and defence of the true religion and liberties of the kingdoms.' 4. The 'discovery of such as have been or shall be incendiaries, malignants, or evil instruments, by hindering the reformation of religion, dividing the King from his people, or one of the kingdoms from the other.' 5. The maintenance of peace between the kingdoms. 6. The assistance and defence of all who should enter into the League and Covenant. This instrument was immediately sent over to Ireland, and not a little of the persecution of after years was suffered for the taking of it. Ministers came from Scotland in April 1644 to administer it over all Ulster, and during the next few months gatherings of the people were being held to hear it read, and to subscribe it. In that time of danger and uncertainty, both to Church and State, men felt the need of some means of banding themselves together in support of their liberties and their faith, and so 'the Covenant was taken in all places with great affection.'[1] Remarkable scenes were witnessed at the taking of it. From Carrrickfergus the ministers charged with its administration went to Belfast, Comber, Newtownards, Bangor, and then to Ballymena, Coleraine, Derry, Letterkenny, Ray, and Enniskillen. In the light of the narratives of the period we seem to see them riding briskly along from place to place, with a guard of cavalry escorting them, preaching to large and deeply interested audiences, now in the parish church, now in the street, explaining the Covenant, and calling on the people to take it with uplifted hands. Their mission accomplished the desired results. The Covenant 'ascertained and united the friends of civil and religious liberty, and inspired them with fresh confidence in the arduous struggle in which they were engaged. It diffused extensively through the province a strong feeling of attachment to the Presbyterian cause. It opened the way for the introduction of the Presbyterian Church into districts where it had been previously opposed, and facilitated its

[1] Adair's *Narrative*, 103.

re-establishment in places where it had been violently overthrown. But what was of still higher moment, the Covenant revived the cause of true religion and piety, which had lamentably declined under the iron sway of the prelates and amidst the distractions and discouragements of intestine war. From this period may be dated the commencement of the second Reformation with which this province has been favoured—a reformation discernible not only in the rapid increase of churches and of faithful and zealous ministers, but still more unequivocally manifested in the improving manners and habits of society, and in the growing attention of the people to religious duties and ordinances.'[1]

In October, 1645, the Parliament, now supreme in England, sent over three 'governors of the province of Ulster' to take charge of affairs in the North of Ireland. These gentlemen recognised the Presbytery, sat in it, and encouraged and countenanced its proceedings. The commander of the forces usually sat with them, as did others of the officers. The parochial tithes were given to the ministers, who were thus fully recognised again as the State Church. They had much to do at this time. They were few in number, and there were many places asking for religious ordinances. But by dint of careful and energetic organization and unsparing labour, they managed to meet all the demands made upon them, establishing Sessions in the several parishes, supplying them with preaching, and fostering them as far as in their power. The Church gradually grew in strength, until in the beginning of 1647 there were nearly thirty ordained ministers permanently settled in Ulster, in addition to the chaplains of the Scottish regiments, which still garrisoned the province.

[1] Reid, i. 456. Readers of Burns's poetry will remember his spirited lines, as true as they are spirited—

'The Solemn League and Covenant
   Cost Scotland blood, cost Scotland tears;
But it sealed Freedom's sacred cause;
   If thou'rt a slave, indulge thy sneers.'

The unhappy Charles, after several battles, was seized by the Parliamentary army, who demanded that he should be brought to justice as the 'capital cause' of all the evils which had befallen the kingdom. The Presbyterians both in Ireland and England were entirely opposed to the violent course into which events now shaped themselves. In the House of Commons the Presbyterian members condemned the seizure of the King as unconstitutional. After a sitting which lasted a long winter night, till five o'clock next morning, a resolution was carried, by a majority of 46 in a House of over 200 members, to the effect that negotiations should be continued between the Parliament and the King. But this was not to be. The day after, a detachment of soldiers, horse and foot, is placed in Palace Yard and Westminster Hall. In the colonel's hand is a list of members, who, as they come in, are seized and carried off. Forty-one are so treated this day. Next day many more are arrested, sent to the Tower or anywhere out of the way.[1] Thus took place the famous 'Pride's Purge.' What remained of the Parliament, (historically known as the Rump), now cleared of that intelligent and staunch Presbyterian element, which has always been troublesome to tyrants on the one hand and to mobs on the other, continued to sit and act as if it had been a fully and legally constituted legislative chamber. Charles was now arraigned, tried, and found guilty, and on 30th January, 1649, beheaded at Whitehall. The Presbyterians of Ireland joined with their co-religionists in England in condemning and protesting against this act. They did not hesitate to denounce it in plain terms as a murder. They had no belief, indeed, in the absurd doctrine of the divine right of kings, nor in the equally absurd principle of passive obedience. Episcopalian bishops might preach that the execution of Charles was a more criminal act than the crucifixion of Jesus Christ![2] The

---

[1] Carlyle's *Cromwell*, i. 99.
[2] See *The Martyrdom of King Charles; or, his Conformity with Christ in his Sufferings*, a sermon by Henry Leslie, bishop of Down and Connor, preached in June, 1649.

Presbyterians talked no such impious nonsense. They protested against the deed, 'not upon the ground of the servile figment that a king is above law and not amenable to justice; ... but when the nation, by its legal governors and representatives, the Lords and Commons in Parliament assembled, had freed itself from the yoke of despotism attempted to be imposed upon it, and was able to dictate satisfactory terms of peace and ensure their observance, they conceived it to be a monstrous violation of all liberty and law, and a more arbitrary and dangerous exercise of power than any which could be laid to the charge of the King, for an armed force to expel with violence out of the House of Commons the majority of its members,—to abolish the House of Lords by the mere right of the sword,—and then to execute the King and wholly alter the frame of the Government, in opposition to the overwhelming majority of the nation, who beheld with amazement, but were unable to resist, these tyrannical acts of a military usurpation.'[1]

The Presbytery which met at Belfast on 15th February, 1649, drew up a 'Representation,' which they ordered to be read from every pulpit, in which they condemned the execution of the King in the strongest terms. The ability of this document, and the importance attached to it, may be inferred from the fact that no less a personage than John Milton was commissioned by the Council of State to answer it. He did so in a paper in which, with a strange ferocity and scurrility, which sit ill on the author of *Paradise Lost*, he denounces the 'devilish malice, impudence, and falsehood' of the remonstrance sent up from Belfast, which he calls 'a barbarous nook of Ireland.' But the Presbytery, with a loyalty to the principles of constitutional government, which was all the more admirable because it was so disinterested (they had received no favours from Charles, and were running the risk of suffering under the hands of the Parliament by opposing their proceedings), continued to protest against the conduct of the party whom they denounced as usurpers.

[1] Reid, ii. 87.

It is not surprising, therefore, that the Parliamentarians, who soon became all-powerful, treated them with scant favour.

Oliver Cromwell by and by appeared upon the scene. On 15th August, 1649, he landed at Dublin, and in one short but tremendously vigorous campaign, the memory of the severities of which still lingers in the traditions of the country, he put down the Royalist and rebel forces, descending upon them like the hammer of Thor. Drogheda, or Tredah as it was then called, was taken by storm.[1] Dundalk was speedily occupied. Newry surrendered to Colonel Venables. Belfast followed suit after a three days' siege. Carrickfergus held out longer, but was finally also taken. In the end the power of the Royalists and the confederate Irish was completely broken, and Cromwell, who after the victory of Worcester, when Charles II. fled from the kingdom to the Continent, was left complete master of the situation, in the enjoyment of almost unbounded power and popularity, expelled the Parliament, dispersed the Council of State, and finally was proclaimed Lord Protector, becoming undisputed master of both England and Ireland.

The known sympathy of the Irish Presbyterians with the royal cause, and their disapproval of the measures adopted by the Parliamentary party, exposed them now to serious trouble. An oath, called 'The Engagement,' binding all who took it to 'renounce the pretended title of Charles Stuart and the whole line of the late King Charles, and every other person as a single person pretending to the government,' and binding them also to be true and faithful to the Commonwealth against any king or other person, was ordered to be taken. The Irish Presbyterian ministers refused to take it, being conscientiously persuaded that Charles II. was lawful king, and his father's execution a murder. Whatever our opinion of their rightness or wrongness,

---

[1] Romish writers speak of the severities inflicted on the garrison of Drogheda as specimens of the ill-treatment which the Irish have always received from the English. The fact is that the garrison consisted in good part of Englishmen. See Ludlow's *Memoirs*, i. 301, and Carlyle's *Cromwell*, ii. 163.

we cannot but admire the firmness with which these plain, sober men took their stand upon principle, and prepared themselves to bear the consequences.

These consequences were in many cases very severe. The ministers were summoned before the governors—soldiers were sent to their churches to overawe them—they had their houses surrounded by dragoons, and were arrested and thrown into jail. Some fled to the woods, or hid themselves in other places where they could find concealment, or escaped to Scotland—anything but do what in conscience they felt to be wrong. In the end they were ordered to leave the kingdom. It was a trying time. Only six or seven of them dared to remain in Ireland, and these disguised as farmers or peasants. Sometimes a congregation would be seen, or the sound of their voices heard, as they sang their psalms, and listened to some outed minister, in a field or secluded mountain glen, by the light of the stars or the moon. Baptist and Independent ministers were brought over by the Government from England to occupy the various pulpits. Finally, unable altogether to silence the Presbyterian clergy, and angry at the influence which they exercised over their people, a plan was devised which it was hoped would effectually rid Ulster of them. This was no less than to banish all the leading Presbyterians of Antrim and Down, ministers and people alike, to Munster. A proclamation was issued, containing a list of them, and ordering them within a specified time, and under severe penalties, to remove to the counties of Kilkenny, Tipperary, and Waterford.[1] Fortunately for Ulster this atrocious project miscarried. Had it succeeded, the history of part of Munster might have been different from what unfortunately it has been. But the development of the North of Ireland, which owes so much to the Presbyterians, would have been brought to a stand, and its history altogether altered. Once more, however, Providence interposed, as He had done several times before, to prevent their being rooted out of the country.

[1] This list can be seen in Reid, ii. 552.

Cromwell, when he felt the reins of power securely in his hands, changed the order of things in Ireland. He saw that the Presbyterians, though they and he did not agree on many points, were peaceable, well-disposed people, not likely to give him much trouble. So the persecutions ceased, and not only ceased, but all their ministers who applied for it were granted a State endowment, and this without any conditions being imposed, or any limitations put upon them in the exercise of their ministry. This endowment was not, if possible, to be below a hundred pounds per annum, which Reid reckons to have been equivalent to £1000 a year now.[1] Thus encouraged, the Presbyterian Church recovered its strength. Its one Presbytery increased to five. Parts of the country which had hitherto been unoccupied were taken in charge. Congregations multiplied, and ministers increased in numbers until there were soon some eighty congregations and seventy pastors, all under the government of a General Synod, which was now established, and which met for deliberation four times every year. These were halcyon days for our forefathers.

But Oliver Cromwell died in 1658, on what he considered his 'lucky day,' the 3rd September. After a short period, during which his eldest son, Richard, tried to succeed him in the protectorate, and succeeded only in affording another illustration of the truth that genius is not necessarily hereditary, the eyes of the nation turned again to the son of the late King.

[1] Dr. Killen thinks this estimate much too high.

CHAPTER IX.

UNDER CHARLES II.

IN the negotiations which were opened with the exiled son of Charles I., with a view to his being called to the throne, Irish Presbyterians took a conspicuous part, for they conscientiously regarded him as the rightful sovereign. A Convention was called meanwhile in Dublin to settle affairs, which chose the Rev. Samuel Cox, a Dublin Presbyterian minister, to be its chaplain. The Presbyterian clergy were now permitted to receive formal induction into the parish churches, and were allowed once more the tithes of each parish for their support, as they had been long ago, while the Baptists were degraded and deprived of their salaries. But this change was not to last long. Charles came to the throne amid general rejoicing. But his professions of regard for Presbyterianism were soon forgotten. Prelacy was re-established. Bishops were appointed to the Irish dioceses, among the rest Jeremy Taylor to that of Down and Connor, and the poor Presbyterians who had suffered so much for the King, and taken the lead in bringing him to his father's throne, now, as the Duke of Ormond truly expressed it, had to suffer under him, and that with no small severity. Meetings of Presbytery were prohibited. Troops of cavalry were sent to scatter them where any attempt to hold them was heard of. The streets of Ballymena rang with the clatter of dragoons sent to break up a meeting of Synod. Moreover, the Presbyterian clergy must either submit to the Prayer-Book and swallow Prelacy, or be turned houseless and homeless on the world. Jeremy Taylor specially distinguished himself in this persecution. The author of a book on *The Liberty of*

Prophesying, he displayed his love of the liberty he had written about by harassing his Presbyterian brethren to the utmost, and making life a burden to them; for it need hardly be said they refused to buy their liberty at the cost of principle. Taylor had no mercy. In a single day he declared thirty-six of their churches vacant. Curates were sent to take their places; and if any attempted to go to their loved pulpits, violent hands were laid upon them, and they were pulled down. Other prelates followed suit. The ministers were not only ejected from their parishes, but deposed from the ministry, and forbidden under heavy penalties to preach. Presbyterians may remember with some pardonable pride, and with deep thankfulness to God, that of all the clergymen who at that time constituted the Synod, only seven purchased immunity from persecution by giving up their principles. Sixty-one calmly made their choice to suffer rather than sacrifice the truth. In the persecution for conscience' sake which now swept over the three kingdoms, Irish Presbyterianism led the van. These sixty-one ministers were ejected from their benefices in 1661, whereas the similar ejections in England and Scotland did not take place till the following year. So they bade adieu to the pulpits and the churches where they had so long broken the bread of life,—sorrowfully closed their manse doors behind them, and with wives and children 'went out not knowing whither they went,'—and were henceforth in their poverty and distress watched as if they had been so many thieves lest they should say a word for Christ.[1]

Many of the congregations of the present day can boast of having had their ministers in this glorious ejection for conscience'

[1] These ejections were not in all cases effected without opposition. The spirit of Janet Geddes extended to Ireland. At Comber, where the minister was ejected and an Episcopal successor appointed, a number of women pulled him from the pulpit and tore his surplice to ribbons. One of them, when tried for the offence at next Downpatrick Assizes, confessed what she had done without much apparent compunction, saying, 'These are the hands that pu'd the white sark ower his heid.' M'Creery's *Presbyterian Ministers of Killyleagh*, 142.

sake—among the rest Bangor, and Newtownards, and Portaferry, and Comber, and Castlereagh, and Killinchy, and Saintfield, and Dromore, and Rathfriland, and Magherally, in Down; and Belfast, and Carnmoney, and Ballycarry, and Larne, and Donegore, and Connor, and Ballymena, and Broughshane, and Ballymoney, in Antrim; and Dungannon, and Minterburn, and Brigh, in the then Presbytery of Tyrone; and Strabane, and Glendermot, and Letterkenny, and Omagh, and Ballykelly, and Aghadoey, and Raphoe, and Ray, and Ramelton, in Route and Lagan. It was not the first time nor the last time at which Irish Presbyterian ministers have shown their readiness to make sacrifices for the cause of God and truth. We may well thank God to-day that they faced their trials and scorned the temptations of worldly preferment and aggrandizement which were freely held out to them, preferring to 'suffer affliction with the people of God' rather than barter conscience and truth for gain and worldly ease. Had they not stood firm, where would be the Presbyterianism of Ireland to-day? And what would its Protestantism be like?

An untoward event which now occurred threatened to bring the Presbyterians into further trouble. In December, 1662, a serious conspiracy against the Government was formed in Dublin. The plot seems to have had its origin among some of the old Irish Cromwellians. Their leader was one Thomas Blood, who had been an officer in the army, and was brother-in-law to the Rev. Mr. Lecky, a Presbyterian minister in Dublin. These two, after long consultation, resolved to endeavour to get the powerful assistance of the Presbyterians, and with this purpose they came to the North. They made but little way with them, however. Ulster Presbyterians are not of a rebellious turn. They have borne patiently where men of another disposition would have risen in arms. But the fact of their having been approached by Blood and Lecky was sufficient in those perilous times to throw suspicion on them, even though only one or two of their number gave any heed to the overtures with which they were plied. As usual in Irish conspiracies, there was an informer among Blood's associates, who kept the Government fully posted up in all their proceedings, and on the 22nd May, 1663, the day on which they had arranged to attack Dublin Castle and seize the Lord-Lieutenant, several of the leaders were arrested and thrown into prison. Blood made his escape. The papers which were discovered showed that there had been correspondence with some of the Presbyterian ministers, and several of them were arrested and imprisoned. Seven were shut up in Carlingford Castle, where they suffered much privation. Others were imprisoned elsewhere. Ultimately, many of them were obliged to go to Scotland—all on account of 'a plot which they knew nothing of.'[1] By and by, however, they went quietly back to their old parishes, one by one, and resumed their pastoral work among their people.

In some places, however, the bishops took up again the scourge of persecution. Thus Bishop Leslie of Raphoe first excommunicated and then imprisoned four Presbyterian ministers, the Revs. John Hart of Taughboyne, Thomas Drummond of Ramelton, William Semple of Letterkenny, and Adam White of Fannet. It may seem astonishing to this age, but it is nevertheless true, that for six years these men were kept in confinement at Lifford on his warrant, for the solitary crime of being Presbyterian ministers! In like manner, the Rev. Thomas Kennedy of Carland was imprisoned in Dungannon by the Primate for nonconformity.[2]

[1] Adair's *Narrative*, 281.
[2] A curious story is told in connection with his imprisonment. His faithful wife daily visited the jail, and, being forbidden permission to see him, left food and other supplies for his use in charge of the jailer. It comforted her greatly to think that, though deprived of his liberty, he was kept so well supplied. On his release, however, she discovered that the perfidious jailer, in addition to treating his prisoner with great harshness, had appropriated all her presents to himself. Years passed, and one day a wretched beggar came to the minister's door. What was Mrs. Kennedy's astonishment when she recognised in him her husband's cruel and faithless jailer! He, too, recognised the woman he had wronged, and quailed before her, not knowing what revenge for his conduct she would take, now that she had him in her power. She left him and ran upstairs, he not knowing what was about to happen, and trembling as he saw her reappear with some-

But, notwithstanding these persecutions, the Church throve. The ministers were shut out from their pulpits. But many a friendly farmer gladly gave his barn; and where there was no roof to shelter them, was there not the open field to stand in, and the blue sky to cover them? They had some solemn gatherings at this trying period. At times they ventured in defiance of the bishops to observe the Lord's Supper together. With fear and trembling, the poor persecuted people gathered from farm-house and cottage under the shelter of night to the appointed rendezvous, and, with sentinels warily posted to tell them of the approach of the enemy, they broke the Bread and drank of the Cup which told them of the Saviour whom they loved.[1] Gradually gathering courage, they began about the year 1668 to build humble places of worship. The rude plainness of many of the older Presbyterian churches of Ireland, and the obscure backward sites which they occupy, are easily accounted for when we remember the untoward circumstances of the times. It was not that our forefathers were lacking in taste, or had any love for ugliness or meanness. But necessity was laid upon them, and they could only do the best that was in their power.

There were several reasons why they were allowed now to raise their heads again for a little. It had been found that the suspicions of their loyalty were quite unfounded. Hence, though the bishops were as anxious as ever to annoy them, the Government grew less and less willing to assist these worthies in their persecuting work. Thus Boyle, who succeeded Jeremy Taylor as bishop of Down in 1667, summoned twelve Presbyterian ministers to appear before him to answer for their nonconformity. It was his intention to excommunicate them, and likely to proceed to still severer measures, such as his brother

thing in her hand. It was a large dishful of meal which she poured into the beggar's wallet, quietly saying, 'This is my way of revenge.' (*Vide* Witherow's *Presbyterian Memorials*, i. 281.) Carland had at least one woman in it in those days who knew the way to heap coals of fire on an enemy's head.

[1] By an Act passed in 1665, any Presbyterian minister who administered the Lord's Supper was liable to a penalty of £100.

prelates had frequently adopted. But the threatened ministers found a friend in their straits, as on many other occasions, in Sir Arthur Forbes, the ancestor of the Granard family. Through his representations in high quarters the persecution fell through, and other persecutions which Boyle had intended, in case this succeeded, were prevented. God had His hand over His suffering servants, and did not suffer them to be tried 'above that they were able.' The feeling towards them may be judged, however, from the following incident:—A fine new theatre had recently been erected in Smock Alley, Dublin, a building 'unto which,' says Adair's *Narrative,* 'the bishops contributed largely.' It was thought that the Dubliners would be vastly entertained in the Christmas holidays if a play were put on the boards ridiculing the Presbyterians. So, on 26th December 1670, a great audience assembled to see the drama of *The Nonconformist* acted. A poor minister is represented,—a humble man who dares to keep a conscience,—and uproarious is the fun among the audience as he is held up to scorn, and at last brought to the stocks. It was quite a piece that the right reverend bishops, who had contributed so freely to the erection of the theatre, and the clergy under their supervision, who sat among the ladies and gentlemen of the audience, would be sure to appreciate and enjoy. The lesson of it they would hope would be learned all over the country. But, lo! just as the merriment is at its height, a great crash echoes through the building. The topmost gallery, crowded with spectators, has fallen. Its weight coming on the gallery underneath, brings it also to the ground, and there, amid broken beams and choking dust, the lords and ladies and fine gentlemen and clergy, who had come to mock at their Presbyterian brethren, are mixed up in one horrid undistinguishable mass of destruction. A fearful scene ensued. In the end, corpse after corpse was dragged out of those terrible ruins, and not a few who escaped with life bore to the grave the marks of that unfortunate day when they held up to mockery the Presbyterian ministers.

It is not a little remarkable that the endowment which afterwards became so well known under the name of the 'Regium Donum' dates from the troublous days of which we now speak, and was first granted by a man apparently so unlikely to favour Presbyterianism, or any kind of earnest religion, as Charles II. Its bestowal was due in no small measure to that staunch friend of the Church, Sir Arthur Forbes. Being in London in 1672, he had a conference with the King; one result of which was a grant of £1200 per annum. When the state of the treasury came to be exactly ascertained, it was found that only £600 were available, and the grant was accordingly made at that amount.[1] This was the origin of the endowment which the Irish Presbyterian Church enjoyed from this time onward, with the exception of some intervals, until the passing of the 'Irish Church Act' in 1869.

About this period the Irish Presbyterian Church had the advantage for a time of the presence and ministry of the celebrated John Howe, whose *Living Temple* and *Blessedness of the Righteous* are among our noblest Christian classics. He came to Ireland in 1671 as chaplain to Lord Massareene, and for five years he lived with him at Antrim Castle. We picture him to ourselves wandering along the shores of Lough Neagh, and through the bosky woods from which one of the mysterious round towers still rises above the trees, as when he lived close by. While here he sat with the Presbytery, and regularly preached weekly in the parish church by special favour. One of his best books, that on *Delighting in God*, was published during his residence at Antrim. With the sanction of the Presbyterian Church he also taught in what may be called the Presbyterian College of the period. For, in conjunction with the Rev. Thomas Gowan, minister of Antrim, he instructed students at that place in theology and philosophy,—doubtless a most valuable service at a time when there was no other means in Ireland of training candidates for the Presbyterian ministry than such a 'school of philosophy.'

[1] Kirkpatrick's *Presbyterian Loyalty*, 384.

Persecution still blazed out, however, at fitful intervals against the little flock. The people were bound by law to attend the Episcopal Church, and the records of the period tell us of multitudes of them summoned before the bishops' courts for their non-attendance, and subjected to such heavy fines as entirely to exhaust their means. Spies watched ministers and people, ever ready to give information of their proceedings. About the year 1684 we find the little liberty which the bishops had been forced to give to them withdrawn, their churches forcibly closed, and their preaching again prohibited. For two years they had to worship once more in barns and secluded glens, and all who were faithful to conscience were oppressed with ruinous and repeated fines for the crime of not using the Prayer-Book. Very strange it seems to us, that a Church whose clergy had been endowed by the King, in token of his appreciation of their sufferings and services, should be so treated. But in the confusion of the times so it was.

An event, little noticed at the time, occurred now, which was destined to bear splendid fruit in after days. The largest, and in many respects the most powerful Presbyterian Churches in the world, are those of the United States of America. They number in all at the present day nearly 14,000 congregations.[1] The Irish Presbyterian Church has the high honour of having given them the founder of their first Presbytery. The name of the Rev. Francis Makemie deserves to be held in constant remembrance for this service, by which, as the Church of Scotland became the mother of the Irish Presbyterian Church in the beginning of the seventeenth century, the Irish Presbyterian Church, in her turn, when the course of empire westward took its way, became in some sort the mother of the Church of the United States. Makemie was a Donegal man, having been born in the neighbourhood of Ramelton. He was licensed by the Lagan Presbytery in 1681, and appears to have proceeded to America shortly after. He settled in eastern Virginia, where he died in 1708. If he

[1] *Proceedings of Third General Council.* Appendix, p. 30.

hoped by emigrating to escape the prelatic persecution which was raging at home, he was disappointed, as we find him imprisoned in New York in January 1707 for preaching without the permission of the Episcopalian governor; nor was he released until he had paid costs amounting to upwards of £80.[1] Makemie was by no means the first Presbyterian minister whom Ireland gave to America. In 1668 we find 'a young man from Ireland who hath already had good success in his work,'[2] but whose name we do not know, labouring in Maryland. During the troublous times from 1670 to 1680, many families emigrated to America from the North of Ireland, most of whom settled in Maryland and Virginia, and these seem to have looked to the Presbytery of Lagan for ministers. The Rev. William Trail, minister of Lifford in that Presbytery, and also its clerk, went to Maryland about 1682, and officiated there for some years. Makemie also went first to Maryland, and thence to Virginia. The Rev. Josias Makie, a St. Johnston man, went out about 1690. In Delaware, the pioneer Presbyterian minister was the Rev. Samuel Davis, who seems also to have been an Irishman.[3] Before the close, therefore, of the seventeenth century, in three of the present States, Maryland, Virginia, and Delaware, Irish Presbyterian ministers were at work. It was in the spring of 1706 that Makemie organized the first American Presbytery—the Presbytery of Philadelphia. It consisted of seven ministers, of whom two others besides Makemie were Irishmen, Davis, already mentioned, and John Hampton, a Burt man, who came out in 1705. Subsequently, four other Irishmen became members of it, making seven in all. In 1716 a remarkable North of Ireland Presbyterian arrived on American soil, William Tennent, destined to become the 'father of Presbyterian colleges in America.'[4] Webster says of him—'To William Tennent, above all others, is owing the prosperity and enlarge-

---

[1] Note by Rev. Dr. Killen in Reid, ii. 342.
[2] Letter from Matthew Hill, Maryland, to Richard Baxter, written in 1669, in Briggs's *American Presbyterianism*. Appendix, p. 42.
[3] Briggs, 124.   [4] Briggs, 187.

ment of the Presbyterian Church.'[1] His famous Log College at Neshaminy, which to Whitfield seemed to resemble one of the schools of the prophets more than any seminary that he had ever seen, did mighty service to the cause of religion in America. The Synod of Ulster gave it its imprimatur in 1754, and Irish Presbyterians sent £500 to its help.[2] In 1718, Mr. M'Gregor, minister of Aghadoey, went out with a number of his people to New Hampshire, and founded a city, which they called, in patriotic recollection of the county they had left, Londonderry. It is a pleasant memory to us, and no small honour, that we were enabled to take so prominent a part in laying the foundations of a Presbyterianism which has become so potent for good as that of the United States.

[1] Webster's *History of the Presbyterian Church in America*, p. 367.
[2] Davies's *Journal* in Foote's *Sketches of Virginia*, pp. 267, 275.

CHAPTER X.

UNDER JAMES AND WILLIAM.

CHARLES II. died in 1685, and the ill-starred reign of his brother James II. began. The sceptre was not long in his hand until he made it manifest that he intended to make Romanism the national religion. In Ireland the steps which he took for this purpose were as decided as they were undisguised. Tyrconnel, a zealous Romanist, who was commonly called by the sufficiently descriptive sobriquet of 'Lying Dick Talbot,' was installed in supreme authority, and soon showed that if James was zealous for Rome, so was he. Protestant judges were superseded by Romanists. Romanists were thrust into the Privy Council, into the municipal corporations, into the magistracy. The Irish army was Romanized to the utmost, Protestant officers and soldiers ousted, and their places filled with Romanists, while the chaplaincies were given to priests. One Romanist was made Lord Chancellor, another Attorney-General. The high offices about the Court and in the Executive were in like manner given to Romanists. High Sheriffs of the same persuasion were appointed. Without doubt the complete ascendancy of Romanism was aimed at, and would have been accomplished, had not Providence in His own strange way frustrated a design which would have turned the whole of both Ireland and England into an appanage of the Pope. The events, by means of which this came about, form one of the most stirring and instructive epochs in our national history.

One December day, in 1688, a letter was seen lying in the street of the quiet little County Down village of Comber, within a few miles of Belfast. It was picked up by a passer-by, and seen to be addressed to the Earl of Mount-Alexander, who lived in the neighbourhood.[1] When opened by the Earl it was found to be anonymous, and evidently the work of some illiterate person, the grammar and composition being execrable. Its purport was to warn Lord Mount-Alexander that a general massacre of Protestants had been planned for the 9th December, six days from the date of the letter, and to bid him take measures for his own safety and that of his friends. Copies of this mysterious missive were soon sent hither and thither through the country, and in the excited state of public feeling they produced the utmost alarm. Among other places, the news reached Derry on the morning of the 7th December, and, by a curious coincidence, on the same morning came a letter from Limavady announcing that a regiment of Roman Catholics, recently raised by Lord Antrim, had arrived there the previous day on their way to the Maiden City, where they might be expected at once. The two communications, arriving simultaneously, produced the deepest excitement. Soon groups of the inhabitants were seen standing about the Derry streets discussing them. The 9th of December was now but two days off, and it was believed that Antrim's regiment of Redshanks was coming to take its part in the general massacre. The ferment in the little city was intense. Business was all but suspended, and the whole talk was of the impending attack. While the situation was being discussed, word came that the vanguard of the expected regiment was already in sight, and, looking from the walls across the Foyle, several companies of it were to be seen over at the Waterside. Already some were crossing the ferry, and two of the officers were at the gates, demanding admittance for the troops in King James's name. What was to be done? Alderman Tomkins, the Mayor's deputy, was in a quandary. He consulted the Rev. James Gordon, Presbyterian minister of Glendermot, who was in the city (Derry Presbyterian Church happened to be vacant at the time). 'Shut the gates and keep them out,' was the short and bold advice which he received. But the

[1] This title became extinct in 1757.

Episcopalian bishop, Ezekiel Hopkins by name, strongly disapproved of such a step. They were King James's troops, and King James ought to be obeyed. He was 'the anointed of the Lord,' and subjects should under all circumstances submit to their sovereign. The Alderman was quite nonplussed amid this contradictory advice. But there are times when aldermen and bishops, and all such importances, if they choose to oppose themselves to common sense, must be quietly left standing in their dignity, while others, who, though they may have no titles to their names, have got the gift of mother wit, act. Five minutes will settle the matter now one way or other, for the Redshanks are by this time within sixty yards of the Ferryquay Gate. Fortunately for Derry, for us all, the wise advice of the Presbyterian minister was taken. Eight or nine young men, apprentices of the city, ran to the gate, at which the measured tread of the advancing troops could already be heard. In a trice they had raised the drawbridge, shut the gate, and locked it, leaving the astonished Redshanks to stand outside in wonderment at their boldness, and Bishop Ezekiel Hopkins to go to his palace astonished too, and in sore dudgeon at the disrespect shown to his reverend authority, —the authority of the consecrated bishop, and to his royal master King James.

But Antrim's men are still at the gate, and showing no disposition to retire. They must be got out of that. 'Bring a great gun this way!' cries James Morrison, one of the citizens, loud enough for the Redshanks to hear. The hint is enough. In the twinkling of an eye the whole party are seen scampering down the hill, scattered by the bare mention of a shot. It is a race who will reach the ferry first, to be out of the reach of those determined Derry men.

No reader will grudge the little space required here for a record of the names of the thirteen Apprentice Boys (for three or four joined the eight or nine who actually closed the Ferryquay Gate, and assisted in securing the others). They deserve to be held in honour by all Ulster men, by all Irishmen, the world over. They were—Henry Campsie, William Crookshanks, Robert Sherrard, Daniel Sherrard, Alexander Irwin, James Steward, Robert Morrison, Alexander Cunningham, Samuel Hunt, James Spike, John Cunningham, William Cairns, and Samuel Harvey. No wonder their memory is cherished in the Maiden City, and far beyond it. It should be specially cherished by all Presbyterians. For these young men who saved the city that day were almost all, perhaps all, Presbyterians, and more than one Presbyterian minister has been proud to be able to trace his ancestry to a Derry 'Prentice Boy.

But the Bishop has not yet got over his horror at the temerity of these Presbyterian lads. So he comes down to the Diamond and makes a speech, descanting on the enormity of what has been done, and on the want of reverence for 'the Lord's anointed' of which the 'Prentice Boys have been guilty. The people, however, are in no mood for hearing him. 'My Lord,' cries young Irwin out of the crowd, 'your doctrines are doubtless very good, but just at present we can't hear you out.' Alderman Tomkins sides with the Bishop, and tries to get the brave deed undone. Fortunately in vain. The gates are kept closed. The Apprentice Boys mount guard upon them. They arm themselves from the magazine. Next day Bishop Ezekiel finds he has been long enough in Derry. Remarkable to relate, the city was able to get on without him.

It was on a Friday that Derry thus took up her determined attitude. The following Sabbath was the date named in the Comber letter for the massacre of the Protestants, and we may imagine the dread with which its approach was awaited all over Ulster. But the day passed without the expected scene of blood. The warning of the Comber letter proved happily false. But, whatever had been the purpose of its author, it had the effect of closing the gates of Derry.

'Lying Dick' was furious when he heard of the behaviour of the Derry men. As his manner was, he wreaked his vengeance on his wig, flinging it in a passion into the fire. He gave immediate orders that Lord Mountjoy and Colonel Lundy (whose name was destined to be bracketed with that of Bishop Hopkins in an evil fame) should go down with troops and occupy the refractory city. But one thing Derry had made up its mind about, —it would allow no Papist, on any pretext whatever, to enter its gates. Lundy was an Episcopalian, however, and he was admitted as governor, with two companies of Protestant soldiers. But the citizens took good care to keep up at the same time their own six companies of guards, which they had formed immediately after the closing of the gates, and to keep up also a sharp lookout on matters in general, and the new governor in particular. Meanwhile James II. has fled from England. The news of the landing of William of Orange at Torbay, of his triumphal march to London, and of his being already in occupation of St. James's Palace, has travelled slowly over to Ireland. Sides must definitely be taken, and taken at once, for James is coming up to Ulster with an army. Lieutenant-General Hamilton is in the North already, and the Protestants have not been able to make good their stand against him. At 'The Break of Dromore' the Williamites, headed by Sir Arthur Rawdon, have fled before superior numbers. Hillsborough Castle has fallen and been plundered. The same fate has overtaken Lisburn and Antrim. The Protestant troops, under Rawdon and Baker, have been obliged to fall back on Coleraine. Here, protected by a mud wall and a ditch on three sides, with the Bann defending the fourth, Hamilton's forces are gallantly repulsed. But a line of defence, some thirty miles in length, was too much for the comparatively few Protestant troops to hold, and it soon became necessary to evacuate Coleraine. So, on Sabbath, April 7th, the whole Protestant forces marched out of it across the mountains to Derry, burning up all supplies which might be useful to the enemy as they went along, and thus it came to pass in the end that almost the whole Protestantism of the North of Ireland concentrated itself on that little city on the banks of the Foyle. Derry was the last hope of Irish Protestantism. Its fate was to be settled behind those old grey walls. If Derry can hold out—well. If she falls—woe, woe, woe to Ulster and the kingdom !

Lundy, the Governor, who had now charge of the city, was one of the falsest of men. He professed fealty to William, while he did his utmost for James. He was a Protestant Episcopalian, yet all the while the best friend of the Romanists. It would take long to rehearse the story of his conduct, his pretences of activity, his secret plottings, his base and dishonourable temporizing. After having induced every Ulster garrison to retire upon Derry, until the whole contest between William and James, between Protestantism and Popery, between constitutional liberty and tyrannical oppression, was staked upon its fate, he suddenly discovered that Derry was untenable, and advised its surrender. Through his influence the principal gentry who had come in took their departure, and the English officers who had been sent over with troops for the assistance of the city sailed away back with them to England. Fortunately the governor's falsehoods were found out by the citizens. When King James was already in person before the gates, and Lundy's whole efforts were directed towards a surrender, the spirit of the people rose again to the occasion. As, before, they had turned deaf ears to the aldermanic and episcopal counsels which would fain have prevented them closing the gates, so now they refused to open them at the bidding of the Governor or any one else, and the last that was seen of Lundy in Derry was when, one evening, disguised as a private soldier, with a load of matchwood on his back, he slunk along the streets in the gloaming, got down to the river, and embarking, stole away from a city, the intelligent, determined spirit of whose inhabitants had proved more than a match for his cowardly plots, as it had for the pusillanimity of its bishop and Alderman Tomkins. To this day the memory and the name of Lundy are execrated in Derry, as well they may be.

Lundy being got rid of, the question was who should be appointed to fill his place. Captain Adam Murray, a Presbyterian elder, and a singularly brave man, who had taken the lead in opposing Lundy's traitorous machinations, would have been rapturously chosen. But he declined the honour, and at a council of the officers Major Baker was elected, and held office till his death. The Rev. George Walker, rector of Donoughmore, and also, it would appear, incumbent of Lissan, and perhaps of a third parish,[1] was at the same time appointed assistant governor, and placed in charge of the provisions. Walker managed, when the siege was over, to take all the honour and glory of the defence of the city to himself. He represented himself as the Governor, ignored everybody else, and trumpeted his own praises so persistently and skilfully, that not a few people to this day regard him as the real hero of the siege. He was nothing of the kind, however. From the glimpses which we get of him in the diaries of the period, he seems to have been a small-minded and pompous old man, intolerably vain and egotistical, bigoted, fonder of his glass than he should have been, not above altering a letter or official document when it suited his purpose, and rather economical of truth. He was not even regarded with the most implicit confidence by the garrison. On one occasion a number of charges were brought against him, in the prosecution of which over a hundred officers, some of them, like Murray, men of the highest position and reputation in the city, were agreed. He was accused of planning the surrender of the city, and even of embezzling the stores. It is not fair to the memories of the brave men who did the real work at Derry, to allow him to clothe himself in the glory which really belongs to them. He had charge of the stores, oversaw the weighing and serving out of the bread and meat to the garrison. But with the military proceedings he had simply nothing to do, and he was certainly not the Governor. It does not appear that he ever commanded in so much as a skirmish.[2] Major Baker held command till he died, and after him Colonel Mitchelburn. Walker was never anything but assistant in charge of the stores.

[1] *Ulster Journal of Archæology*, ii. 132.

[2] He talks, in his account of the siege, of his military exploits. But no one was aware of them but himself. 'As to the enemy, he was a man of peace all the time, and was guilty of shedding no other blood to stain his coat but that of the grape.'—*Invisible Champion*, 8.

HORRORS OF THE SIEGE OF DERRY.

The city was now closely invested without,[1] and the strictest arrangements were maintained within. Every man had his post, and his clear instructions as to his duty. Walls and bastions were carefully manned. Two cannon were planted on the top of the Cathedral tower. There were cannon at the gates and cannon in the Diamond. The street pavements were torn up, and the stones piled along the walls, for use against the enemy. Soon James's cannonade opens furious and heavy. Shells, large and small, are thrown in in multitudes. Roofs and walls of houses come crashing down on the tenants. Graves in the Cathedral burying-ground are torn up, and corpses thrown out of them, sometimes even over the surrounding wall. People are killed as they pass along the streets. The worst was that the garrison could not return this fire in kind, having neither mortars nor bombs. But they annoyed and seriously injured the enemy by repeated sallies, in which conspicuous daring was shown. Murray was a leading spirit in these onsets. In one of them he slew the French general Maumont with his own hand. Murray, indeed, was the real hero of the siege.

As the weeks rolled on, the scanty supplies of food in the city began to run alarmingly low. The garrison was reduced to shorter and shorter allowance, and by and by famine, with its usual concomitant, disease, began to work even sadder havoc in the city than the bombs and cannon-balls of the besiegers. Everything that could be eaten was seized on with avidity. Dogs, lean, skinny, half-starved horses, cats, rats, mice, and tallow were consumed, and even sold at high prices. Yet, terrible as the suffering was,—the fire of the enemy dealing constant destruction, and sickness and starvation daily thinning the ranks, and reducing the living to walking skeletons,—there was no thought of surrender. The very word was forbidden to be uttered, under penalty of death. The ammunition began to fail, and brickbats, coated with lead, had to be used for cannon-balls. But no

---

[1] The siege proper commenced on 18th April, 1689.

straits would induce the Derry men to entertain the thought of capitulation. That was one thing they had sternly and determinedly made up their minds about.

In June, General Rosen was sent by James, who was growing impatient, to take the command, and push forward the siege with greater vigour. His name will be for ever associated with an act of horrible barbarity, of which only a fierce savage could have been guilty. Infuriated at the refusal of the garrison to yield, he ordered a message to be shot into the city in an empty shell, informing the Derry men that if they did not open the gates within twenty-four hours, he would gather all the Protestants on whom he could lay hands in the surrounding country, sparing neither age nor sex, and drive them under the walls, leaving them there to die in sight of their friends. It was a terrible threat, well calculated to stagger brave men. No great wonder if it had proved unendurable. But the answer was a stern refusal. Perhaps there was some lingering thought that cruel and relentless as Rosen was known to be, he would yet not carry out his proposal in all its force. If this idea was entertained, the Derry men were soon undeceived. One Monday evening they descried from the walls a motley crowd advancing towards them, with a gang of soldiery behind, driving them on. It was a piteous sight to see the aged patriarch tottering wearily along on his staff —the mother with her infant in her arms—and to hear the cries of the poor children, as hungry, and tired, and terrified, they clung to their parents; and still more piteous to watch them as darkness fell, lying on the bare ground without shelter, and to hear their cries all through the night. Next morning a still larger crowd of a similar kind appeared, until altogether some twelve hundred hapless people were massed together round the beleaguered city. What made the sight more trying, was the fact that, looking down from his guard-post, the soldier could recognise in that throng the face of his own aged mother or father, or his sister, or his wife. It was an awful trial; but, melting as the sight was, it did not move the men of Derry from their stern watchword of 'No Surrender!' And to the honour of their friends be it told, from that miserable crowd itself went up a cry to the garrison on the walls, begging them not to be moved, out of pity for them, to yield. So those nights and days went on—the starving Protestant garrison within, their starving mothers, and wives, and sisters, and children without, and the cruel enemy all round. But still no man suggested surrender.

What did the Derry men do? They raised the biggest gallows they could build on one of the bastions, in full view of the Romish army, and told some twenty prisoners whom they had captured to prepare for death. The prisoners ask leave to write to Rosen, and a letter goes out signed by five of them in the name of all, begging the general not to have them put to a criminal's death. The determination of the garrison wins the day. The cruel stratagem, which would have disgraced a Turk, is abandoned. The poor people are allowed to go home; and when the last of them is seen safely on the way, the gallows comes down from the Double Bastion. It had done its work well, though not a victim had swung from it.

So the siege went on, matters growing worse and worse in the city, hunger raging fiercely, and hunger and loathsome food together producing terrible sickness and many deaths. 'Oh, none will believe,' says John Hunter of Maghera, who served during the siege, 'but those who have found it by experience, what some poor creatures suffered in that siege. . . . I was so weak from hunger that I fell under my musket one morning as I was going to the walls, yet God gave me strength to continue all night at my post there, and enabled me to act the part of a soldier, as if I had been as strong as ever I was. Yet my face was blackened with hunger. I was so hard put to it by reason of the want of food, that I had hardly any heart to speak or walk; and yet when the enemy was coming, as many a time they did, to storm the walls, then I found as if my former strength returned to me. I am sure it was the Lord that kept the city, and none else, for there were many of us that could scarcely stand on our feet before the enemy attacked the walls, who, when they were assaulting the out-trenches, ran out against them most nimbly and with great courage. Indeed it was never the poor starved men that were in Derry that kept it, but the mighty God of Jacob, to whom be praise for ever and ever!'[1]

All this time ships loaded with ammunition, with meal, and beef, and biscuit had been lying for weeks down Lough Foyle, sent from England for the relief of the garrison. From the tower of the Cathedral their tall masts were plainly visible. But the command of this relief expedition had been entrusted to a man, Major-General Kirke, who, whether from lack of pluck or lack of will, was evidently wholly unfit for his charge. There he lay with his cargoes of provisions and war material, watching the daily signals of distress which were made to him, but all the time making no earnest effort to reach the quay. True, there were difficulties in the way. At Culmore, where the Lough narrows so that a man on one shore can easily hail a friend on the other, stood a fort of which the Jacobites had gained possession, and any ship which sought to make her way up to Derry must face the fire of its guns. Besides, the besiegers, determined to bar all communication with the city, had stretched a formidable boom, constructed of great beams of wood, fastened together with chains, and cables twelve inches thick, across the river. But these obstacles, formidable though they were, were not insurmountable, as the sequel showed, and it is a soldier's business to expect to meet difficulties, and, at least, do his best to overcome them. Kirke did nothing. There he lay with his ships full of food week after week for seven weeks, which must have seemed to the Derry men like the seven years of famine in Egypt, while they starved and died, till the living were scarcely able to bury the dead. At length the same intrepid Presbyterian clergyman who had given the advice to shut the gates in the faces of the Redshanks, the

---

[1] Graham's *Ireland Preserved*, p. 355, quoted in Witherow's *Derry and Enniskillen*, p. 158. The Rev. James Hunter, 3rd Coleraine, was great-grandson of this John Hunter.

Rev. James Gordon of Glendermot, got somehow on board Kirke's squadron, had an interview with him, and gave him very plainly a piece of his mind on the delay which had taken place. Whether it was the influence of this remonstrance, or the reception of more peremptory instructions from England that now moved him, at all events orders were at length given that the passage of the river should be attempted. It should have been done weeks before.

It is a Sabbath day, and the July sun shines on the waters of lovely Lough Foyle, as four ships are seen detaching themselves from Kirke's flotilla. One, the *Dartmouth*, is a frigate, commanded by Captain Leake, who has sailed round from Carrickfergus along the Antrim coast, to assist in this enterprise. The other three are provision-ships—the *Mountjoy*, of Derry, commanded by Captain Micaiah Browning ; the *Phœnix*, of Coleraine, with Captain Andrew Douglas in charge of her; and the *Jerusalem*, Captain Reynell. On they move till they are abreast of the fort at Culmore, which no sooner sees the business they are at than it opens fire. Leake sails the *Dartmouth* between the fort and the provision-ships, receiving all the fire, and returning it with interest. While fort and frigate are battering away at each other, the *Mountjoy* and the *Phœnix* (the third vessel having orders not to move forward until the others are seen to have got a clear passage) are taking full advantage of the rising tide, and sailing on. But soon the wind dies away into a calm, and all along the shore on both sides of the river the enemy swarm down thick as bees. They bring their batteries to bear upon the ships. They rake them with a determined fire of musketry. The air of the Sabbath evening resounds with the hoarse shouts of the Jacobites, with the roar of cannon, and the rattle of small arms. Still the ships hold gallantly on. Now the *Mountjoy*, which leads the way, is approaching the boom. She strikes it, but, recoiling from the blow, runs fast aground. The whole shore from bank to bank now re-echoes to the wild cheering of the Jacobites. Volley on volley is fired into the stranded ship, and, sure of making her their own, they rush to board her. But she is not theirs yet. Captain Browning orders all the ship's guns on the land side to be simultaneously discharged. By the recoil of this broadside she is thrust out into deep water, and floats again. Meanwhile a picked crew on board a small boat have been hewing at the boom with hatchet and hammer. The *Mountjoy* makes for it again. This time she crashes clean through it as through a wall of paper. Her brave captain at this moment falls dead on deck, shot through the head. But slacking no speed, she sails on, and the *Phœnix* coming close in her wake, the two ships are soon in full sail for Derry quay. By ten o'clock they are moored, and it is not long till a liberal ration is served out to every one. Brave Derry is at last saved. James's army quickly took in the whole situation. On Thursday, 1st August, they were in full retreat. The siege was over, after having lasted a hundred and five days.[1]

We have lingered somewhat long over the story of this memorable siege, because, though so often told, it occupies such a unique position in the history of Ulster that its people never weary of hearing it,—because the accounts which are periodically given of it are not always distinguished by their fidelity to historical accuracy,—and because the defence of Derry was very largely a Presbyterian exploit. It was a Presbyterian minister, as we have seen, who counselled the shutting of the gates, and the same spirited man who urged Kirke to relieve the garrison. Most if not all of the Apprentice Boys were Presbyterians. Episcopalians and Presbyterians united in the defence. But the vast majority of those who stood behind the walls were Presbyterians. Murray, to whose prowess and determination it owed so much, was a Presbyterian. 'Among the superior officers of the garrison the Episcopalians and Presbyterians were nearly equal; among the inferior officers the latter were in the majority; but among the ordinary soldiers they were more than ten to

[1] For a detailed account of the siege, see Witherow's *Derry and Enniskillen*.

one.'[1] It is not the least of the honours which Irish Presbyterians can justly claim—that it was they that bore the brunt of the siege which saved Derry and Ireland for King William, and in the end saved much more than either Derry or Ireland for Protestantism and freedom. There were eight Presbyterian ministers in Derry during the investment of the city. Presbyterians and Episcopalians both used the Cathedral for worship, the latter in the morning, the former in the afternoon, 'besides two or three other meetings in other parts of the city.'[2] A quaint old poem of the period says—

> ' The Church and Kirke did jointly preach and pray
> In St. Columba's Church most lovingly,
> Where Dr. Walker, to their great content,
> Preached stoutly 'gainst a Popish Government.
> Master Mackenzie[3] preached on the same theme,
> And taught the army to fear God's great name.
> The Reverend Rowat[3] did confirm us still,
> Preaching submission to God's holy will.
> He likewise prophesied our relief,
> When it surpassed all human belief.
> The same was taught by learned Mr. Crooks ;[3]
> And Master Hamilton[3] showed it from his books.
> Then Mills,[4] a ruling elder, spoke the same
> Of our relief, six weeks before it came.
> From sunrising to sunsetting they taught,
> While we against the enemy bravely fought.'[5]

It is a pity that this beautiful harmony, which might have been the precursor of a united Irish Protestantism, disappeared with the raising of the siege, that the Episcopalians recommenced at the first opportunity their malevolent persecutions of their co-religionists, and so handed down to us the legacy, not only

---

[1] Witherow, 255. Mackenzie, in his *Narrative of the Siege*, reckons the Presbyterian soldiers as fifteen to one.

[2] Mackenzie.

[3] Presbyterian clergymen.

[4] William John Foster, Esq., J.P., Derry, is a lineal descendant of this worthy elder.

[5] *Londerias*, iii. 5.

of a divided Protestantism, but of embittered memories and wounded feelings. They had a grand opportunity, but they threw it away.[1]

Enniskillen's gallant stand against the Jacobite troops on its island home in Lough Erne must not be passed over in silence. The conditions there were different from those in Derry. It had no walls, as Derry had, nothing save the Erne to defend it, and there was no siege, properly so called, at Enniskillen. The tactics pursued by its garrison were to prevent the possibility of a siege by continual raids on every considerable body of the enemy of which they heard as being in their vicinity. In these sallies they were uniformly successful. Nothing seems to have been able to withstand their sudden and determined onslaughts. As one result, the town was kept well supplied with provisions by the booty which was brought in. The chronicles of the period tell of thousands of cows and sheep captured in some of these fierce sallies; and so, while the Derry men were prolonging a miserable existence on tallow and dead dogs and cats, the Enniskilleners had more food than they knew what to do with. We read of good milch cows sold on their streets at the time of their worst troubles for eighteenpence, and dry cows for sixpence each. In other respects there was a considerable similarity between the circumstances of the two defences. It was the Comber letter which first alarmed Enniskillen, as it did the people of Derry. A copy of it reached the former town on the 7th December, the day on which the gates of the northern fortress were closed by the Apprentice Boys, and, four days after, they received the news that two companies of Romish soldiers were coming to take up quarters among them. They resolved to refuse them admittance, set carpenters speedily to work to complete a drawbridge, expelled every Roman Catholic from the town, in a word, made up

---

[1] It ought to be mentioned that the glory of the defence of Derry cannot be monopolized by Derry men. Within the walls were men from Antrim, and Down, and Armagh, and Monaghan, and Tyrone, and Donegal, who had fled thither, and joined in making a stand against the common foe.

their minds to hold Enniskillen, at all odds, for Protestantism. In Enniskillen, as in Derry, a Presbyterian clergyman was foremost in encouraging the people to stand boldly against the common enemy—the Rev. Robert Kelso, minister of the town. Not only did he urge them to defend the place against the emissaries of Tyrconnel, but he himself took up arms and marched at the head of the inhabitants who enrolled themselves in the garrison. Yet it seemed a mad resolve to face the Government and the troops of James with eighty men, twenty guns, and ten pounds of powder—the entire strength which Enniskillen could muster.[1] Nevertheless they resolved to do it. The Romish troops came on. It was the Sabbath day, and most of the people were at church. But on the tidings of the approach of Tyrconnel's men, out they sallied, and the first sight of them struck terror into the intended garrison, who turned tail and fled, officers and all, to Maguiresbridge, eight miles away. The first step was thus taken, and Enniskillen, now committed to resistance, took proper measures for maintaining its position. Gustavus Hamilton was chosen Governor. The townsmen were organized into two companies of foot, one of which consisted mostly of sturdy Presbyterians. It would take long to tell of the brave conduct of this little island garrison, of their vigorous sallies all over the surrounding country, wherever they heard of the enemy appearing in force—sallies which they seem to have thoroughly enjoyed—of the 'Break of Belleek,' in which Colonel Lloyd and a party of his men chased the troops of James and relieved the Protestant garrison of Ballyshannon; of the raid, under the same brave commander, into Cavan and Meath, in which they swept the whole country before them, penetrated to within thirty miles of Dublin, and returned without the loss of a man, bringing with them an enormous booty; of their attempt to relieve Derry, which, however, proved a task too great for such a comparative handful of men, though it is hard to say what might have been its result had Lloyd been the leader on this occasion as before; of the 'Battle of Belturbet,' in which

[1] Witherow's *Derry and Enniskillen*, 177.

they routed Brigadier Sutherland and his forces, and carried back to Enniskillen some twenty tons of provisions, besides many prisoners and a good store of ammunition ; of the 'Battle of Lisnaskea,' in which, about nine o'clock one July morning, they charged through a bog on Colonel Anthony Hamilton and his forces, and chased the whole of them like sheep through Lisnaskea and a mile beyond it; and of the 'Battle of Newtonbutler,' in which, on the same day, to the watchword of 'No Popery,' they routed General Macarthy and his men, and, hunting all night through bush and bog, left by morning scarce a foot soldier out of 3000 alive or uncaptured. This day of double triumph closed their brilliant record. It was the 31st July, 1689, the day on which James's army fled from before those frowning walls from which the voice of 'Roaring Meg' and her noisy sisters had thundered their 'No Surrender.' Scouts brought the Enniskilleners the news of the clouds of dust which they had seen at Castle-caulfield, within three miles of Dungannon, marking the march of the Duke of Berwick's rearguard. So, almost simultaneously, the two northern strongholds of Protestantism finished their memorable campaigns.

While matters had thus been progressing in Ireland, the Revolution had been quickly and successfully accomplished in England. On 18th December, 1688, James had finally left London, and amid as profuse a display of orange ribbons as marks an Ulster Twelfth of July, William had entered St. James's Palace. As he subsequently figures conspicuously in Presbyterian history, it may be well to say a word or two of him here. By his mother he was grandson of Charles I., and by his father great-grandson of that noble specimen of a man, William the Silent, 'the first prince in Europe who avowed and practised those principles of toleration which lie at the foundation of all religious freedom.' His wife, Mary, was a daughter of James II. King William was a Presbyterian. He was brought up in that faith in Holland, and taught by it in those Scriptural principles which, once imbibed, are sure to keep any man, prince or peasant, right, so long as he holds by them.[1] It is a curious fact that the two kings who have done most to make Ulster what it is, James I., to whom we owe the Plantation, and William III., from whose reign we date the foundation of our civil and religious liberties, were both born and brought up in the Presbyterian fold.

William was also a strong Calvinist. 'The tenet of predestination was the keystone of his religion. He often declared that if he were to abandon that tenet, he must abandon with it all belief in a superintending Providence, and must become a mere Epicurean.'[2] It was largely owing to his hearty Calvinism that 'through a life which was one long disease,' with a sickly body, asthmatic and consumptive, tortured by headaches and racked by coughs, and living in the midst of constant peril, his spirit never sank, and he was able fearlessly to pursue whatever he saw to be the path of duty.

William was a stout Protestant, but nothing of a bigot. He did his best to have such changes effected in the polity and ritual of the Church of England that Nonconformists might be included within its pale. Episcopal narrowness defeated this favourite project of his, which, if it had succeeded, would have put an entirely different face on the subsequent ecclesiastical history of both England and Ireland. Scotland owes to him the establishment of her Presbyterianism on the basis of the 'Revolution Settlement.' There were no more attempts to force Prelacy on her after he came to the throne.

Popular idols do not always deserve the adulation which they receive. But King William III. was unquestionably one of the noblest men that ever wore a crown.

One June day, in 1690, Belfast Lough presented such a stirring sight as plainly told that something unusual was in the wind. From the Gobbins on one side and Donaghadee on the other,

---

[1] 'He had been heard to utter an ominous growl when he first saw in his wife's private chapel an altar decked after the Anglican fashion.'—Macaulay, *History of England*, chap. xi.

[2] *Ibid.* ii. 3.

right up to Carrickfergus, the waters were covered with ships. Nearly 700 vessels lay at anchor on them—the largest fleet that they have ever borne. They had come to escort King William to Ireland. Schomberg, his favourite general, had come over the preceding year with an army and prepared the way, and now the King himself was about to enter on an Irish campaign. On Saturday, 14th June, he landed amid great enthusiasm from the yacht *Mary* at Carrickfergus, where the stone on which he first set his foot still forms part of a flight of steps leading down to the water. From Carrickfergus he rode towards Belfast, accompanied by his suite and a great crowd. At Whitehouse he was met by Schomberg's carriage, 'drawn by black Barbary horses,' which had driven from Belfast along the strand to meet him. At the north gate of Belfast[1] (which stood near where now Royal Avenue intersects North Street) he was received by the Sovereign (Captain Robert Leathes) and burgesses and a great crowd of the populace, who rent the air with their acclamations. After the usual formalities, he was conducted to the Castle,[2] then tenanted by Sir William Franklin, second husband of the Countess of Donegal. That night all the streets were illuminated. The red glare of bonfires gleamed from the surrounding hills, and cannon thundered from point to point, telling of the arrival of the King. He remained in Belfast five nights. On the Sabbath he went to church. On Monday he was waited upon by a deputation of Presbyterian ministers, who presented him with a loyal address of welcome. The deputation was headed by the Rev. Patrick Adair, minister of Belfast, Rev. Archibald Hamilton, Armagh, and Rev. William Adair, Ballycaston. On Thursday he left Belfast and passed on by Lisburn to Hillsborough, where he issued his celebrated order to Christopher Carleton, Collector of Customs at Belfast, authorizing him to pay £1200 per annum to the clergy of the Presbyterian Church, being assured, as he said,

---

[1] Belfast was then surrounded by ramparts, with regular gates.
[2] It stood on the ground now occupied by Castle Market and the surrounding buildings.

'of their constant labour to unite the hearts of others in zeal and loyalty towards us.' This may perhaps be taken as the real commencement of the *Regium Donum*, the previous grant of Charles II., already mentioned, having been irregularly paid, and latterly stopped altogether. From Hillsborough he joined the army then encamped beside Lough-brickland, and numbering about 36,000 men. On the 25th June he marched with these troops to Newry. On the 27th they were beyond Dundalk, for the King said he had not come to Ireland to let the grass grow under his feet. On the 29th they passed Ardee, and on the 30th they reached the banks of the famous Boyne, where the next day was to be fought the battle which more than any other is remembered in Ireland to this hour. By six o'clock on that memorable Tuesday morning, the 1st July, the troops were in motion, every man wearing a green sprig in his cap, the soldiers of James putting a bit of white paper in theirs. We need not rehearse the oft-told story of the famous fight which raged all through that long summer's day. Both sides fought with signal bravery. But nothing could withstand the disciplined valour of William's troops. The day became his, though with the loss of Schomberg and many another, old George Walker of Derry (who had just been promoted to the bishopric of that place) among the rest. The King, when told that he was killed, showed his opinion of the man by asking what business he had to be there. James fled to Dublin, and as soon as he could to France. He felt that the war was virtually over; and he was right, for though it lingered on all through the following winter, the ultimate triumph of William's army was secured by the victory at the Boyne.

The success of William was rather an awkward circumstance for the Episcopalians. When he reached Dublin they sent a deputation to him, acknowledging him as their king, and fervently praying 'for the consummation of the good work' which he had undertaken.[1] Yet a few months before, with the same prelate, Bishop Dopping of Meath, at their head, they had

[1] Appendix to Leslie's *Answer to King*, 29, quoted by Reid.

appeared in just the same manner before King James, and presented him with an address, in which they expressed their 'resolution to continue firm' in their loyalty to him.[1] A more wretched spectacle of inanity and contemptible time-serving was never presented than those bishops and clergy now exhibited. The glorious doctrines of passive obedience and of the divine right of kings, to which poor Ezekiel Hopkins was so faithful at Derry, and to which his brethren on the bench still clung, made fools of them. But they knew well how to trim their sails so as to suit the wind. 'While James's power was in the ascendant in Dublin, they prayed for King James and his reputed son, the Prince of Wales, for confusion on all his enemies, William included, and for deliverance from the heinous sin of rebellion. Bishop Dopping and the metropolitan clergy had so prayed on the last Sunday of June; but on that day week, when William's forces had removed from among them their rightful sovereign, whom they were never to forsake or oppose, they at once adopted the new collects in use in England, praying for King William as their lawful king, whom they had a few days before denounced as a usurper, and imploring the divine blessing on the very same enterprise which they had just been reprobating as an unnatural rebellion. In Ulster these fluctuations in the public prayers of the Established Church were still more numerous; for, as one of themselves afterwards stated, the Episcopalian clergy in many parts of Ulster, according as the adherents of James or William obtained the ascendancy, had been "four times in one year praying forward and backward, point blank contradictory to one another."'[2]

It might have been thought that the loyalty of Presbyterians had now been so well and so often proved, and that the services which they had recently rendered at Derry, Enniskillen, and elsewhere, had been so conspicuous and valuable that the least they could expect would be liberty to live, and exercise their

---

[1] Appendix to Leslie's *Answer to King*, 23.
[2] Reid, ii. 409.

religion according to their conscience. But it was far otherwise. The treatment they received now at the hands of the Episcopalians forms a most melancholy chapter in the religious history of Ireland. It has left behind it bitter memories of wrong not easily to be erased, and is largely responsible for the want of cordial union which exists to this day, to a greater or less extent, between these two great branches of Protestantism, a want of union which would be sad anywhere, but which in a country like Ireland is simply ruinous.

In March, 1692, the Presbytery had sent a probationer named Ambrose to officiate at Hillsborough. But the Episcopal incumbent, who was also chancellor of the diocese and an archdeacon, Lemuel Matthews by name, swore an information against him for having had the temerity to conduct worship without the aid of the Book of Common Prayer, procured a warrant, and actually had him committed to prison for the atrocious crime of which he had been guilty! In October of the same year the bishops succeeded in obtaining a vote of the Irish House of Lords' 'Committee for Religion,' providing that there should be no toleration conceded to Presbyterians or others in Ireland, unless the English Test Act were brought into force here, forbidding any one to hold any public office whatever who did not become a communicant in the Episcopal Church. At their instigation the Lord-Lieutenant was induced to recommend to King William the enaction of the Test. But, as might have been expected, the wise and tolerant monarch refused to sanction any proceeding of the kind. If the bishops, instead of persecuting their neighbours, had looked a little more diligently into their own ecclesiastical affairs, they would have found quite enough to occupy their time. The *morale* of the Episcopal Church at this period seems to have been frightful, if one may judge from the testimony of the official records. Thus, in 1693, a memorial to the Lord-Lieutenant called attention to the scandalous state of matters in the diocese of Down and Connor, and a Royal Commission was sent down to investigate it. The results of this visitation speak for themselves. The bishop, Hackett, was deposed for selling the livings and preferments, and 'for many other crimes.' The archdeacon of Down, our friend Lemuel Matthews, who was so scandalized by a Presbyterian presuming to officiate without the Prayer-Book, was deprived of his archdeaconry, and suspended from his other offices, for enormous neglect of duty, and 'other things acted and committed by him.' The Dean of Connor, Ward, was dismissed from his deanery for adultery. The prebendary of Kilroot, Milne, was convicted of intemperance and incontinence; and so on with a melancholy list. A nice body of dignitaries these, not only to preside over the affairs of a Church of Christ, but to hinder true and faithful ministers of God from preaching the gospel in the district cursed by their presence!

Irish Presbyterians at this period enjoyed no legal toleration. Had the law as it stood been rigidly enforced, their worship and discipline might have been completely put down. Such were the thanks they received for their heroic defence of the kingdom. King William, true to his principles, wished the fullest protection extended to them by law; but all he was able to do was to prevent the scandalous statutes which still existed from being carried out. The Irish bishops determined to keep the Presbyterians down, and at every attempt to relieve them from the opprobrious position in which they were placed, these worthies were found insisting that instead of their circumstances being improved, the whips with which they had been hitherto chastised should be changed into scorpions. In the Irish House of Lords there were sometimes twenty-one bishops present in a House of forty-three members,[1] so that it can easily be seen how they were able to make their influence felt. In other ways they did their utmost to harass the Presbyterians. Thus, in 1698, the Rev. John M'Bride, minister at Belfast, was summoned to Dublin, on the

[1] This was the case on September 24, 1695, when the House rejected the 'heads of a bill for ease to the Dissenters.'

complaint of Walkington, the bishop of Down and Connor, for a sermon which he had preached before the annual meeting of the Synod of Ulster, in which he had asserted the right of Church Courts to meet without the authority of the civil magistrate. He was also charged with calling himself, on the title-page of the sermon, 'minister of Belfast,' and the meeting a 'provincial synod.' The bishops failed to do the good man any harm, the Lords Justices dismissing the complaint. But the failure was not for want of perseverance on the part of his right reverend lordship to press his case. In Cookstown, the rector actually had the Presbyterian church pulled down in the year 1701 ! Fortunately there was connected with it one of those 'honourable women,' of whom Irish Presbyterianism has had 'not a few' in the course of its history—Mrs. Stewart of Killymoon. At once she set about building a new church at her own expense for the outed people, planting it within the walls of her own demesne, where she thought the intolerant rector would scarcely venture to interfere with it ; and so energetically did she do the work, that the building was ready for occupation in three weeks !

Away in the West of Ireland, Episcopacy manifested the same intolerant spirit as in Ulster. In the year of the complaint against Mr. M'Bride, the Rev. William Biggar, minister at Limerick, having gone to Galway occasionally to minister to some Presbyterian families which had settled there, was arrested, carried before the Mayor, and thrown into jail for his action, and the Lords Justices were petitioned to prohibit the establishment of a Presbyterian congregation in Galway. Strangely as it may sound in our ears, they actually did direct that no Presbyterian minister should for the present preach in Galway.[1] They had the letter of the law on their side in issuing this prohibition, for, as we have said, the Presbyterians were without legal toleration.

[1] The prohibition must soon have been either disregarded or removed, for in 1700 there was a Presbyterian congregation in Galway with a minister.

The Episcopalians also sought to deprive Presbyterian ministers of the right to solemnize marriage. They did not hesitate to stigmatize marriages celebrated by them as invalid, to apply the most insulting terms to the persons so united in wedlock, and to their children, and they summoned the ministers before the ecclesiastical courts for exercising the right to unite their people in wedlock. King William did his utmost to put a stop to such proceedings. But the power of a constitutional sovereign is limited, and William could not do all that he wished. In March, 1702, he died, and the Presbyterians lost the best friend whom they had ever had on the British throne. No wonder they venerate his name and memory to this day.

CHAPTER XI.

THE REIGN OF QUEEN ANNE.

WILLIAM was hardly cold in his grave when King, bishop of Derry, wrote to London urging that the *Regium Donum* should be stopped, or if continued, so managed 'as to be an instrument of division and jealousy' among Presbyterians.[1] A noble and high-minded suggestion truly! A change was now accordingly made in the distribution of this grant, the Lord-Lieutenant being empowered to keep it in his own hands, and give or withhold it as he pleased.

Notwithstanding all the troubles in the midst of which she was called to walk, the Presbyterian Church prospered marvellously.[2] She seems to have contained the only real salt of true religion in the land, and God blessed her accordingly. In 1702 the Presbyteries had grown to nine—viz. Belfast, Down, Antrim, Coleraine, Armagh, Tyrone (sometimes called Cookstown), Monaghan (or Stonebridge), Derry, and Convoy. These were superintended by

[1] King's *MS. Correspondence.*
[2] The Rev. Richard Choppin, Dublin, writing from Derry to a friend in 1712, speaks of the large Presbyterian congregations of the north-west :— 'In a little country place, where few would hardly expect to see the face of a Christian, you shall have on the Lord's day an auditory of 600 to 700 people. Most of the ministers of whom I have inquired concerning the numbers of their people have told me that they have upon their list 1000 examinable persons, and some 1500, some 1800, while at the same time the Established minister has not above six or seven, and not above three or four persons to attend the service of the Church. Since I have made these observations, I cease to wonder at the jealousy and rage of the clergy in these parts, and of all that they can influence. For the truth is, they make a very contemptible figure.' Quoted by Witherow, *Presbyterian Memorials,* i. 326.

three sub-Synods—viz. those of Belfast, Monaghan, and Lagan, and all were under the jurisdiction of the General Synod, which met annually in the first week of June. These various Courts were most sedulous in attending to the interests of the Church. Special attention was paid to the superintendence of students. We have already mentioned the 'School of Philosophy' for their training at Antrim. There was another at Killyleagh, superintended by the Rev. James M'Alpine; and in 1709 the Synod granted £10 per annum to the Rev. Fulk White,[1] minister of Broughshane, 'to encourage him in teaching Hebrew.' But many of the Irish students went for their education to Glasgow, and some to Edinburgh and St. Andrews. In 1698 it had been enacted that no young man should be licensed without signing the Westminster Confession of Faith. Nor was this a mere form. The orthodoxy of the Church was strenuously guarded. In 1703 the Rev. Thomas Emlyn, minister of Wood Street, Dublin, was deposed for Arianism[2]—the first indication of the appearance of that baleful heresy which was afterwards to cause such trouble.

The year 1704 is memorable in the history of Irish Presbyterianism as that in which the iniquitous Test Act was introduced into Ireland. It had long been eagerly longed for by the bishops, and now it came. By this law it was enacted that all persons holding any public appointment whatever must take the Communion in an Episcopal Church within three months after their appointment, or lose their office. Viewed in itself, a more monstrous law could scarcely be conceived. But towards the Irish Presbyterians —who had served the State so long and well in many an hour of trial — it was especially unjust and insulting. It was hoped, doubtless, that this infamous Act would gain many of them to Episcopacy; that rather than lose their

---

[1] Ancestor of the Whites of White Hall.

[2] As an illustration of the temper of the times, it may be mentioned that he was indicted by Government for blasphemy, and imprisoned for two years.

position, or their hopes of preferment, they would conform. If the enemies of Presbyterianism thought so, they soon found their mistake. Our forefathers had a staunch attachment to their Church, for which we cannot too highly venerate them, and, to their honour be it told, very few of them were led to turn their backs upon her by this law. Their behaviour at this trying juncture, when expediency whispered temptation in every ear, and when loss and degradation threatened them as the penalties of fidelity, is a standing lesson for all time to us their children. In Derry, of the 12 aldermen, 10 were Presbyterians, and they were turned out of office. Of the 24 burgesses, 14 were Presbyterians, and were expelled. This in a city which some of these very men had contributed to preserve by their services and sufferings to the British Crown! In Belfast, of 13 burgesses, 9 were Presbyterians, and forfeited their seats. So it was over the country. The Presbyterian magistrate was put off the bench, the Presbyterian postmaster or postmistress out of the post office, the Presbyterian town councillor out of the corporation. No wonder Daniel Defoe lashed with his powerful pen an age which could lend itself to such infamous proceedings.[1] But, outrageous as this Act and the proceedings connected with it were, all the influence that the Presbyterians could employ, and all the petitions that they could send forward, were powerless to obtain them redress. They had once again to

'Know how sublime a thing it is
To suffer and be strong.'

During the entire reign of Queen Anne, Irish Presbyterians were down-trodden beneath the feet of Episcopacy. It is sickening to read of the intolerance and hatred which bishops and clergy alike manifested towards them. They had no legal toleration, and every attempt to give it to them was frustrated. They were excluded from all public offices, down to the very humblest. Their pittance of *Regium Donum* was incessantly

[1] Vide *The Parallel; or, Persecution of Protestants the shortest Way to prevent the Growth of Popery in Ireland.* London, 1704.

inveighed against by the bishops, and the Government urged to take it from them, which was actually done before the close of the reign. It was made penal for a Presbyterian even to teach a school. Landlords were induced to refuse them as tenants on their estates, or, if accepted, to charge them higher rents than their neighbours of other denominations; and the bishops, in leasing Church lands, inserted clauses prohibiting under severe penalties the erection on them of Presbyterian churches, or the letting of any farm to a Presbyterian tenant. The press was employed to circulate pamphlets, bitter with scurrilous abuse of them. Jonathan Swift, dean of St. Patrick's, Dublin, and Tisdall, vicar of Belfast, were specially prominent and vigorous in this wicked warfare. Not content with such measures, wherever a favourable opportunity presented itself, the law was appealed to, to prevent Presbyterian worship. Thus, in 1708, the Rev. James Fleming, minister at Lurgan, who had been sent by the Synod to officiate to the Presbyterians at Drogheda, was summoned at the instigation of the rector of the town, and informed that if he persisted in preaching there, the law would be put in execution against him. Undismayed by this threat, he appeared in the pulpit on the following Sabbath, and the rector, true to his word, had him summoned again, along with three of the congregation, and bound over to stand trial at next assizes, where a true bill was found against them. The Rev. William Biggar, now loosed from his charge at Limerick, next came to take up the supply of Drogheda. The rector, well upon the watch, had him arrested and committed to jail for three months. The Lords Justices, however, interfered to protect these godly men from the malignant persecutions of their enemies. Mr. Biggar was ordered to be set at liberty after an incarceration of six weeks' duration, and the prosecution of Mr. Fleming was directed to be withdrawn. But it was not the fault of the rector that his intended victims thus escaped, nor the fault of the Episcopalians if the Presbyterian Church was not completely stamped out of the province. At Belturbet, proceedings equally high-handed and scandalous were taken. In 1709 the Presbyterian inhabitants of this town set about the erection of a church, and the Presbytery of the bounds met to confer with them on the matter. But a number of Episcopalian ministers, accompanied by several justices of the peace, assembled at the place, and as soon as the Presbytery had entered on business, had them arrested, and informations laid against them on the monstrous charge of holding an unlawful and riotous assembly. Notwithstanding the absurdity of the charge, a true bill was found against them at next Cavan Assizes, and, to pacify their persecutors, they had to promise not to build the proposed church within a mile of Belturbet, and 'resolve never to give any uneasiness to the town on that account.' In other places matters even went further. In the towns of Antrim, Downpatrick, and Rathfriland, the dominant party actually had the doors of the Presbyterian churches nailed up, so that no service could be held in them. Swift did the same with the Presbyterian church at Summerhill. Such was the state of matters all through the reign of Queen Anne.

A source of trouble which also affected a few of the body was the Nonjuring Controversy. There were some ministers who refused to take the oath of abjuration, not because they had the smallest sympathy with the cause of the Pretender, but from scruples as to the phraseology of the oath. Three of these, the Rev. Messrs. M'Bride[1] of Belfast, M'Cracken of Lisburn, and Riddel, had warrants issued against them, and were compelled several times to leave the country. In 1713, Mr. M'Cracken was arrested and sent to Carrickfergus jail. At the next assizes he was fined in £500, and ordered to be imprisoned for six months, and then to take the oath. He was thus kept in confinement for nearly two years and a half altogether.

Notwithstanding all this harsh treatment, in spite of the want

[1] A portrait of Mr. M'Bride hangs in the session-room of the First Unitarian Church, Belfast, with the mark still visible of a sword-cut through the 'bands,' where a soldier, on the occasion of one of the searches for him, enraged at not being able to find his prey, thrust his sword through the picture, then hanging in the manse.

even of legal permission to be in the country at all, Presbyterianism not only held its ground, but made steady progress. In 1710 the Synod of Ulster formed a plan for the preaching of the Gospel to the Irish-speaking Romanists in their own tongue. Seven ministers and three probationers[1] were at this time able to preach in Irish, and arrangements were made for providing Bibles, Catechisms, and copies of the Confession of Faith, in that language. Another important movement was the establishment of the 'General Fund' in the same year 'for the support of religion in and about Dublin and the South of Ireland.' By means of it many congregations were established in that part of the country, and a beginning made towards the transformation of the Synod of Ulster into the Presbyterian Church of Ireland. Some notable literary ventures also, which were now given to the press, prove to us that among the ministers of that day were men of no small ability. Two of these works, called forth by the misrepresentations of the Episcopalian party, deserve especial mention. The first bore the vigorous title, *A Sample of Jet-black Prelatic Calumny, in answer to a Pamphlet called 'A Sample of True-blue Presbyterian Loyalty,'*[2] by the Rev. John M'Bride of Belfast. This work is not, however, so well known as another, *An Historical Essay upon the Loyalty of Presbyterians in Great Britain and Ireland from the Reformation to this Present Year*, 1713. This was written by the Rev. James Kirkpatrick, although his name for obvious reasons does not appear on the title-page. He had been minister at Templepatrick, whence he was translated to Belfast to be colleague to Mr. M'Bride in the ministry of the First Congregation. When, in 1708, that congregation was divided by the Synod, and a portion of the people erected into the Second Congregation, he became their first minister, and this work of his, under its popular title of

---

[1] One of these Irish-speaking probationers was the Rev. Patrick Plunket, who subsequently became minister of Glasslough. He was ancestor of Lord Plunket, archbishop of Dublin.

[2] It was published in Glasgow in 1713. Pp. 218.

Kirkpatrick's *Presbyterian Loyalty*, soon became, and is still, widely known.

On the 1st August, 1714, Anne died—the very day, as Providence would have it, on which the Schism Act, which would have rendered the position of Irish Presbyterians still more intolerable than it had been, was to come into operation. George I. ascended the throne, and under his sway their position much improved. The *Regium Donum*, the withdrawal of which the malevolence of the bishops had secured, was restored, and in 1718 increased by an additional grant of £800 per annum. In the following year a Toleration Act was passed, notwithstanding the strenuous opposition of the majority of the bishops, exempting our forefathers from the penalties to which they had hitherto been legally liable for the celebration of their worship. All their efforts to obtain a repeal of the Test Act, however, were unavailing. Even a Bill exempting them from penalties for serving in the militia without communicating in the Episcopal Church, was opposed by the prelatists, although, to the honour of our Presbyterian forefathers be it told, when the North of Ireland was threatened by the Pretender, they stood forward nobly in defence of king and kingdom, notwithstanding the legal penalties which they incurred in so doing.

The Synod now contained eleven Presbyteries and one hundred and forty congregations; and not only was there this gratifying increase in numbers, but a spirit of deep religious earnestness pervaded the body, which, had it continued, augured well for the future of both the Church and the country.

CHAPTER XII.

THE 'NEW LIGHT.'

IN the beginning of the eighteenth century a cloud appeared on the Church's sky, which, though apparently no bigger than a man's hand, was destined in the end to breed much mischief. Hitherto the Synod's troubles had all come from without. Her own ministers and people had stood firmly and compactly together, one in doctrine, as in polity and worship. This happy condition of things was now to be changed, and changed in a very simple way.

In 1705 a number of young clergymen in the neighbourhood of Belfast formed themselves into a clerical club, for the discussion of theological and other topics. The leading spirit among them was a clever young 'son of the manse,' a conspicuously able and cultured man, the Rev. John Abernethy of Antrim.[1] He associated with himself such men as the Rev. William Taylor of Randalstown, Rev. Alexander Brown of Donegore, the Rev. James Kirkpatrick of Templepatrick (afterwards of Belfast), the Rev. Thomas Orr of Comber, the Rev. Alexander Colville, some probationers, theological students, and a few laymen. They called their club 'The Belfast Society,' and ultimately it became a most influential body. Unfortunately, its influence was by no means for good. Strange views were propounded at the

---

[1] Mr. Abernethy was a son of the Rev. John Abernethy, successively minister of Brigh, Moneymore, and Coleraine, where he died in 1703. He was born in 1680, and ordained in Antrim in 1703, the year of his father's death. In 1730 he became minister of Wood Street, Dublin. He published a large treatise, entitled, *Discourses on the Being and Attributes of God.* The celebrated London surgeon, Abernethy, was his grandson.

meetings—views which had never hitherto been broached by any minister of the Synod of Ulster, such as that sincerity was the great test of a man's religious condition; that erroneous opinions were only hurtful when wilful; that it was unwise to place too much stress on positive enunciations of doctrine, and that subscription to creeds or confessions should not be required by the Church. At each meeting of the society a sermon was preached. On Wednesday, 9th December, 1719, it fell to Mr. Abernethy to discharge this duty. The title of the sermon (which was subsequently published), *Religious Obedience founded on Personal Persuasion*, will give a sufficient idea of the nature of the views inculcated by the preacher, views which gradually came to be known as 'New Light,' a designation not yet forgotten in the North of Ireland. This sermon was the first note of a sad controversy which raged for seven long years, partly in Church Courts and partly through the press,[1] and which agitated almost every congregation within the bounds of the Church. To meet the emergency which thus arose, the Synod in 1720 passed what became known as The Pacific Act, a measure intended, as its title indicates, to reconcile the contending parties. On the one hand, it declared that the Synod firmly adhered to the Westminster Confession of Faith and Catechisms, and enjoined these to be observed. But, on the other hand, it enacted that 'if any person called on to subscribe shall scruple any phrase or phrases in the Confession, he shall have leave to use his own expressions, which the Presbytery shall accept of, providing they judge such a person sound in the faith, and that such expressions are consistent with the substance of the doctrine.' This Act was undoubtedly passed with the best intentions; but in the first place it was not firmly carried out, for immediately after its being made law, a signal violation of it was permitted; and secondly, like most compromises, it failed in the end to give satisfaction to anybody, and was found to be only the means of opening a

[1] More than fifty publications of various sizes were issued in connection with it.

wider door for the admission into the Church of men holding the most erroneous views. The Act was passed at the meeting of the Synod in June, 1720. On the 28th of July following, the installation of the Rev. Samuel Halliday,[1] a member of the Belfast Society, in the old congregation of Belfast took place. He refused altogether to subscribe the Confession of Faith in any form, tendering instead a declaration of his own. The majority of the Presbytery approved of this declaration as satisfactory, and in defiance of the protest of four members, the installation was proceeded with. No small alarm was naturally aroused among the orthodox members of the Church by this proceeding, and all eyes looked anxiously to see what action the superior Courts would take in the case. The sub-Synod of Belfast assembled in January, 1721. It was noted at the time as a significant circumstance that Mr. Halliday found it convenient to be in England at the time of its sittings. A very animated debate took place regarding the conduct of the Presbytery. The discussion began on Tuesday, and was continued until four o'clock A.M. on Friday morning. In the end the members of the Presbytery who had proceeded with the installation were publicly rebuked. But the deep-seated nature of the mischief which had already begun was proved by the fact that they as publicly informed the Synod that 'their conscience would not allow them to subscribe the Confession nor submit to the Act of the Synod.' Yet no steps were taken to bring them to the bar for this declaration. The sub-Synod over, Mr. Halliday was soon back in Belfast, and the members of Presbytery who had protested against his installation now called upon him to subscribe the Confession. But he resolutely refused, and the majority, who sympathized with him in the position he had taken up, managed hastily to adjourn the meeting without any formal decision on the matter being arrived at. The annual meeting of the General Synod now came on, amid general uneasiness. A very large attendance of the members indicated the anxiety felt for the safety of the Church.

[1] Or Hollyday, as he himself spelt the name.

The ruling elders especially mustered in great force, there being a hundred of them present,[1] and a hundred and twenty ministers. Seventeen memorials were presented from as many sessions, asking that 'all the members of the Synod, and all inferior judicatories of the Church, may be obliged to subscribe the Westminster Confession of Faith as the confession of their faith.' It would have been well if the Court had adopted the firm course thus urged. But again a temporizing spirit manifested itself. To allay the suspicions which had become prevalent regarding the orthodoxy of its ministers, the Synod declared its belief in 'the essential deity of the Son of God.' But the members of the Belfast Society refused to support this declaration, not, they said, 'because they disbelieved the article of Christ's supreme deity . . . but because they are against all authoritative human decisions as tests of orthodoxy.' The Synod further resolved, in order to dispel the alarm felt throughout the Church, not to enjoin but to permit all members of the Court who were willing, to subscribe the Confession. The Belfast Society argued strenuously against even this voluntary subscription, but it was carried against them by an overwhelming majority, and almost all the members in attendance affixed their signatures. Hence originated the names Subscribers and Non-Subscribers, by which the two parties began now to be known.

The case of Mr. Halliday also came before this eventful Synod. Strange to say, although, on being asked, he still refused to subscribe the Confession, the consideration of his case was quietly allowed to drop, and the law, made a solitary year before, to be trampled on. Discreditable as this action of the Court undoubtedly was, it led to one important result. A number of the members of the First Congregation of Belfast were so deeply dissatisfied with Mr. Halliday, and so unwilling to sit under his ministry, that they asked the Synod to erect them into a separate

[1] A hundred years later the ruling elders rendered similar good service by their large attendance at the Synod when the question of subscription was again agitating the Church.

charge. Mr. Halliday opposed the application, and was joined in his opposition by Mr. Kirkpatrick, the minister of the Second Congregation. But in the end, after a hard struggle, the prayer of the memorialists was granted. In August, 1721, a Third Congregation—that now known as Rosemary Street—was erected by the Belfast Presbytery, and its organizers set about the building of a new church.[1]

Into the war of words and pamphlets into which the subscription controversy resolved itself, it is not necessary to enter here at length. At each successive meeting of the Synod the question came up again in one form or another. Lengthened and sometimes acrimonious debates took place. Public meetings, attended at times by crowded audiences, discussed the question at issue, and the Belfast press was kept busy by the issue of controversial pamphlets. On the orthodox side the leading men who spoke or wrote were the Rev. John Malcome, Dunmurry; Rev. Gilbert Kennedy, Tullylish or Donacloney; Rev. Matthew Clerk, Boveedy or Kilrea; Rev. Charles Mastertown,[2] Connor, afterwards of Belfast; Rev. John Hutcheson,[3] Armagh; and Colonel Upton, Templepatrick; while on that of the Non-Subscribers were Rev. John Abernethy, Antrim; Rev. Samuel Halliday, First Belfast; Rev. James Kirkpatrick, Second Belfast; Rev. Thomas Nevin,

---

[1] Large part of the subscriptions for building the church were obtained in Scotland, Mr. Samuel Smith, a Belfast merchant, one of the elders, having gone over there on several occasions for the purpose of soliciting aid. Among others, the Magistrates and Town Council of Glasgow sanctioned a collection in the city churches for the object. The Synod of Glasgow and Ayr ordered a similar collection in their bounds. In return for this kindly and seasonable aid, three pews in the gallery of the new building were set apart for the use of strangers from Scotland visiting Belfast. The Rev. Charles Mastertown of Connor was installed as the first minister in February, 1723. Mr. Mastertown's farewell sermon to the people of Connor, from Acts xx. 32, was 'published by Eliza Vance, Bridge Street, Belfast, 1753.'

[2] An excellent treatise on *The Doctrine of the Holy Trinity*, by Mr. Mastertown, has been several times republished.

[3] Mr. Hutcheson was father of the famous Dr. Francis Hutcheson, Professor of Moral Philosophy in Glasgow.

It was during the erection of a new church in Armagh for Mr. Hutcheson

Downpatrick; Rev. John Elder, Aghadoey; and Dr. Victor Ferguson, Belfast. During the course of the debates the Rev. Thomas Nevin was brought to trial for having, as was reported, said on a certain occasion that it was no blasphemy to say that Christ is not God. The case against him broke down, but the Synod having required of him an immediate declaration of his belief in the Supreme Deity of Christ, and he having refused to comply with this demand, on the usual ground of the Non-Subscribers, that such declarations were wrong, adding that his refusal did not proceed from disbelief in the doctrine, it was carried that the Synod should hold no further ministerial communion with him—a peculiar and awkward sentence, inasmuch as he was neither deposed, nor suspended, from the ministry, nor disjoined from his congregation. It is not to be wondered at that it led to confusion and disorder. The Synod of 1725, for the purpose of putting an end to the collisions which were now of frequent occurrence between Subscribers and Non-Subscribers, adopted the expedient of separating all the non-subscribing ministers from the Presbyteries with which they were connected, and putting them into one—the Presbytery of Antrim, 'which expedient,' the resolution on the subject says, 'is to be continued until the God of peace shall mercifully remove the present mis-

that the well-known humorous incident, in which Dean Swift figures, occurred. The new building was partly built with stones taken from the ancient church and monastery of St. Peter and St. Paul, which had stood near. Swift, happening to pass by during the operations, found the masons busily smoothing a number of the carved stones, which had been adorned with cherubim and other figures. 'See,' said he, 'how these fanatical Puritans are chiselling the Popery out of the very stones.' (It might have been better for some other bodies if the Popery had been a little more completely 'chiselled' out of them.) 'Pray,' said the Dean to a sawyer who was busy cutting timber, 'how much do you earn per day?' 'Fifteenpence, please your reverence.' 'Fifteenpence!' he replied; 'why, I can get a better sawyer in Dublin for tenpence.' 'And I,' said the workman, 'can produce a parson who preaches better sermons than the Dean of St. Patrick's though he is only paid £40 a year and the Dean receives £700.' It is creditable to Swift's good nature, that, so far from being angry at the man's plainness of speech, he was so pleased with his ready wit that he gave him half-a-crown.

understandings.' It was evident, however, that some more decisive step must be taken before peace could be restored to the Church. The various temporizing resolutions that had been passed on the question at issue had by no means settled it. Accordingly, at the Synod of 1726, held in Dungannon (where for half a century the annual meetings were held about this period), an overture was passed, largely by the votes of the ruling elders, refusing to hold communion with the Non-Subscribers any longer in Church Courts. So this seven years' conflict was terminated by the members of the Presbytery of Antrim being separated from the Synod. It was a very partial separation, however. They were still at liberty to preach, if invited, in the Synod's pulpits, and administer ordinances to the Synod's members. It was merely in the Church Courts that they were declared incompetent to sit, while even here any ministers who secretly held their views, of whom there were not a few, were allowed to remain as an evil leaven to imbue their brethren insidiously with their opinions, and to produce in the sequel further trouble. Thus was consummated the first exclusion of the Non-Subscribers from the Synod of Ulster, which was destined to be followed, about a hundred years later, by another more complete and more significant, and on a larger scale.

CHAPTER XIII.

THE SECEDERS.

WHILE the 'New Light' was working to the detriment of Irish Presbyterianism, a counteractive was being prepared by the King of the Church in His own mysterious way. This was the introduction into Ireland of the body called Seceders. To understand their appearance in Ulster at this juncture, we must glance again for a moment at Scotland, which had given Ireland in 1642 the first Presbytery of the Synod of Ulster, and now, about a hundred years afterwards, gave her, as a new gift, the first Seceders.

In 1707 the union between England and Scotland took place. Before this union was consented to north of the Tweed, stringent provisions were insisted on and secured, safeguarding the rights and liberties of the Church of Scotland. It was enacted that the Confession of Faith and the Presbyterian form of church government were 'to continue without any alteration to the people of this land in all succeeding generations.' But only five years had passed till a most serious change was made in the ecclesiastical arrangements of the country by the passing of an Act of Parliament reimposing lay patronage on the Church,—an Act which, for a century and a half, was to breed controversy and mischief. For some years it seems to have lain a dead letter on the statute-book. But moderatism by and by began to shed its chilling influence over Scotland, and this law chimed in so well with its well-known spirit that in the end it came about that ministers began to be imposed upon vacant congregations against the will of the people, and where Presbyteries refused to have any share in giving effect to unpopular presentations, the General Assembly superseded them by 'Riding Commissions,' composed of men who had no scruples in the matter, and the obnoxious settlements were effected. The first case of such an intrusion of a minister into a parish against the will of the people took place in 1725, and from this time onward case after case occurred, and the General Assembly would listen to no remonstrance and give no redress. Matters came to a crisis in 1732. In that year the famous Ebenezer Erskine preached a sermon before the Synod of Stirling, in which he emphasized the need for reform in the Church. For this he was called to account, and, in the end, first suspended and then deprived of his congregation. Three other ministers united with him in protesting against this high-handed proceeding,—viz. Messrs. Fisher of Kinclaven, Moncrieff of Abernethy, and Wilson of Perth,—but all three were served in the same manner. The four then formally withdrew from the jurisdiction of the Church of Scotland, and, constituting themselves into 'The Associate Presbytery,' formed the nucleus of that dissent which is now embodied in the United Presbyterian Church.

While it was the question of patronage that was thus the immediate cause of this secession, there was much more than patronage involved in the movement. The Seceders were men deeply imbued with a love of sound evangelical doctrine, and with a burning desire for the spread of true religion, as opposed to the cold moderatism which was now in the ascendant. To this is largely to be attributed the success which attended their labours.

The state of things in several parts of Ulster was now such as to require the infusion of just such a curative element as the Seceders were fitted to supply. Laxity of doctrine and of practice were creeping all too quickly into the Synod. The infection of Scottish moderatism had appeared in it, and for this malady it was fitting that Scotland should supply the remedy. The first planting of Secederism in Ireland was not, however, directly due to the prevalence of unsoundness in the faith. Lylehill, in County Antrim, within three or four miles of Templepatrick, has the distinguished honour of having been the first spot in Ireland where it took root. It is a quiet rural district, lying high behind the mountains which guard Belfast on the west, and is still the abode of a staunch Presbyterianism worthy of the antecedents of the place. At the time we speak of, the people of Lylehill belonged to the congregation of Templepatrick, whose minister, the Rev. William Livingstone, was a sound and energetic pastor, and whose session had as one of its elders the excellent Colonel Upton of Castle Upton (ancestor of the Templetown family), who manfully opposed in the Synod the insidious efforts of the Belfast Society to weaken the defences of orthodoxy. It could not therefore have been on the ground of dissatisfaction with the soundness of either minister or session that the Lylehill people sought the erection of a new congregation. Several other causes for their action are mentioned, among the rest their distance from the church in Templepatrick.[1] Whatever were the reasons, however, which actuated them, in 1741 they applied to be taken under the care of the Associate Presbytery in Scotland. More than one memorial on the subject was sent to that body, and in August 1742, Messrs. John Gibson[2] and Samuel Henderson went over to them as commissioners from Lylehill, 'earnestly requesting supply of sermon.' After several temporary supplies, the Rev. Isaac Patton, a licentiate of the Associate Presbytery of Dunfermline (for the original Presbytery had already grown into three, which were united under the care of 'The Associate Synod'),

---

[1] A dispute about a farm in Rickamore, which, on the expiration of a lease, Colonel Upton gave either to Mr. Livingstone or his son, is alleged as one of the causes.

[2] This John Gibson married the daughter of his brother commissioner, Samuel Henderson, and among their great-grandchildren were the late Rev. John Barnett, D.D., Moneymore, and the late James Gibson, Esq., Q.C., County Court Judge of Donegal, and one of the most faithful ruling elders that the Irish Presbyterian Church ever had.

described as 'a little, active, sharp-eyed man,' was finally ordained over them on 9th July, 1746. A humble church was soon erected for the accommodation of the people, and so, within sixteen or seventeen miles, as the crow flies, from the spot where Edward Brice, in 1613, planted the standard of Presbyterianism, originated the cause of the Secession in Ireland,—a cause which was to exercise so useful an influence in the province during a separate existence of a hundred years, and finally to merge its life, along with the Synod of Ulster, in the united General Assembly of the Presbyterian Church, where to this day its influence lives, and the power of its principles is felt.

Some of the people of Lisburn who were dissatisfied with the state of matters there had applied to the Associate Presbytery for supplies before those of Lylehill, their application dating from 1736, and Mr. Patton, though ordained at Lylehill, had also charge for a time of the Seceding interest in Lisburn, and in Belfast as well—a pretty large parish for a single minister! But labourers were then scarce, and the Associate Synod had so much to do in Scotland, that it could afford no more than the one man to Ireland. By and by, however, as the cause in Scotland progressed, larger aid was forthcoming, and congregation after congregation sprang up on this side the Channel. Among those earliest organized may be mentioned Markethill, Ballyrashane, Roseyards, Boardmills, Moira, Ray, Ballyroney, Newtown-Limavady, Ballibay, Bangor, Armagh, Aghadoey, Ballykelly, Balteagh, Dunboe, Kilraughts, Ballymoney, and Derrykeighan.

The Seceders had their own troubles. The body had not long been organized in Scotland until it was rent in twain by a controversy as to the lawfulness of its members taking a certain oath required to be sworn by those who were elected to serve in town councils in several Scottish burghs. This oath pledged the swearer to the maintenance of 'the true religion presently professed within this realm, and authorized by the laws thereof,' which one party affirmed meant the Protestant religion, the oath having, they said, been framed to prevent Romanists from being elected as burgesses; while another held that it involved the recognition of patronage and the other abuses of the Church of Scotland as by law established. The controversy ended in 1747 in the rending of the Secession into two Synods, the one popularly known as the Burghers, who defended the taking of the oath, the other, consisting of those who objected to it, being named the Anti-Burghers. Though Ireland had no concern in the world with this oath, the Seceders here must needs take sides also. So Mr. Patton and the Lylehill congregation joined the Anti-Burghers, others sided with the Burghers, and thus, almost at the very inception of its history, Secederism began to present a divided front to its enemies. Its ministers met also, as might be expected, with opposition from members of the Synod of Ulster, who naturally did not relish their intrusion upon what they had come to regard as their own private preserves. Pamphlets were written against the newcomers, sermons preached, and on one occasion a set discussion between two champions of the rival denominations created no small excitement. The scene of this debate was the quiet, rural district of Ballyrashane, between Coleraine and the Giant's Causeway, whose snug and snowy farm-houses and well-tilled fields are still the abodes of as fine a body of Presbyterian people as could anywhere be found. Here, on a platform erected in the open air, the Rev. Robert Higinbotham, minister at Coleraine, and Mr. John Swanston, a probationer of the Secession, hammered at each other during the length of a summer day, in the presence of a prodigious assembly of people, both combatants, as usual, claiming the victory. This mode of settling controversies was evidently in favour in those days, as we read of similar discussions being held at Aghadoey, Clontibret, and other places. In spite of all opposition, however, the cause of the Seceders throve. It is quite certain that it did Ireland good service. We owe to it such men as the three Edgars,—Samuel of Ballynahinch, whose academy, long before Boards of Intermediate Education were dreamt of, sent to college youths well grounded in classics and mathematics, some of whom afterwards rose to great eminence,[1] and Samuel of Armagh, author of *The Variations of Romanism*, and John of Belfast, to whose enlightened Christian philanthropy Ireland owes so much;—Robert Wilson, author of one of the best extant treatises on *Infant Baptism;* the Rogerses of Cahans, and Glascar, and elsewhere; the Rentouls, and many others. Better still, it gave Ulster, in a time of need, a leaven of gospel truth and vital godliness, the traces of which can be seen to this day.

[1] See a little work by Rev. W. J. Patton, Dromara, entitled, *Three Ballynahinch Boys*, in which he traces the careers of three men taught at this school,—Professor James Thomson, author of many valuable educational works, and father of Sir William Thomson of Glasgow; the Rev. David Hamilton of Belfast, whose godliness and high services to the Church of his fathers have been so often spoken of; and Dr. John Edgar, mentioned above.

CHAPTER XIV.

A TIME OF DEADNESS.

THE latter part of the eighteenth century enjoys an evil reputation in the annals of religion. All over Europe it was a time of looseness of thought and coldness of heart. In France, it was the age of Diderot and the *Encyclopédie*. In Scotland, the moderatism represented by Robertson and Jupiter Carlyle was in the ascendant. In England, Deism and deadness prevailed; and the Church over here in Ireland did not escape the prevalent infection. The Westminster Confession of Faith began to be thrust more and more into the background. The practice of requiring subscription to it from licentiates and ministers fell into abeyance. Most of the Synod's theological students received their education at Glasgow College, and here the prevailing influences were all on the side of moderatism, or something worse. Professor Simson, who occupied the chair of Divinity in Glasgow for several years, was a man deeply imbued with the prevailing spirit. Dr. Leechman, who afterwards filled the same chair, is believed to have been at heart an Arian. And in another chair which, though not strictly theological, deals with questions so closely allied with religion that it is not easy to be right in it if they are wrongly solved, the chair of Moral Philosophy, a brilliant young Irishman was delivering lectures which crowded his class-room with students from all the three kingdoms, such was the beauty of his theories and the fascinating eloquence with which he expounded them. This was the famous Francis Hutcheson, the son of an excellent and godly father, the Rev. John Hutcheson, Presbyterian minister of Armagh. But, though the lectures were eloquent and all the more popular because, discarding the custom of the day, Dr. Hutcheson addressed his students in English instead of Latin, and though his theories were very beautiful, he taught a philosophy which sapped the foundations of evangelical religion, and which was the more dangerous because of the glitter which his beautiful speculations and eloquent Irish tongue threw around it. With such professors poisoning, at its fountainhead, the stream of the ministry, it is not to be wondered at that the pulpits of the Synod of Ulster began to give a very uncertain sound on the great verities of the faith, and in some cases to ignore them altogether. Little by little the orthodox band, which had turned a stern face towards non-subscription, waned and dwindled away; and as the old heads disappeared, and a new generation arose trained under Hutcheson and Simson or Leechman, the former majority sank into a minority which was powerless against the rising tide of error, until in the end 'New Light' principles gained a complete ascendancy. Life seemed now to leave the Synod almost entirely. There was none of that 'outward propagation' of the faith which is as essential to the life of a Church as 'inward preservation.' The erection of new congregations was discouraged, no matter how urgent the necessity for them. Friendly overtures were made to the Non-subscribers who had been excluded from fellowship in a more strenuous age. The gold had indeed become dim since the days when Blair, and Brice, and Livingstone preached Christ in the towns and villages of Down and Antrim, or since at a later date godly men had refused to sit in the same Synod with those whose fidelity to Bible truth they doubted.

The Seceders were for some time a happy counteracting influence to the evils which thus sprang up. When the Synod of Ulster refused to permit the erection of a new congregation in a district where it was needed, it very frequently happened that the sister Church took the disappointed applicants under its care. In many places also where ministers were starving their people by giving them the cold stone of morality in place of the bread of the gospel, the Seceders were at hand to feed them. On the 12th April, 1750, the first Irish Associate Presbytery met at Arkilly, near Newtown-limavady. It consisted of three ministers, the Rev. Messrs. Patton of Lylehill, Arrott of Markethill, and Stewart of Drumachose. On 24th July, 1751, the first Irish Burgher Presbytery was constituted in 'Wm. M'Kinley's field' at Ballybay, as it is described with fond minuteness in the old Session-book of the congregation of Cahans (to the pastoral charge of which Mr. Thomas Clark had on the same spot been ordained the previous day,—a man who was to become one of the most eminent of the fathers of the Secession, and whose tall and gaunt figure stands out prominently before us, as he rode rapidly about from place to place through the country, with his Highland bonnet and his homely attire, the zeal of the Lord eating him up). This Presbytery also consisted of three members, the Rev. Messrs. Black, Boardmills; Mayn[1] of Ballyroney, and Clark. When the Burgher Presbyteries had grown to three, viz. Derry, Monaghan, and Down, containing in all twenty ministers, they formed a Burgher Synod, which met for the first time at Monaghan on 20th October, 1779. When the Presbyteries of the Antiburghers numbered four, viz. Belfast, Markethill, Derry, and Templepatrick and Ahoghill, with seventeen congregations, they formed an Antiburgher Synod, which met for the first time in Belfast on the third Tuesday of August, 1788. These old distinctions, which once meant a good deal, are now almost forgotten. The Reformed Presbyterians, or Covenanters, as they are popularly called, may here be mentioned. Their first Presbytery in Scotland, consisting originally of two ministers and some ruling elders, dates from 1743. In 1752 two missionaries of the body appeared in the North of Ireland, and preached for some time. But their first Irish minister was not ordained until 1761,

[1] Mr. Mayn was grandfather of the Rev. Thomas Mayne Reid, long senior Clerk of the General Assembly, and great-grandfather of Captain Mayne Reid, the novelist.

when the Rev. Matthew Lynd, a native of Larne, was inducted into the pastorate at Vow, near Rasharkin. Their first Presbytery was organized in 1792.

The state of the Episcopal Church at this period was very bad. 'There was not one active minister in every county who preached evangelical doctrine, and scarcely one bishop could be named who laboured to promote the spiritual interests of his diocese. The Primate, Dr. George Stone, a man of great talents and unbounded ambition, was completely immersed in politics, and according to the testimony of a respectable historian who was a member of his own communion, was so bent on the maintenance of his party, that he sacrificed religion and morality in the most abominable manner that he might gain and confirm adherents. Several of the inferior clergy held Arian sentiments, and at least one dignitary, who wore an Irish mitre for nearly thirty years, was an avowed and zealous Unitarian.'[1] Almost the entire Protestantism of Ireland was thus at this period honey-combed with error. It was indeed a dark night in our religious history.

About this time began that full tide of emigration to the Western World, which was destined to produce such marked effects both on Ireland and on America. We have already noticed the fact that the Rev. Francis Makemie, a licentiate of the Lagan Presbytery, went to America about the year 1681; and from that time onward we find Ulstermen leaving their native province for the New World in larger or smaller numbers. But about the year 1729 this tide of emigration began to set with a persistency and a force towards the other side of the Atlantic which, considering the tediousness and hardships of the voyage in those days, and the uncertain prospects presented to the new settlers, cannot but be looked upon as remarkable. Year after year, from the second quarter of the eighteenth century, it is estimated that twelve thousand people annually sailed for America from the North of Ireland — an astonishing

[1] Killen continuation of Reid, iii. 302.

number, considering the population of Ulster at the period. Such was the drain, indeed, that it was computed that in 1773 and the five preceding years the North of Ireland lost by emigration to America 'one-fourth of its trading cash, and the like proportion of the manufacturing people.'[1] The large body of those who thus left the country were Presbyterians. Many causes combined to send them away. One of these was an intolerant landlordism. Bishops, as we have already seen, in leasing their lands, bound up the lessees under heavy penalties to permit the erection of no Presbyterian Church upon the property, and the residence of no Presbyterian tenant within its bounds. Episcopalian landlords followed the unchristian and intolerant example set by their 'right reverend fathers in God,' refusing either to let land on any terms to a Presbyterian, or if given at all, charging him a higher rent than his neighbours. The falling in of leases was a favourable opportunity with them for thus venting their miserable spleen on their unfortunate tenants who had the boldness to keep consciences of their own. It was hard to bear all this. But Presbyterians have always been a long-suffering race, very slow to wrath; and besides, what redress had they? To add to their troubles, some most unfavourable seasons reduced many of them to abject poverty, and so they began to pour out of the country across the ocean in their thousands. By a strange Nemesis, the nation which denied them the means of earning an honest livelihood within its borders was sorely punished for casting them out, for these sturdy Irish Presbyterians, who thus sailed from Belfast, and Carrickfergus, and Derry to America in the eighteenth century, were the main instruments in wresting that country from the rule of Britain.[2] Indeed it was a colony of Ulstermen in Mecklenburg County that first proclaimed the doctrine of American Independence, before Charles Thomson of

---

[1] *Historical Collections relative to the Town of Belfast*, 114.

[2] 'Most of the early successes in America were immediately owing to the vigorous exertions and prowess of the Irish emigrants, chiefly from the north, who bore arms in that cause.'—Plowden, *Historical Review*, i. 458.

Maryland, and Thomas Jefferson of Virginia, reduced it to writing in Philadelphia. 'We can name twelve Ulster to one English general around Washington. The ministers of the gospel in whom he most confided during the great revolutionary struggle were John Rodgers, James Caldwell, Alexander M'Whorter, George Duffield, and Patrick Allison, all sons of Ulstermen.'[1] But if this transfusion of Ulster blood in the eighteenth century into America wrested it from Britain, it gave to it a strength and a religiousness it has never since lost, and which have helped largely to make it the great land it has become.

Towards the close of the eighteenth century the social status and political privileges of Irish Presbyterians were largely improved. At its beginning, as we have seen, they did not even enjoy a legal toleration. Even so late as 1745, when the Pretender raised the standard of rebellion in Scotland, and when Ulster Presbyterians, true to their traditional loyalty, published a 'Declaration,' dated 24th August, 1745, announcing their determination, 'at the hazard of their lives and fortunes, to oppose all attempts against His Majesty's person and Government,' they petitioned in vain to be relieved of the odious Test Act; and even when they enrolled themselves in the militia for the defence of the kingdom, which they might have well excused themselves from doing, seeing that by accepting commissions therein, without being communicants in an Episcopal Church, they exposed themselves to the penalties of the Act, all that was done to relieve them was the passing of an Act of Indemnity, saving them for the time from these penalties. In 1780, however, when George III. had been twenty years on the throne, this most monstrous and iniquitous measure was at length repealed, after having galled the most loyal subjects of the Crown for nearly eighty years, and done no good, but much evil, to the cause it was meant to serve. Two years afterwards, Presbyterians obtained yet another boon of no small importance. For years their ministers had been subjected to prosecution and annoyance for

[1] Professor Croskery in *Presbyterian Churchman* for 1881, p. 155.

celebrating marriage between members of their congregations. Bishops and rectors seemed to take a delight in showing their power over them in this matter, and many were the fines and great the suffering endured owing to it. In 1782, however, an Act was passed, notwithstanding the strong opposition of the bishops (thirteen of whom caused their protest against it to be entered on the journals of the Irish House of Lords), declaring the perfect validity of all such marriages, and thus a wearisome controversy which had been a source of great distress came to an end. The *Regium Donum* also was twice increased about this time, £1000 per annum having been added to it in 1784, and £5000 per annum in 1792. The Seceders, who had previously enjoyed no State endowment, were granted £500 per annum in 1784, largely through the influence of the Earl of Hillsborough, ancestor of the Marquises of Downshire, and they received a proportionate share of the increase of £5000 above mentioned.

CHAPTER XV.

FROM THE RISE OF THE VOLUNTEERS TO THE LEGISLATIVE UNION.

WHEN the war with America broke out, followed by that with France, and when all the British troops that could be spared were required to meet these formidable antagonists, Ulster, left almost destitute of military protection, and with French men-of-war hovering about her coasts, was obliged to take measures for her own defence. These assumed the shape of a Volunteer movement, which rapidly became immensely popular. Belfast took the lead in it, two companies having been enrolled here on Patrick's Day, 1778, with the Rev. James Bryson,[1] one of the Presbyterian ministers of the town, as their chaplain. Thousands of Protestants, (no others were allowed at first to be members,) enrolled themselves in the various corps. Clergymen exchanged the sober black for the military scarlet, and in some cases so far forgot themselves as to appear at the Presbytery or Synod, or even in the pulpit, in regimentals. Reviews were held amid great enthusiasm, and by and by meetings for the discussion of political grievances began to take place among the members. The people came thus to feel their power, and Government came to feel it too. Demands made in the name of 100,000 armed men can never be lightly treated, but at a time like the closing quarter of the last century, when there were not 5000 regular troops in all

---

[1] He was at this time minister of the Second Congregation. In 1792 he became the first minister of Donegall Street Presbyterian Church, now demolished.

Ireland, they could not easily be refused. Such demands were made by the Volunteers at their meetings. One such meeting lives in history. It was held on 15th February, 1782, in Dungannon. The quiet old borough must have worn an unwontedly gay and stirring appearance that day, as delegate after delegate alighted from mail coach and post-chaise, or dismounted from horseback, and all made their way in full military attire to the Episcopal Church, where, with a strange sense of the fitness of things, the meeting was held. There were 143 corps represented. The large body of those present were Presbyterians, as indeed the large body of the Volunteers throughout the province were. Resolutions in favour of the independence of the Irish Parliament were passed amid immense enthusiasm, the Rev. Robert Black, D.D., a leading Presbyterian minister, being one of the chief speakers, and making a deep impression by his eloquence, as he usually did.[1] The Dungannon resolutions were re-echoed at similar meetings held throughout the country, and, before many months had elapsed, the demand for the independence of the Irish Parliament, so loudly made, had to be conceded, and for eighteen years the country was enabled to try the experiment of a certain kind of Home Rule. If any one wishes to know how the experiment succeeded, he has only to read the history of the country during that period to see for himself that it was a failure. The splendid Parliament House in College Green no doubt echoed to the eloquence of a race of orators of whom Ireland may well be proud. Few public speakers like Grattan, and Flood, and Curran have ever graced any assembly in the world, and there was a galaxy of such men in the Irish Parliament of that time. But it was a hopelessly corrupt body, and refused to reform itself. Of the 300 members in the House of Commons only 72 were returned

---

[1] Dr. Black was for long the leader of the Synod of Ulster. He is said to have been a man of remarkable eloquence. He was born in 1752, was ordained in Dromore, County Down, in 1777, installed in Derry in 1784, and elected agent for *Regium Donum* in 1788. Unhappily his mind gave way, and in December 1817 he threw himself into the Foyle from the parapet of Derry Bridge, and was drowned.

by the free choice of the people. Rotten boroughs, and pocket boroughs, and boroughs without any inhabitants, were the rule. Belfast had a population of 15,000 at the time. Thirteen persons, only five of whom were residents, elected its two members. Other places were even worse off. The venality of the Parliament is sufficiently proved by the history of the means by which its independence was bought from it, and, if we are to judge a tree by its fruits, the state of the country during those eighteen years, going as it did from bad to worse, until its miseries culminated in the terrible outbreak of 1798, sufficiently proves that such a Parliament is not a possession which Ireland need be anxious again to enjoy.[1]

The Volunteers had another still larger meeting in 1783. Again the place of assembly was Dungannon, this time, however, the Presbyterian Church, instead of the Episcopal, receiving the delegates. The representatives of 272 companies were present. Parliamentary independence having been achieved, a loud demand for Parliamentary reform went up from this meeting, to emphasize which a National Convention was summoned to assemble in Dublin, composed of delegates from every county in Ireland. The Convention accordingly met amid extraordinary excitement, but nothing came of it, and the Volunteer movement, which thus began to grow troublesome, came to an end in 1793. It had served its generation, and it was as well that it should fall on sleep.

Disaffection had now for years been growing in Ireland. The example and the success of the American colonies in shaking off the British yoke and establishing a Republic, and the example still nearer home of the French Revolution, lent it courage and hope, while the Volunteer movement, which had shown the people their strength, which had put arms into their hands, and taught them how to use them, suggested the means of carrying out its designs. The 'Society of United Irishmen' was formed, and soon, all over the country, the ramifications of a deep-laid and

[1] Grattan's Parliament was exclusively composed of Protestants.

dangerous conspiracy were spread. Secret meetings were held. Each parish, townland, barony, county, was organized. Efforts were made to corrupt the military, efforts which in not a few cases were successful. The smithies were busy forging pikeheads, and the farmers' daughters making cockades. The leading spirits of the movement, such as Theobald Wolfe Tone, Thomas Russel, and Lord Edward Fitzgerald, met frequently to organize and arrange details, and, we must not forget to add, to indulge in deep potations of Irish whisky. One such meeting (where no drink, for a wonder, is mentioned) lives in popular tradition. Tone, Russel, and others ascended the Cave Hill, near Belfast, on a May day in 1795, and, standing on M'Art's Fort, its highest point, swore with hands uplifted to heaven that they would never rest till Ireland was free. In June, 1798, the insurrection broke out. In Ulster it was confined to the three counties of Antrim, Down, and Derry, and even there it was foredoomed to failure from the first. The marvel is that the crowds of farmers and labourers who assembled at Roughfort, and on Donegore Hill, and at Saintfield, and Ballynahinch, did not themselves see the ludicrous hopelessness of an enterprise whose supporters were a motley crowd of untrained ploughmen, many of them with reaping-hooks or scythes tied to poles as their only weapons, a bag of oaten cakes their simple commissariat, and their confidence in their own cause so tremulous, that when in the act of assembling, the distant sound of horses' feet, as a few farmers trotted home from a fair, was sufficient to send a whole regiment of them to the right-about, in full belief that the dragoons were upon them. The British power in Ireland was not very likely to be overthrown by such foes. In the North, therefore, the whole movement ended in a miserable fiasco. Men gathered, in some cases to the number of several thousands, at appointed rallying places, marched with drums beating and flags (such as they were) flying, along the country roads. In Ballymena and Larne and Randalstown there were brisk encounters with the King's troops. At Antrim the fight assumed some dimensions. Henry Joy M'Cracken, with a courage and bravery worthy of a better cause, led the insurgents, and there was sharp firing in the street, and from behind Lord Massereene's garden wall. Lord O'Neill met his death there that day. But a few troops of cavalry and yeomanry sufficed to bring the business to an end, and poor M'Cracken, after hiding in the rugged recesses of Slemish, along with some followers, for several days, was finally taken, and his head impaled on Belfast Market House.¹ A more formidable encounter took place at Ballynahinch, the only one in the North which deserves the name of battle. Here the rebels, under Henry Munroe, were drawn up on Ednavady Hill, and courageously stood their ground for some time. But the Battle of Ballynahinch ended, like all the other encounters with the rebels, in their complete defeat. A day or two sufficed to put down in the North of Ireland the whole rising, which had been looked forward to as certain to realize the dream of Irish independence, which had been plotted for years, and on which many misguided men had staked their all.

In the south of the island the insurrection assumed much more formidable dimensions, and was not crushed before much blood had been shed. It assumed here the form of a religious war. Romanism was for the time in the ascendant, and in a delirium of fierce joy feasted gluttonously on Protestant blood. The fury of the outbreak culminated in County Wexford. Under the leadership of a Romish priest, Father Murphy of Boolavogue, the most horrid atrocities were here perpetrated. They began on a Sabbath morning. A Protestant clergyman named Burrows was brutally murdered. His son was mortally wounded, and when seven of his parishioners had been also despatched, his poor wife was left sitting on the lawn among the bleeding bodies, beside her dead husband and her dying boy, with her home in flames behind her. Similar brutalities day after day marked

¹ The Market House stood on the site at the corner of High Street and Corn Market, now occupied by the establishment of Messrs. Forster Green & Co.

the path of this bloodthirsty ecclesiastic. He hounded on his followers to deeds at which humanity blushes. A camp was formed at Vinegar Hill, and its record is simply sickening. A windmill stood on the top of the hill and a barn at the foot. The country was scoured for miles round, and all the Protestants on whom hands could be laid brought in, and crowded into these buildings. From the windmill they were brought out in batches to be piked. The windmill was kept filled from the barn, and the barn from the surrounding country, and so every day, like tigers which had tasted blood and could not be satisfied, Father Murphy and the horde of other Romish ruffians whom he had collected, feasted on the slaughter of Protestants, while, to give the proceedings the solemn sanction of Mother Church, twenty priests said mass at regular intervals in different parts of the camp, and a great tub of holy water was daily blessed, that the murderers might sprinkle themselves with it and go to their work feeling that they had the blessing of the Church in their pious work.[1] It would take too long to tell here all the other horrors of that awful time in the South of Ireland, the fearful scenes which were enacted at Enniscorthy, and in the town of Wexford, and elsewhere. One place lives in infamy in the memories of many, the barn of Scullabogue. Into this 184 Protestants, chiefly old men, women, and children, were driven at the pike's point. By and by, in obedience to an order for their massacre signed by a priest, they were brought out one by one and shot or piked, while their murderers actually licked up the blood which ran from their wounds. This mode of despatching their victims, however, did not prove rapid enough. So the doors of the barn were nailed up, and a burning faggot applied to the thatch roof. Soon the whole building was in a blaze, and the ruffians yelled with joy as the shrieks and cries of the hapless people within rose to heaven

---

[1] It is surely no wonder that Irish Protestants dread the establishment of any Romish ascendancy in the country, when they know that on every single occasion since the Reformation, at which Popery has gained the upper hand in Ireland, it has persecuted to the death.

amid the crackling of the flames. It is still remembered how, when one little child tried to crawl out beneath the door from the burning barn, a pike was stuck into its flesh as coolly as a farmer would put his fork into a sheaf of corn, and it was tossed back into the fire ![1]

As might have been expected, the outbreak received no countenance from either the Synod of Ulster or the Secession Synod. Both acted throughout the trying crisis with the loyalty for which Irish Presbyterianism has always been famous, and of which we have seen example after example as we have traced its story. Individuals connected with both no doubt sided with the rebels. Several ministers of the former Synod were deeply implicated. The Rev. James Porter of Greyabbey, an Arian, was tried by court-martial at Newtownards, and executed close to his own church on 2nd July, 1798. He was the only minister of the body who suffered capital punishment. The Rev. William Steel Dickson, D.D., of Portaferry,[2] also one of the New Light party, was arrested and kept in confinement for three years at Fort George, in Scotland. The Rev. Sinclair Kelburn[3] of Belfast, the Rev. Samuel Barber of Rathfriland, and the Rev. John Smyth of Kilrea, were also imprisoned for longer or shorter periods, and the Rev. James Simpson of Newtownards,

---

[1] Froude's *English in Ireland*.

[2] Dr. Dickson was a man of remarkable ability. Had he devoted himself to the duties of his calling, instead of being led away by the pursuit of politics and the carrying out of visionary schemes, he would undoubtedly have risen to great eminence in the Synod. He was born near Templepatrick, educated at Glasgow, licensed in 1767, ordained in Ballyhalbert (now Glastry) in 1771, and in the same year, as he tells us himself, 'became a husband and a farmer.' In 1780 he was installed in Portaferry, where he was minister at the time of the rebellion. After his liberation he became minister of Keady; but Government refused him the *Regium Donum*, and in 1815 he resigned the congregation and lived in Belfast, supported by the kindness of friends. He died there on 27th December, 1824. He was the author of several works, the best known of which is *A Narrative of the Confinement and Exile of W. S. Dickson, D.D.*

[3] Mr. Kelburn was the immediate predecessor of Dr. Hanna in Rosemary Street Presbyterian Church. He published several sermons.

Rev. John Glendy of Maghera,[1] and the Rev. Thomas L. Birch of Saintfield, who were also implicated, left the country, and went to America. But, in all, only eight ministers of the Synod of Ulster, out of a total of about two hundred, were convicted of complicity in the rebellion, and at its first meeting, held immediately after the suppression of the outbreak, the court emphatically condemned the movement, and enjoined the several Presbyteries, 'under penalty of severe censure,' to 'institute a solemn inquiry' into the conduct of any ministers or licentiates charged with 'seditious and treasonable practices.' At the same time it adopted an earnest address to the people under its care, remonstrating with those who had been 'led into open outrage and rebellion,' and urging all to loyalty and a peaceable demeanour. This address was ordered to be read from every pulpit, and as 'the contribution of the members of the body towards the defence of the kingdom,' the sum of £500 was voted to the Government. Of the Seceders, not a single minister seems even to have been accused of treason. On the contrary, one, the Rev. Francis Pringle, Gilnahirk, resigned his charge owing to the discomfort which he suffered on account of his opposition to members of his congregation who sympathized with the views of the United Irishmen, and other ministers, who remained, found themselves very unpleasantly situated from the same cause. Most of the leading spirits in the movement were Episcopalians, and the first person convicted of carrying on a treasonable correspondence with France, and condemned to be hanged, was a minister of that body, the Rev. William Jackson. But it would be as unfair to charge the Episcopalians with the guilt of the rebellion as it would be to fasten it on the Presbyterians, or to accuse Trinity College, Dublin, of sympathy with it, because individual fellows and scholars were implicated.

No sooner had the insurrection been quelled than the project of a legislative union between Great Britain and Ireland was urged

[1] The Rev. Dr. Cooke was baptized by Mr. Glendy, and brought up under his ministry for a time.

forward. It is unnecessary here to rehearse the various means employed to bring this union about. Suffice it to say, the measure, after fierce debates, and an agitation which convulsed the entire country, was at length carried, and from 1st January 1801 the United Kingdom of Great Britain and Ireland has been under the rule of one Imperial Parliament. If this were the place to treat of the advantages which have flowed to Ireland from this union, it might easily be shown that it has conduced immensely to the prosperity of the country in every way, and that its repeal, or the passing of any measure which would have the effect of weakening the connection between the two countries, could only issue in disaster to both.

In 1803 the *Regium Donum*, which had been so long enjoyed by the Synod of Ulster, was increased by a very large amount. Up to this time each minister had only received about £32 per annum from this source. Now the 186 congregations of the Synod and the Presbytery of Antrim were divided into three classes, containing sixty-two each, the classification being made according to the size and importance of the congregations, the largest being put in the first class, the ministers in which were to receive £100 per annum, those of the second class £75, those of the third £50, all Irish currency. The Synod strongly objected to this system of classification, but their objections were overruled. The Seceders did not share in the increase, and they strenuously denounced the principle of classification on which the grant was now made, at the same time urging their claims strongly for an augmented endowment. In 1809 their request was granted, but, to their great chagrin, on the same principle of classification, only with this difference, that their ministers were to be paid on a lower scale than those of the other body, the three classes receiving respectively only £70, £50, and £40 per congregation per annum. Both bodies, however, accepted the grant, with the exception of one minister, the Rev. James Bryce of Killaig, near Coleraine, who remained firm in his opposition, and seceding from his brethren, became the founder of a separate Presbytery, now the United Presbyterian Presbytery of Ireland.[1] In 1838, we may here mention, the principle of classification was done away with. The *Regium Donum* was in that year equalized, each minister, both of the Synod of Ulster and the Secession Synod, receiving £75 per annum, Irish. At this figure the endowment continued till it was abolished by the Irish Church Act in 1869.

[1] Mr. Bryce was a Scotchman, having been born at Airdrie in 1767. The Rev. Dr. Bryce of Belfast is one of his sons, and James Bryce, Esq., M.P., author of *The Holy Roman Empire*, his grandson.

CHAPTER XVI.

THE EVANGELICAL REVIVAL.

WITH the commencement of the nineteenth century a notable change in the religious condition of the Synod of Ulster began to manifest itself. Signs of returning life and earnestness appeared, which gave intense joy to those ministers who had not ceased to maintain a faithful testimony amid general defection, and who had long waited and prayed for the coming of such a time. In 1810 a case came before the Synod which brought the undoubted fact of the existence of Arianism within its bounds formally before it. A minister, during the hearing of an appeal which he had brought, boldly acknowledged himself an Arian. No proceedings were taken against him for the avowal; but it is worthy of notice, as indicating a spirit of dissatisfaction with the toleration of error, that a protest against the conduct of the Synod in the matter was entered on the minutes, and signed by seventeen ministers.[1] Another sign of reviving vigour was the re-

---

[1] The names of these protesters were James Elder, James Brown, Richard Dill, Samuel Dill, John Hall, Solomon Brown, Charles Kennedy, William Wright, Thomas Greer, W. D. H. M'Ewen, Richard Dill, jun., James Marshall, James Goudy, James Horner, Samuel Hanna, John Thomson, and Joseph Harrison. James Elder, whose name heads this list, was minister of Finvoy. His evangelical fervour earned for him the sobriquet of 'The Gun of the Gospel.' The three Dills belonged to a family which has given a large number of notable ministers to the Irish Presbyterian Church. Solomon Brown was minister of Castledawson, brother of the late Rev. John Brown, D.D., Aghadoey, and father of Dr. Samuel Browne, the well-known Belfast surgeon. Thomas Greer, minister of Dunboe, was father of the late Mr. S. M. Greer, Q.C., Recorder of Derry, and of the late Rev. Thomas Greer of Anahilt. James Goudy of Ballywalter was father of the late Rev. Dr. Goudy of Strabane. James Horner was colleague of Rev.

appearance of a missionary spirit. In 1812 the well-known Rev. Dr. Waugh of London appeared before the Synod at Cookstown, to plead the cause of the London Missionary Society. Several of the leading ministers objected to his being heard, and actually denounced the idea of attempting to convert the heathen as absurd and visionary. But other members as strenuously supported his application, and he obtained leave to speak and produced such an impression by his address that tears glistened in the eyes of his auditors, and the pulpits of the Synod were freely placed at his disposal for the advocacy of the cause which lay so near his heart. It is surely instructive to note that three-quarters of a century ago the idea of missions was scoffed at among us as a wild dream, and their advocate only granted a hearing through the earnest intervention of a few good men.

An event occurred about this time in Belfast which was destined to be fraught with important issues to the cause of Irish Presbyterianism. This was the opening of the Academical Institution, founded by a number of public-spirited men, and opened in 1815 as a college, with a Government endowment of £1500 per annum.[1] Both the Synod of Ulster and the Seceders agreed, at the solicitation of the Managers of the Institution, to recognise the new college, and to receive its 'General Certificate' as equivalent to a university degree. The Synod of Ulster also appointed the Rev. Samuel (afterwards Dr.) Hanna as its Professor of Divinity and Church History,[2] to lecture in

Dr. M'Dowell in Mary's Abbey, Dublin, and a man of kindred spirit. Samuel Hanna was the Rev. Dr. Hanna of Rosemary Street, Belfast; and John Thomson was the venerable minister of Carnmoney.

[1] There was also from the first a school department, which still continues. The collegiate department was closed on the opening of Queen's College, Belfast, in 1849.

[2] The Rev. Samuel Hanna, D.D., was one of the ministers most intimately concerned in the evangelical revival in the Synod of Ulster. He was born at Kellswater, near Ballymena, in 1771, ordained minister of Drumbo in 1795, and translated to Rosemary Street, Belfast, in 1799. He died in 1852. The late Rev. William Hanna, D.D., LL.D., son-in-law and

the Institution to its theological students,—a significant appointment, Dr. Hanna being a strenuously orthodox and excellent minister. The Burgher Synod also appointed a professor to instruct its candidates for the ministry—the Rev. Samuel (afterwards Dr.) Edgar of Ballynahinch, and from this time forward the tide of Irish student life, which had used to set strongly towards Glasgow at the beginning of each winter, began to flow instead to Belfast. This connection of the Presbyterian Church with the Institution was destined to be the cause of no small amount of irritation and contention. Arianism became dominant in the management of the new seminary, and no small part of the Arian controversy in the Synod of Ulster arose out of the relations between that body and the Belfast College.

There was now being trained, unnoticed by the world, in a secluded spot among the Derry mountains, a man destined in the Providence of God to be the means of freeing the Synod of Ulster from the trouble of Arianism. This was the afterwards illustrious Henry Cooke, a man whose name and fame will last as long as the Presbyterian Church endures, or Protestantism exists in Ireland. He was born on 11th May, 1788, at a place called Grillagh, near Maghera, in the county of Derry. His father was a plain, honest, hard-working farmer, who had for his second wife a godly woman, of great strength of character and natural mental capacity, a Howie, of the same stock as the author of *The Scots Worthies*. His school days, spent in the thatched cabins which then did duty for school-houses in Ireland, with stones or black oak sticks from some neighbouring bog for seats, and a great fire, to which every boy contributed a daily turf, smoking in the middle of the floor, were soon over, and at the age of fourteen he entered Glasgow College. His course here

biographer of Dr. Chalmers, colleague of Dr. Guthrie in Free St. John's, Edinburgh, and author of *The Last Day of our Lord's Passion* and five other volumes, forming together a complete life of our Lord upon the earth, was one of his sons.

finished, in 1808 he was ordained as assistant minister of Duneane, near Randalstown, where his entire income amounted to £25 a year, Irish currency. In 1811 he accepted a call from Donegore, and here he continued for seven years honestly discharging the duties of his ministry, and at the same time setting himself to systematic and thorough study of the theological questions of the day. His fame as a pulpit orator of rare power soon spread far and wide, and in 1818 he accepted a call to Killyleagh. He had been about three years here when a Rev. J. Smethurst was brought over from England to the North of Ireland by the New Light party to infuse life into their cause, which was evidently fast waning before the rising evangelical spirit of the time. In the course of an itinerant preaching tour he made his appearance in Killyleagh. Cooke attended his meeting, and, when he had done, invited the whole assemblage, Smethurst included, to his church the following Sunday, where he pledged himself to refute every dogma which the commissioned advocate of Arianism had propounded. Sunday came, and a tremendous crowd thronged the edifice. Cooke, according to promise, took up the Arian arguments, and tore them to shreds. He then announced his intention of following Smethurst from town to town, and from village to village, wherever he should go, and refuting his unscriptural heresies as soon as they were uttered. A chase more exciting than any fox-hunt ensued. From district to district Cooke pursued the apostle of Arianism, until the leaders of the party perceived that his mission was doing their cause far more harm than good, and he fled back to England. We do not hear of him revisiting Ireland on a similar mission. The Arian controversy was now begun in earnest,[1] and for seven years every annual meeting of the Synod of Ulster saw Cooke determinedly battling for the truth. In

---

[1] Dr. Cooke himself stated that the first time that he felt alarm for the situation of the Synod was 'on listening to an Arian prayer from the pulpit of Dr. Hanna's Church many years ago.'—*Speech at Academical Institution* in 1841.

1822 the court met at Newry, and he brought under its notice the influence which Arianism was exerting in the Belfast Academical Institution. But he stood almost alone. His brethren were not yet prepared to follow his lead, and, to add to his embarrassment, the very elements seemed against him. As he spoke, a terrific thunderstorm burst over the town and almost drowned his voice. It was a scene which would have disconcerted less able orators. 'I seem,' he said, 'this day to stand alone. Yet I am not alone. Men may draw back in fear, but God and truth are with me.' Ere long his brethren found that he was right.

In the same year the Rev. Dr. Bruce published a volume of sermons which created no little noise. The character of their theology may be guessed from the name of the author, who was long one of the Arian leaders in Belfast. Belonging as he did to the Presbytery of Antrim, the Synod had no jurisdiction over him, and could take no cognizance of his book. But as in the preface of the volume he stated that Arianism was making extensive though silent progress in the body, it publicly contradicted him, as it was bound to do in the interests of truth, for New Light principles, instead of advancing, were gradually and surely on the decline. In 1824 Cooke was elected Moderator of the Synod. In this capacity it fell to his lot to give evidence before a Royal Commission on the state of education in Ireland. Some statements which he made here regarding Arianism gave deep offence to its abettors, and round them battle after battle raged in the Synod and in the columns of the public press. The controversy approached a climax in 1827. In that year the Synod met in Strabane, with the Rev. J. Seaton Reid (afterwards D.D.), Carrickfergus, author of the well-known *History of the Presbyterian Church in Ireland*, as Moderator. Two important discussions took place on the burning question of the day. The Clerk of the Synod, the Rev. Wm. Porter, Newtown-limavady, had declared himself an Arian before the Royal Commission on education, and it was now moved by the Rev. Robert Magill of Antrim,[1] that in consequence of this avowal he should no longer be continued in the clerkship. A long and fiery debate took place on this motion. It was the evening of the second day before it terminated. An amendment, drafted by Dr. Stewart of Broughshane, was then carried, highly disapproving of Mr. Porter's evidence, yet, as his removal from the clerkship on this ground 'might be construed into persecution for the sake of opinion,' declining to take that step. Cooke approved of neither motion nor amendment. They were mere half measures, and he felt that the Synod should purge itself completely, not of the presence of an Arian clerk, but of the whole taint of Arianism which clung to it. He accordingly moved that the members of the Synod should be called upon to declare whether or not they believed the answer to the sixth question of the Shorter Catechism, viz., 'There are three persons in the Godhead, the Father, the Son, and the Holy Ghost; and these three are one God, the same in substance, equal in power and glory.' A debate took place on this motion, which is admitted to have been one of the finest displays of oratory which ever took place in the Synod. It began on a Thursday, and lasted during the following Friday and Saturday. Every one felt that the marrow of the question had now been reached, and the leaders on both sides put forth all their energies. Cooke delivered one of his most splendid speeches. Stewart, who all through the controversy rendered noble service, proved himself a most skilful lieutenant. He was unquestionably one of the most gifted of the many eminent men whom the Irish Presbyterian Church has produced. In acute logical power, and cool, cogent argumentative ability, he was a perfect master. He could dissect an opponent's argument with the skill and impassiveness of an anatomist. Unlike Cooke, he was not an orator, nor were there about him any graces either of person or manner to render what

---

[1] Mr. Magill was one of the most popular preachers of his day, and a man of great warmth of heart. He was also a poet of no mean ability. He died in 1836, after a brief ministry of less than sixteen years.

he said attractive. But, notwithstanding these deficiences, few antagonists had any chance against him in debate.[1] His speech on this occasion was one of his best efforts. It was 'calm, cold, and as usual brief. But every sentence told.'[2] On the Arian side, in this as in all the debates, Mr. (afterwards Dr.) Montgomery was the champion. He was minister at Dunmurry, a small village close to Belfast, and at the same time head master of the English Department in the Academical Institution. He was a man of remarkable power, a ready debater, and a speaker of singular eloquence.[3] On this occasion he made one of his most brilliant speeches. But Cooke and Stewart completely demolished his arguments. The motion was carried by an overwhelming majority. No more solemn scene was ever enacted in all the history of the Synod than that old church in Strabane then witnessed. The building was crowded with a deeply interested audience, and, as the roll was called, and each member stood up in answer to his name and declared whether he believed the doctrine of the Trinity or not, the excitement was intense. Of those present, 117 ministers and eighteen elders declared their belief in the doctrine. Only

---

[1] Dr. Stewart was born in April 1783, at Tullybane, in the parish of Clough, County Antrim. In 1803 he matriculated in Glasgow College, where he was a fellow-student of Cooke. At the close of his curriculum he was licensed by the Presbytery of Connor, and next year was called to Broughshane. Here the poll for him was taken on a Sabbath, and the voting did not terminate till ten o'clock on the night of the sacred day. This is the last Sabbath poll on record. He was ordained in 1809, and continued minister of the parish till his death in 1852.

[2] *Life and Times of Dr. Cooke*, by J. L. Porter, D.D., LL.D., p. 107.

[3] Dr. Montgomery was born at a place called Boltnaconnell, in the parish of Killead, on 16th January, 1788. In his boyhood he had for one of his teachers the Rev. Isaac Patton, the first Seceding minister who settled in Ireland, and he often spoke of the lessons he learned from him 'in his little old parlour, where he sat for upwards of fifty years.' He entered Glasgow College in 1804, was licensed by the Templepatrick Presbytery in 1809, and in the same year was ordained minister of Dunmurry—the charge which he held till his death. In 1817 he was appointed head master of the English Department in the Royal Academical Institution, Belfast, an office the duties of which he discharged for many years.

two ministers indicated their disbelief, and eight declined to answer. At the Synod of next year, which met at Cookstown, those who had been absent from the Strabane meeting were called upon to declare themselves, with the result that thirty-eight more ministers and fifty-nine elders declared their belief in the doctrine, four ministers and fourteen elders their disbelief, one minister withdrew, three ministers and two elders did not answer to their names, and two elders protested against the question altogether.[1]

At this Cookstown Synod of 1828, of which the Rev. Patrick White[2] was Moderator, Cooke proceeded a stage further. He brought forward a series of overtures providing for the establishment of a committee for the examination of all candidates for the ministry, with a view to the exclusion from the office of all persons holding Arian or other unsound sentiments. Another tremendous debate took place on these, distinguished as before by fierce encounters between Cooke and Montgomery. The overtures were carried by a sweeping majority, 99 ministers and 40 elders voting in their favour, and only 40 ministers and 17 elders against them.

Victory had now unmistakably seated herself on the banners of Cooke. The Arians saw that they were beaten, and the question with them was what they were to do. If they remained in the Synod, it was evident that they must submit to a process of gradual extinction, for the establishment of the new Theological Committee rendered it impossible for any addition to be made to their numbers. Accordingly they held a meeting for consultation in Belfast on 16th October, 1828. Here they drew up a 'Remonstrance,' intended to be laid on the table of the Synod, protesting against its recent action. This was soon published in the newspapers, and in pamphlet form, and circulated over the country.

---

[1] Reid, iii. 449.
[2] Mr. White was the excellent minister of Bailieborough. He died in 1862, leaving behind him several sons who have risen to eminence in the Church.

All through the winter and spring the excitement on the subject continued. Scarcely anything else occupied the attention of the Presbyterian public. All eyes were directed to the next meeting of Synod, for it was evident that matters could not remain much longer as they were. The Court met in Lurgan, with the Rev. Robert Park of Ballymoney[1] as Moderator. It was evident from the very commencement of the proceedings that great issues were pending. There had recently been elected as Professor of Moral Philosophy in the Belfast Institution a Mr. Ferrie, who was strongly suspected of holding Socinian views, and this further indication of the predominance of Arian influence in a seminary where the larger number of the candidates for the ministry of the Presbyterian Church received their training, could not pass unnoticed.[2] Mr. Cooke brought forward the subject of the election, and moved a series of resolutions. The Arian leader had come up fully prepared for this, and fully prepared also to make a final and, as he hoped, crushing attack on his opponent. He had gone carefully into the history of many past years, ransacking bluebooks and volumes of minutes for material wherewith to confound him. In his hand, as he rose out of the pew in which he had taken his seat, and stepped out in front of the pulpit, he held the ponderous report of the 'Commission on Education' containing Cooke's evidence. Amid loud plaudits he began his speech. In a short time he proceeded to assail Cooke, who sat in a pew close by, with terrific vehemence. 'His face put on a sallow paleness,'[3] and his voice became deeper, as with mingled sarcasm and invective he launched out into a tremendous philippic against the

---

[1] Mr. Park was ordained in Ballymoney in 1817. He succeeded Dr. Reid in the clerkship of the Synod of Ulster, and at the Union became one of the clerks of the General Assembly. He died in 1876. He was one of the godliest and most faithful men whom the Irish Presbyterian Church has ever had in her ministry. John Park, Esq., D.Lit., Professor of Logic and Metaphysics in Queen's College, Belfast, is one of his sons.

[2] Cf. *Minutes of an Inquiry respecting the Moral Philosophy Class.* Belfast, 1835.

[3] *Life of Dr. Montgomery*, by his son-in-law, Rev. J. A. Crozier, Newry.

orthodox leader, contrasting his statements with regard to the case of Mr. Ferrie with his sworn evidence before the Education Commission, and maintaining that the one flatly contradicted the other. As he insisted on his successive points, he raised the heavy blue-book in his hand and waved it in the face of the Synod, exclaiming—'This, remember, is his sworn testimony,—sworn upon the holy Evangelists!' When he had in this manner inveighed against Cooke, with looks, gestures, and words almost appalling, until the only person in the great audience who seemed unmoved was the object of his denunciations, he changed his tone with the consummate skill of the practised orator, and, in a voice tremulous with emotion, contrasted the scene of bitter conflict in which they were now engaged with the peace of heaven, until every hearer was melted into admiration. When he sat down, after holding his audience almost spell-bound for nearly three hours, an adjournment of half-an-hour followed. On the resumption of business, Cooke took the floor to reply to his assailant. It was no easy task. In fact, many of his friends trembled for him. They did not see how it was possible to meet the terrible charges which had been hurled at him. But he had not been long on his feet until their apprehensions on his behalf were completely dissipated. The dense audience listened with mingled astonishment and admiration as, to use his own impassioned language, he 'dashed to atoms the vile accusation,' as he 'smote and shivered the atrocious calumny with the talisman of truth.' It would be impossible to describe the speech. Competent judges who heard it pronounce it one of the most marvellous displays of eloquence to which they ever listened. Although, unlike his antagonist, he had had no time for preparation, and was called upon without warning to reply to grave charges founded on evidence given more than four years before, he not only completely vindicated himself, but, what was even more important, gave the death-blow to the cause of Arianism in the Synod. Montgomery's speech had been the last desperate effort of a failing cause. It was a splendid effort. But it was a failure so far as results were concerned. The Arians themselves felt that all was lost. Their last card was played, and they were beaten men.

A special Synod was held at Cookstown in the following August. The Arians absented themselves, with the exception of the Clerk, Rev. William Porter, who in their name formally laid their 'Remonstrance' on the table, together with an 'Address' which they had adopted. All that remained now was to arrange the terms of separation. These were soon agreed upon, and seventeen ministers left the Synod and formed themselves into a separate body, taking the name 'Remonstrant Synod,' and the Synod of Ulster was at last finally free from the taint of an unscriptural and God-dishonouring heresy.

The after histories of the separatists and the Church which they left are instructive. The Arian cause, left to itself, steadily declined, until as a system it is now practically moribund in Ireland. On the other hand, the Synod of Ulster, when the poison of Arianism was extruded from it, put on new life and vigour. The blessing of heaven seemed to attend all its movements. In ten years it had grown more than during the whole previous century. New and tasteful churches took the place of old and dilapidated buildings all over the country.[1] Better still, a spiritual life manifested itself, which was as gratifying as it was real. The modern prosperity of Irish Presbyterianism dates from the Arian separation, and, it may safely be added, would never have been attained had that happy event not taken place.

To complete here the history of the Arian controversy and its results, it may be mentioned that in 1835, on the motion of the Rev. John (afterwards Dr.) Brown of Aghadoey,[2] the Synod agreed to an overture making absolute subscription to the Westminster Confession of Faith requisite on the part of all wishing to

[1] During the ten years ending with 1837 there was expended on church building £107,000 by 170 of the congregations.
[2] Dr. Brown was ordained in Aghadoey in 1813. He died in 1873. He was for long one of the most prominent figures in the Synod of Ulster, and afterwards in the General Assembly.

become licentiates, elders, or ministers. In 1836 this overture was finally confirmed, and the law ever since has been unqualified subscription.

Nowhere did the happy effects of the deliverance from Arianism appear more conspicuously than in Belfast. When the controversies on the subject began there were just two orthodox congregations connected with the Synod of Ulster in the town— Rosemary Street, founded, as we have seen, in 1721, and Donegall Street, founded in 1792 by a secession from the 2nd Congregation. Besides these there was one Secession church in Berry Street. In 1820, the Rev. John Edgar was ordained by the Seceding Presbytery of Down to the pastoral charge of another infant congregation, which met in a hired room in Commercial Court, off Donegall Street. By the energy of its young minister, a small church was built in Alfred Place, and opened for worship in 1821, exactly a hundred years after the erection of Rosemary Street. The feeble cause steadily grew, and became a centre of life and light in the town, under the energetic care of its pastor.[1] In 1828 the Rev. James Morgan[2] was installed as pastor of the newly-erected

[1] He was the son of the Rev. Samuel Edgar, D.D., Ballynahinch. He was born in 1798 at Ballykine, near that town, and received his collegiate education in Glasgow. In 1826 he succeeded his father as Professor of Theology to the Secession Synod, and on the formation of the General Assembly in 1840 he became one of its professors. He died in Dublin in 1866. A memoir of him by the Rev. Dr. Killen has been published.

[2] He was born at Cookstown on 15th June, 1799. His father, a bleacher there, was an Episcopalian, but left the then Established Church and lived and died a Presbyterian. His son James entered Glasgow College in his fifteenth year. Under God, he ascribed his conversion, which he dated from the year 1815, to the conversation and influence of an elder brother. He was licensed to preach in 1820, and in the same year was ordained as minister of Carlow, where he continued five years. His next charge was Lisburn, where he was assistant and successor to the Rev. Andrew Craig, who had long been minister there. The congregation here was greatly blessed under him. In 1828 he was called to undertake the charge of the newly-erected congregation of Fisherwick Place, Belfast. The blessings which resulted from his ministry here it would be difficult to exaggerate. Fisherwick Place became the model congregation of the Church, and its minister the model pastor. Dr. Morgan's work in the cause of church extension, in the establishment and

congregation of Fisherwick Place, commencing thus a ministry in Belfast which was to prove of singular advantage to the town as well as to the whole Church. In 1829, Dr. Cooke was called from Killyleagh to occupy a new church expressly erected for him in May Street, a most important event, not for Belfast alone, but for all Ulster. From this date the erection of places of worship has kept pace well with the gradual increase in the population, so that there are now in the town thirty-one Presbyterian churches under the jurisdiction of the General Assembly, as compared with the three which were all it possessed at the beginning of the century.

working of the Foreign Mission, and on behalf of temperance, can only be properly appreciated by those who are able to compare the state of things sixty years ago with what we have now. He died in 1873. Some of his published works enjoyed a very extensive circulation, among others a treatise on *The Person and Work of the Holy Spirit*, a *Commentary on the First Epistle of John*, and an excellent work on *The Lord's Supper*. His son, the Rev. Thomas Morgan, is minister of Rostrevor.

CHAPTER XVII.

WORK AND WARFARE.

THE year 1829 saw the birth in Ireland of a movement which has been productive of untold good, not only to her, but to the other two kingdoms. From that year dates the Temperance Reformation. The use of whisky was at this time almost universal, and seemed to be rapidly growing. During the ten years ending with 1829, the consumption of intoxicating liquors in the three kingdoms doubled. The bottle was everywhere—on the dinner table and the supper table, at the wedding and the wake, at the baptism and the funeral, produced as regularly as the Bible when the minister called to visit a parishioner, kept in the vestry of nearly every church, and applied to before service or after it, or both. In a word, it was supposed to be an absolute necessary of life—as necessary as the staff of life itself. Ministers and people alike drank. The elders drank. Everybody drank. Yet for long no adequate effort was made to put a stop to the terrible evil.

Dr. Edgar had his attention turned to the matter on this wise. In the summer of 1829 the Rev. Joseph Penny, a young Irish Presbyterian clergyman who had emigrated to the United States from Drumlee, paid a visit to his native country. Among others he called upon Dr. Edgar, and told him of the temperance societies which had been established in America. His hearer saw the thing at once, and with him to see was to act. Opening his parlour window, he emptied out the remains of a gallon of whisky which had been bought for household consumption,[1] and from that hour threw himself with characteristic ardour into the temperance movement. It was not, it is to be observed, total abstinence that he advocated. The temperance pledge of those days merely bound one to abstinence 'from all distilled liquors.' A letter from his pen, advocating the new departure, appeared in the *Belfast Newsletter* on 14th August, 1829. Some who read it thought it the work of a madman—so monstrous did the proposal to abstain altogether from whisky seem. To do without bread would not have appeared much more ridiculous. But the letter was read, among others, by the Rev. G. W. Carr, New Ross, who called upon Dr. Edgar shortly after, and on August 20th, by his influence, the first temperance society ever established in Europe was organized in New Ross. On the 24th September of the same year a few ministers met in a room at the old Tract Depository in Waring Street, Belfast, and founded the Ulster Temperance Society. The first three names subscribed to the pledge taken that day were those of James Morgan, Thomas Hincks, then a curate in Belfast, afterwards archdeacon of Connor, and John Edgar. The last of the three was the apostle of the movement. Letters and publications of all kinds advocating it flowed from his pen—sermons and speeches in multitudes from his lips. Meeting after meeting was arranged, and society after society organized, until an idea, which at first was ridiculed as chimerical, took deep root in the land, and to-day we see the development and fruit of it in the temperance sentiment which is so widely diffused, in the temperance legislation which has been obtained, and in the alteration in our drinking customs which has been brought about,—blessings great in themselves, and certain to be followed in the near future by others still more signal.[2]

---

[1] *Memoir of Dr. Edgar*, by W. D. Killen, D.D., p. 28.

[2] The progress of the temperance cause in the General Assembly has been very marked. Five-sixths of the ministers, and nearly all the theological students, are total abstainers.

The original basis on which the Temperance Reformation was established was, ere very many years had passed, found to be altogether too narrow and too artificial. A pledge which only forbade a man to drink whisky, and left him at liberty to satisfy his craving for liquor with port, sherry, and champagne, porter, ale, cider, or any other intoxicating drink which was not a product of distillation, failed to satisfy the logical convictions of its own advocates, and was soon seen to be an instrument altogether too weak to overcome the intemperance of the age. Hence, while Dr. Edgar and others continued to cling conservatively to the old pledge of abstinence from distilled liquors only, the principle of total abstinence from intoxicating drinks of all kinds ere long came to the front, and it has been almost exclusively under its banner that the modern Temperance Reformation has been prosecuted, and its victories won in the Irish Presbyterian Church and elsewhere. On July 4th, 1850, fifteen ministers united in forming the 'Temperance Association in connection with the General Assembly,' whose pledge is one of total abstinence from all intoxicating liquors as beverages. The membership has grown year by year, until now five-sixths of the clergy have subscribed that pledge. The number is still increasing, almost all the theological students being total abstainers. The entire Assembly in 1876 urged the adoption of the practice of total abstinence on all the people under its care. Such has been the gratifying progress of this great and much needed work, which began in 1829.

Two years after the commencement of the Temperance Reformation an important step was taken in the direction of dealing with the ignorance which, dense as night, overspread a large part of Ireland. In October, 1831, Mr. Stanley, Chief Secretary for Ireland (afterwards Earl of Derby), announced the intention of Government to establish a system of National Education for Ireland. Some of the original provisions of the scheme thus announced met with the utmost disfavour from a large portion of the Protestant public. The Rev. James Carlile,[1] one of the ministers of Mary's Abbey Presbyterian Church, Dublin, was appointed a commissioner for the administration of the new scheme, and ultimately became Resident Commissioner, a position in which he rendered essential service to the cause of education. But the Synod of Ulster in general was entirely opposed to certain features of the system. Much negotiation and discussion ensued. Year after year the Synod was occupied with it in one form or another, and outside the Synod the country was convulsed with the controversy. Nor was it until January, 1840, that the question was set finally at rest by the concession to the Church of such modifications of the scheme as enabled her to avail herself of its provisions. The Rev. Dr. Stewart of Broughshane had the honour of sending up to the Commissioners the 'model application' for aid to one of his schools, from the granting of which may be dated the formal connection of the Presbyterian Church with the Board. The General Assembly has now (1886) 742 national schools in connection with its congregations, and has been the best friend of the system of 'united secular and separate religious instruction' in Ireland. The system has been sadly 'tinkered' of late years in the interests of an unholy Roman Catholic ascendancy, so that it is difficult to recognise in it the features of the scheme of half a century ago. But withal it has been a great blessing to the country.

[1] Dr. Carlile was born in Paisley, in 1784, of the same Dumfriesshire stock from which Thomas Carlyle sprang. For some time he pursued a business career in the establishment of an uncle in London, but strong religious impressions, largely due to the ministry of Rowland Hill, changed the current of his thoughts, and he resolved to enter the ministry. After the usual course of study, he was licensed, and in 1813 received a call to be colleague of Dr. M'Dowell and Dr. Horner in Mary's Abbey, Dublin, and thenceforth his life was devoted to Ireland. His mission work in Birr, which he gave up residence in Dublin to prosecute, was singularly blessed. He died in 1854. We owe to his pen several of the best of the Irish National school-books. He was also the author of several valuable theological works.

CHAPTER XVIII.

THE UNION OF THE SYNODS, AND AFTER.

ONE of the happiest events in the modern history of Irish Presbyterianism occurred in the year 1840. It had for some time been clear that there was no good reason for the Synod of Ulster and the Secession Synod dwelling apart. Both subscribed the same Confession of Faith, held by the same polity, and maintained the same form of worship. The idea of a union between the two began therefore to be mooted among the theological students who were in attendance at the Institution. At one of their prayer-meetings in 1839, the Rev. John Coulter (afterwards Dr. Coulter[1]) of Gilnahirk gave an address strongly urging the advisability of such a step. Memorials praying that it should be taken into earnest consideration, were sent by the students to the next meetings of both Synods. Similar memorials were sent up from various congregations, and from a large public meeting held in Belfast. The question was evidently ripe for settlement, and negotiations were at once entered upon, which progressed so rapidly and satisfactorily that all necessary preliminaries were settled within one year, and on Friday, 10th July, 1840, the two Synods proceeded to the consummation of the union. Belfast has seen few days of such intense interest, and the Irish Presbyterian Church none of such importance. The streets of the town were densely crowded that morning, in expectation of the event. The Synod of Ulster sat in May Street Church, and the Secession Synod in Linen Hall Street.

---

[1] Dr. Coulter was one of the worthiest ministers of the Secession. He was Moderator of the General Assembly in 1851. He died in 1877.

At eleven o'clock the doors of the two churches opened, and a procession of clergymen and elders emerged from each. In front of the members of the Synod of Ulster was seen the figure of the venerable Rev. James Elder of Finvoy, its Moderator, with his snow-white hair and saintly look; while at the head of the members of the sister court walked one of the fathers of the Secession, the aged and deeply-respected Rev. John Rogers of Glascar.[1] The interest grew as the two bodies coalesced, and the two Moderators walked side by side, followed by the long black-coated procession, along Donegall Square and Donegall Place, until Rosemary Street Church was reached. Here an immense congregation had assembled. The two Moderators proceeded to the pulpit together. One gave out the 133rd Psalm, which was sung with deep feeling, the tears standing in many eyes as they saw those who were brethren come now to dwell together in unity. The other Moderator then read the 17th chapter of John, and, prayer having been offered, the Rev. Dr. Reid, Clerk of the Synod of Ulster, twice read over the Act of Union, which had been previously agreed upon by both Synods. The question was then put to the House whether this Act was ratified. All rose, and with uplifted right hand expressed their solemn approval of it. The Rev. Dr. Hanna was then unanimously chosen Moderator of the first General Assembly of the Presbyterian Church in Ireland, and the court was fully constituted.

Let us look round Rosemary Street Church and note the chief actors in the scene of that morning, for it will live in history as one of the red-letter days in the annals of Irish Presbyterianism. There in the Moderator's chair is the venerable Dr. Hanna, at whose feet successive generations of Belfast citizens have sat Sabbath after Sabbath for nearly half a century. At the Clerk's table, beside him, are seated the learned Dr. Seaton Reid, the

---

[1] Mr. Rogers was son of the venerable Rev. John Rogers of Cahans, and father of the late Rev. James Rogers of Glascar, who left two sons in the ministry of the Irish Presbyterian Church.

historian of the Church,[1] and Mayne Reid of Drumgooland, whose name is to be perpetuated in a son, the idol of boys for his tales of adventure. On the platform, too, are three well-known clergymen of the mother Church of Scotland, sent to congratulate the daughter on the auspicious event of the day, —the venerable Patrick Macfarlane of Greenock, who within three years is to give up the richest living north of the Tweed for conscience' sake; James Begg, the sturdy champion of Presbyterianism, and opponent of innovations; and the seraphic M'Cheyne, with the accustomed heavenly look upon a face that is all too soon for the world to be hid in the coffin. Glancing over the pews we see not far from the pulpit the majestic head of Cooke, now just in his prime; and the less conspicuous form of the saintly and sagacious Morgan; and burly, brusque, warm-hearted John Edgar. Near these is the godly and devoted David Hamilton, already fired through his inmost soul with a consuming desire for the salvation of the house of Israel, which ere long is to find embodiment in the Jewish Mission. The mild, hazel eyes of the scholarly Professor Wilson look on

[1] Dr. Reid was born in the eventful year 1798, at Lurgan, where his father, Mr. Forrest Reid, kept one of the best grammar schools of the day. Seventeen children were born to this excellent man, of whom the future historian was the sixteenth. He entered Glasgow College in 1813, was licensed by the Presbytery of Letterkenny (of which his brother, Rev. Edward Reid of Ramelton, was then a member) in 1818, and was ordained in Donegore in 1819. Here, at the age of twenty-three or twenty-four, he conceived the idea of writing the history of the Irish Presbyterian Church. It was not, however, till after his translation to Carrickfergus, which took place in 1823, that the project took shape. In 1834 the first volume was published. The second appeared in June, 1837, and in the following month the author was appointed by the Synod of Ulster its Professor of Ecclesiastical History. Already in 1830 he had been chosen Clerk to that body. In 1841 he was appointed by the Crown Professor of Ecclesiastical and Civil History in Glasgow University. The third and last volume of his great work was little more than half finished when death bade the busy fingers lay down the pen. He died at the seat of Lord Mackenzie, near Edinburgh, in 1851. The unfinished history was admirably completed by his successor in the chair of Ecclesiastical History in Belfast College, the Rev. W. D. Killen, D.D.

interestedly at the scene from underneath his fine forehead; and yonder is the eloquent Josias Wilson, who is soon to exchange the church at the end of the town (Towns-end Street) for a London charge. These from Belfast. From the country, notable men too—the courtly and polished Henry of Armagh, the son and grandson of a clergyman, destined in after years to be first president of the northern Queen's College; and the eloquent young Henry Jackson Dobbin of Ballymena, also a son of the manse; and Coulter of Gilnahirk, one of the best types of the excellent Secession pastor. There are Dills there, John of Carnmoney, and Richard of Ballykelly, Samuel of Donoughmore, and Samuel of Hillsborough, the last by and by to be in Ballymena, and in the end in a college, not yet thought of, on the banks of the Foyle. Rogerses, father and son, come from Glascar. Yonder are Edgar of Armagh, author of *The Variations of Romanism;* and Stewart of Broughshane, Cooke's *fidus Achates,* the fame of whose three days' contest with Father M'Auley of Ballymena has not yet died; the scholarly Barnett of Moneymore and the metaphysical Molyneaux of Larne; James Elder of Finvoy, currently known as 'The Gun of the Gospel,' and Johnston, the savour of whose ministrations and 'gallery meetings' is not yet dead in Tullylish, and who is to leave a son behind him, when he passes away, who is to be known all over Ireland as the orphan's friend. Derry has sent up to take part in the solemn scene the urbane William M'Clure, the senior of an eminent brother not yet come to the front, but destined by and by to do good service in Parliament, and James Denham, the father of his people and the stalwart defender of his Church's polity in the *Plea of Presbytery.* But the time would fail to tell of all the noteworthy men there that day—of the venerable White of Bailieborough, prolific ancestor of pastors; and Brown of Aghadoey, the stout defender of unconditional subscription to the Confession of Faith; and Huston of Macosquin, the staunch presbyter and the faithful minister; the eccentric David M'Kee of Anaghlone, oddest but most original of men;

and the cultured and busy John Weir of Newry, and the aged Horner of Dublin, and the earnest and scholarly Bleckley of Monaghan, and Park, the beloved pastor of Ballymoney, who is by and by to succeed Reid in the Clerkship, and be a familiar figure in the Assembly for another generation. One grieves to think that these are all gone. Among the elders, too, are men not to be passed over in silence. Thomas Sinclair is there from Fisherwick Place, the bearer of an honoured name, and the owner of a great heart, both destined to live on in a son like-minded. Counsellor Gibson sits as the elder from Rosemary Street, and Counsellor Greer from Dunboe—two men whose legal knowledge and public influence were at the service of the Church of their fathers long before and long after. D. K. Clarke has come up from Kilmore, which owed the building of its church to him, as the whole Church is to owe him many another help before he has fallen on sleep. Altogether it was surely a remarkable gathering,—in it men of truest genius, orators able by the spell of their eloquence to move men as by a magician's wand, thinkers of no mean order, authors of books which yet live and are not likely to die, wise and far-seeing educationists, faithful pastors, busy philanthropists, founders of great benevolent enterprises which for years have gone on blessing the world while they have been turning to dust, Christian merchants who struck a new keynote of Christian beneficence at which the old-fashioned held up their hands in astonishment, and Christian lawyers whose delight it was to make the law a handmaid to the gospel. A notable assemblage truly! How solemn the thought that all the worthies we have named—all, all are gone to the narrow house of their rest, and that of the others who joined with them that July day in Belfast in consummating the Union, but a handful are left![1]

---

[1] The congregations of the Synod of Ulster numbered 292 at the Union, and those of the Secession 141, so that 433 congregations in all were by the Act of Union placed under the jurisdiction of the General Assembly. 333 ministers and 135 elders attended this first meeting.

Almost the first act of the newly-constituted Assembly was the establishment of a Foreign Mission, and the designation of two brethren to proceed in connection with it to India, the Rev. James (afterwards Dr.) Glasgow, minister of Castledawson, and the Rev. Alexander Kerr, of Portadown. Thus was initiated a work which has since been greatly extended and greatly blessed.[1] It was not the beginning of Irish Presbyterian missionary enterprise. Long before, both Synods had given no obscure indications of their anxiety to propagate the faith. So far back as the eighteenth century the Synod of Ulster had taken steps to have the gospel preached in Irish to the Irish-speaking population.[2] In 1710, 'The General Fund,' intended to diffuse the gospel through the South of Ireland, was established, a scheme which for many years played an important part in establishing and sustaining Presbyterian congregations in that part of the country. In 1798, 'The Evangelical Society' was organized for the purpose of carrying on a system of itinerant preaching throughout the North of Ireland. Its chief supporters were Seceders.[3] In 1826, 'The Synod of Ulster Home Missionary

[1] Dr. Morgan, the first convener of this scheme, was succeeded in the office by the Rev. William Fleming Stevenson, afterwards D.D., Dublin, under whom it made great progress. He was a native of Strabane, where he was born in 1832. In 1856, after the usual college course, taken partly in Edinburgh and partly in Germany, he was licensed by the Presbytery of Strabane, and shortly afterwards became an agent of the Belfast Town Mission. In 1860 he was ordained by the Presbytery of Dublin as first minister of Rathgar, a suburb of the city of Dublin, where he was the means of establishing a most flourishing congregation, of which he remained the beloved minister till his death on September 16th, 1886. Dr. Stevenson was chaplain to the Lord-Lieutenant of Ireland during the viceroyalty of the Earl of Aberdeen—being the first Presbyterian clergyman who ever held that office. His book, *Praying and Working*, has attained widespread popularity, and his unquenchable enthusiasm in the cause of foreign missions, for the advancement of which he undertook, in 1877, a mission tour round the world, made him known and honoured throughout the whole of evangelical Christendom. He was Moderator of the General Assembly in 1881. His wife was a daughter of the late Mr. John Sinclair, The Grove, Belfast.

[2] *Ante*, p. 114.

[3] The Rev. George Hamilton, Armagh, father of the late Sir James Hamilton, Belfast, was its secretary.

Society' was established, but seems never to have possessed much vitality, and, after a brief existence of only three years, is no more heard of. In 1830, 'The Presbyterian Missionary Society' was formed, which attained considerable vigour, and commanded a large amount of support, its receipts having reached £1200 per annum in 1836. The Seceders, in addition to their efforts in connection with the Evangelical Society, in 1818, immediately after the union of the Burghers and Antiburghers, organized a Home Mission, and established preaching-stations in many places where Presbyterianism had hitherto been almost unknown.

All these efforts and plans show that the duty of sending the gospel to those without was clearly realized from an early period, and that, if greater efforts were not made by Irish Presbyterianism, the will at all events to make them was not wanting. No attempt at Foreign Mission work had indeed been made by either Synod. But Foreign Missions can scarcely be said to have had an existence anywhere a century ago. Now, both bodies being joined together, the first foreign missionaries ever designated by any Church in Ireland were set apart to labour in India. It was surely a good keynote to strike on that eventful day!

The tide of missionary fervour now began to flow with uncommon strength. One new mission had been established, but one was not felt to be enough. The Home field had been provided for. So had the Foreign. But there had been no recognition yet of the claims of the Jews. This, however, was not long to be. The General Assembly of 1841 had two memorials presented to it, praying for the establishment of a mission to them. One of these was from the Presbytery of Belfast; the other came from the laity of the same town, and had so many signatures attached to it, that, when unrolled, it was found to reach completely round Rosemary Street Church. The result was the establishment of the Jewish Mission, with the Rev. David Hamilton as honorary secretary.[1]

---

[1] The Irish Presbyterian people showed their cordial approbation of this action of their supreme Court, by sending in £954 as their first offering

In 1846 another scheme was organized—the Colonial Mission, intended, as its name indicates, to be the means of caring for the multitudes of our countrymen who are scattered abroad in the various colonies of the Empire. Of this the Rev. Wm. M'Clure of Derry was the first secretary. From the same year we find the Assembly interesting itself in the affairs of the Waldenses and other Continental Churches. The Continental Mission was ultimately established to take charge of this field, with the Rev. Professor Gibson as secretary. A Mission to Soldiers and Sailors was the last to be set on foot, with the Rev. Robert Black as first convener. The Church has thus fully taken her stand as a missionary Church, and has had not a few tokens that the Lord of the harvest has acknowledged her labours.

To return, however, to the history of the times succeeding the Union,—the 10th June, 1842, was the two hundredth anniversary of the establishment of the first Irish Presbytery. Dr. Cooke, who was then Moderator, by appointment of the Assembly proceeded on the bicentenary day to Carrickfergus, and preached a sermon from the words in the 51st Psalm, from which the Rev. John Baird had preached on the same day in 1642. It was a most solemn and interesting occasion. As a memorial of the goodness of God to the Church during those two centuries, a Bicentenary Fund was established, which was so heartily supported that £14,000 were contributed to it, a sum which was expended for the benefit of the cause of Presbyterianism in the South and West of Ireland.

The connection of the Synod of Ulster with the Belfast Institution had been attended by unpleasant friction almost from the beginning. Although largely erected by means of money contributed by Trinitarians,[1] the Arian party had managed to obtain a predominant influence in its affairs, and during the dis-

---

on behalf of Israel. See *Faithful unto Death*, a Memoir of the Rev. David Hamilton, by his Son, p. 75.

[1] It is stated on good authority that of the £22,000 expended on the buildings, £17,000 were contributed by Trinitarians.

cussions which eventuated in their separation from the Synod of Ulster, they managed to make that influence very uncomfortably felt. Again and again the Synod and the Board of Managers came into collision, and more than one of the debates, during the Arian controversies, hinged on some new phase of this conflict. From the class of one professor, Mr Ferrie, the Synod withdrew its students altogether, and in the whole seminary there was a want of confidence which was continually breeding irritation. Shortly after the Union, the relations between the two became intolerable, and the General Assembly, at a special meeting held in Cookstown in 1844, resolved on the erection of a college of its own. In a short time a sum of £3000 was subscribed for the purpose, and a beginning having thus been made, Government was applied to for the endowment of certain additional chairs necessary for such a seminary. In 1845, however, the reply came that Government 'would not endow any denominational college in Ireland.'[1] In the same year a Bill for the establishment of three Queen's Colleges in Belfast, Cork, and Galway, was introduced into Parliament by Sir Robert Peel, and speedily became law, and the idea now began to prevail that the best plan for the General Assembly would be to take advantage of one or all of the new seminaries for the literary and scientific training of its candidates for the ministry, and to confine its own operations to the provision of a theological college for their education in sacred subjects. An event which happened in 1846 gave matters, however, a new turn. At the Assembly of that year the Rev. Richard Dill of Dublin announced that Mrs. Magee, widow of the Rev. William Magee, Presbyterian minister of Lurgan, had just died in Dublin, and had left to the Irish Presbyterian Church sums amounting in all to about £60,000, £20,000 of this being for the erection and endowment of a college. This splendid legacy seemed to have come just in the nick of time. But it soon appeared that there were difficulties connected with its use. The trustees of Mrs. Magee's will maintained that the money must be used for

[1] *Minutes of the General Assembly*, i. 413.

the erection of a college affording a literary and scientific as well as a theological education; while, on the other hand, there were many who held that, inasmuch as the Queen's Colleges would now fully and admirably supply this literary and scientific training, it would be better to devote the money to the building and maintenance of a thoroughly efficient theological seminary. Ultimately the view of the trustees, who were left large powers by the will, prevailed, and the result was the erection of two colleges—Magee College, Londonderry, a splendid building with seven endowed chairs, affording a full training alike in secular and sacred subjects, and now affiliated with the Royal University, so that its alumni are able to proceed to the various degrees; and the Assembly's College, Belfast, one of the finest and most completely equipped edifices in the kingdom, with six chairs. The latter was formally opened in 1853 by the celebrated Merle D'Aubigné of Geneva, the historian of the Reformation. Dr. Cooke was appointed its first president. Of late years it has received a number of splendid benefactions, one, the gift of a sum of £10,000, for the completion of the college buildings, from an anonymous donor, since discovered to have been the late Mr. Adam S. Findlater of Dublin, which was the means of raising nearly £11,000 more for the College Endowment Fund.[1] Magee College was opened in 1865. The Rev. Richard Dill bequeathed a large sum to it, and many others gave it gifts or legacies. The Irish Society has also befriended it, and of late a suite of fine residences for the professors has been erected by the liberality of friends of

---

[1] Five gentlemen gave £1000 each to this fund, viz. Sir James P. Corry, Bart., Belfast; Mr. A. S. Findlater, Kingstown; Mr. Charles Wilson, Cheltenham; Mr. William Todd, Dublin, and Mr. Henry Campbell, Belfast. Mrs. Gamble, widow of the Rev. Henry Gamble, Presbyterian minister of Cloughey, County Down, has also been a munificent benefactress to the college. 'The Gamble Library,' on which she expended £1500 in memory of her husband, is one of her gifts. A fine suite of chambers for the residence of students has also been erected as a memorial to the late Professor Gibson, and scholarships and prizes have been founded to the value of about £400 per annum.

the college.[1] In 1881 the theological professors of these two colleges were incorporated by Royal Charter as 'The Presbyterian Theological Faculty, Ireland,' and empowered to grant degrees in divinity. What a change in the entire educational apparatus of the Church since Gowan started his humble 'school of philosophy' at Antrim, for the education of candidates for the ministry in the seventeenth century!

[1] Magee College has recently lost one of its ablest and best known professors, the Rev. Thomas Croskery, D.D. He was born at Carrowdore, a village in County Down, on May 26th, 1830. Brought up a Unitarian, he discovered the unscripturalness of Unitarianism after entering Belfast College, and severed his connection with the body. He was licensed by the Presbytery of Down in 1851, but did not receive ordination until 1860, when he was settled in Creggan, spending the interval in travel and in literary work in connection with the Belfast newspaper press. In 1863 he was translated to Clonakilty, and again in 1866 to Waterside Church, Londonderry. In 1875 he was appointed Professor of Logic in Magee College, and in 1879 transferred to the chair of Theology, which he held till his death on October 3rd, 1886. He was a frequent contributor to the *Edinburgh Review* and other leading organs of public opinion, and was also the author of a very able volume, entitled *Plymouth Brethrenism, a Refutation of its Principles and Doctrines*, and of other works.

CHAPTER XIX.

PRESBYTERIANISM OUTSIDE ULSTER.

OUR history has hitherto been the history almost entirely of the Synod of Ulster and the Secession. But outside both bodies, in the southern portion of the island, there were from an early period a number of Presbyterian congregations of great influence. Presbyterianism made its appearance in Dublin at a pretty remote date. The Rev. Walter Travers, first regular Provost of Trinity College, appointed in 1594, was a Presbyterian minister. So was his successor in that high office, the Rev. Henry Alvey, who also became the first Vice-Chancellor of the University. Its first two elected Fellows — James Hamilton, afterwards Lord Claneboy, and James Fullerton — were also Presbyterians. So that here, from the reign of Elizabeth, was a little knot of Presbyterians settled in Dublin, and we cannot doubt that they established a Presbyterian service for their own worship, and for any that chose to unite with them. From this we may probably date the advent of Presbyterianism to the South of Ireland,—a period, it will be observed, anterior to the date of its appearance in Ulster. During the time of the Commonwealth, Independents and Baptists were the favoured sects in Ireland as elsewhere, and it is an interesting fact that during that period Dublin enjoyed the benefit of the ministrations of two of the most eminent of the Puritan divines—John Owen and Stephen Charnock. The former came to the metropolis in 1647, and in 1649 we find him still there, preaching to a congregation in Wood Street, which subsequently became one of the regular Presbyterian churches of the city. During the Protectorate many officers and soldiers of Cromwell's army, and others from England, settled in the South, and by degrees little Dissenting congregations sprang up here and there owing to this cause. In the last quarter of the seventeenth century we find five Presbyterian congregations in Dublin, viz. Wood Street, Cook Street, New Row, Plunket Street, and Capel Street. The first three of these seem to have been mainly composed of English Presbyterians, the last two of Scotch and North of Ireland people. Dublin being the seat of the Irish Court, and the meeting-place of the Irish Parliament, some of these congregations attained to great conspicuousness and prosperity. The people of Wood Street, for example, must have been a wealthy body, for we find that when the 'General Fund' was established in 1710 they contributed £6750 of the £7670 originally raised for it. In 1738 we find a congregation in Stafford Street, an offshoot from Capel Street.[1] By and by, when Secederism appeared in Ireland, two congregations, the one of Burghers and the other of Antiburghers, sprang up in the city. We find them located in obscure lanes.[2] Some of these Dublin churches had from time to time ministers of no mean celebrity, men like Joseph Boyse, author of the *Vindiciæ Calvinisticæ;* Francis Iredell, who, along with Adair of Ballyeaston, presented the address of the Presbyterians to Schomberg when he arrived in Ireland; and John Leland, whose works on the Christian evidences prove the possession of a mind of conspicuous acuteness, and are still valuable. These old Dublin ministers had not a few notable people among the members of their congregations. Lord Ferrard and his family, Lady Donegal, and the Countess of Enniskillen, sat in New Row in the end of the eighteenth century. The Granard family were connected with Capel Street, and others of the congregations were also attended by persons of high rank.

[1] In 1762, Stafford Street united with Wood Street, and by and by the united congregation built a new church in Strand Street.
[2] Union Chapel, Lower Abbey Street, derived its name from the fact of two congregations of Seceders, one of Burghers and the other of Antiburghers, having united to form its congregation. The congregation in Plunket Street, of which Rev. S. G. Morrison was minister, also joined itself to this charge.

Over the South were not a few Presbyterian churches. That at Clonmel dates from 1673. It was at one time one of the most influential congregations in all Munster. The chief families of the neighbourhood, the Bagwells, Hutchisons, Moores, Ryalls, were all Presbyterians, and belonged to it. Cork congregation must have been nearly as old. We know, at all events, that it had had thirteen successive ministers prior to the year 1710. Limerick probably dates from the reign of James I. or Charles I., Waterford from 1673, Summerhill from 1660, Fethard from 1655, and the united congregation of Sligo and Moywater (now Killala) from 1695. Besides these and other congregations which are still in existence, there were not a few which have quite disappeared, and of which one fails to recognise even the names as possessing any ecclesiastical significance. Such, *e.g.*, were Aughmacart and Ballybrittas, in Queen's County, which in the early part of last century were very considerable congregations, and had large landed properties connected with them, held for a peppercorn each per annum. The congregations disappeared, and the lands were lost to the Church. Again, at Portarlington, Mountrath, Cullohill, The Leap, Rahul, and Edenderry there were congregations, all with landed property, held at nominal rents, belonging to them. But both congregations and property have vanished.[1] Sir Arthur Langford was connected with the congregation of Summerhill, near which he had his country seat, and on which he bestowed many benefactions. Various causes combined to weaken the Presbyterian cause in the South, and in many cases to eradicate it altogether. One of these was the insidious spread of Arianism, with its usual deadening influence. Not being connected with the Synod of Ulster, the evangelical light which in the darkest days of defection continued to shine, however dimly, in the North, failed to be kept burning in the congregations of the South, and so error had its own way among them, with disastrous results. Then the rebellion of 1798, the

---

[1] See *History of Presbyterian Congregations in Ireland,* by W. D. Killen, D.D. 1886.

full fury of which was felt in the South, and whose course was marked by the massacre of Protestants and the destruction of their property, was most destructive to them. The southern congregations grouped themselves for mutual advantage into what was called the Southern Association.[1] In 1809 a Synod of Munster was formed by the union of the Southern Presbytery of Dublin with the Presbytery of Munster. But, Arianism spreading here unchecked, the disastrous results we have mentioned ensued. By and by, with the incoming of the evangelical revival, the orthodox ministers of the Synod withdrew, and the present Presbytery of Munster was established, which in 1854 joined the General Assembly. One cannot contemplate the losses which our Church has sustained in the South without a pang of regret. Many of them, it is true, have been repaired. Within the last fifty years the Presbyterian Church has made most gratifying progress both in the South and West. She has not only 'repaired the waste places, the desolations of many generations,' but has broken much new ground. She is no longer the Synod of Ulster, but the Presbyterian Church of Ireland, having flourishing congregations from Derry to Cork, and from Limerick to Dublin. But the losses which were caused through neglect and error can never be retrieved.

In 1846 a sad calamity fell on Ireland, which was destined to have the most marked influence on its future. This was the terrible potato blight. No more appalling calamity could have befallen the country. On the produce of their potato fields millions had to live. The produce being gone, those millions were face to face with starvation.

There was one noble-minded Presbyterian clergyman who came to the help of the people in this crisis with an alacrity and a helpfulness which can never be forgotten. This was Dr.

---

[1] In 1708, it is to be noted, Queen Anne granted £800 per annum to the southern congregations,—a grant usually known as the 'English Bounty,' inasmuch as it was remitted direct from London to the Irish Treasury,—and this sum was increased from time to time.

Edgar. In September, 1846, he was in Connaught on an evangelistic tour. As he drove through the country, the sight of the blackened fields, and the starving peasantry, and the hopeless, blank looks of despair on the faces of the people, went to his heart. On the spot he penned an appeal to the people of Ulster on behalf of their perishing fellow-countrymen. That letter awoke a sympathetic response in the northern breast. Thousands of pounds were contributed in answer to it and the other stirring appeals written by the same facile pen, all of which were wisely and well expended under Dr. Edgar's care. But he did more than this. With the fine eye of a true patriot, he saw a way of turning this fearful calamity into a means of permanent good. He found Connaught suffering from a worse famine than the loss of bread—a famine of the Word of God. One Bible, given by an English sportsman to a Connaught peasant a short time before his visit, had wrought a religious revolution in Connaught.[1] Man after man had been led by it out of Popery. Dr. Edgar now established the Connaught Irish schools,—nor only Irish schools, but by and by English schools, taught by pious teachers, and thoroughly imbued with Scriptural instruction; then Industrial schools, where useful works were taught. Churches were built, with neat manses beside them, and men of God, like the Rev. Robert Allen, and others of a similar spirit who still live, to labour in them. The result is seen to-day in the fact that 40,000 children have passed through the Connaught schools, all taught in the Scriptures, many of them with blessed results—an Orphanage and Refuge Home in Ballina have sheltered numbers of destitute Roman Catholic children and others fleeing from persecution, and the Connaught Presbytery has more than doubled the number of its congregations. The famine was a terrible evil, but it left more than one good result behind it.

[1] Killen's *Memoir of Dr. Edgar.*

CHAPTER XX.

THE LAST THIRTY YEARS.

ABOUT thirty years ago the first steps were taken in an enterprise to which the Irish Presbyterian Church owes no small measure of its stability. At that time little more than one in twenty of the congregations possessed manses, and very many of the churches were unworthy of the holy purposes for which they were used. The Assembly therefore resolved on the establishment of a Church and Manse Fund. The Rev. David Hamilton, Belfast, was put at the head of this scheme, and the amount of labour which he bestowed on it was almost incredible.[1] The original idea was to raise £5000, £1000 to be spent in aiding the erection of churches, and £4000 in helping to build manses. But when, on an August day in 1853, a meeting of Belfast merchants was held to make arrangements for opening a subscription list for the new fund, the late Mr. John Sinclair, one of two brothers who did more during their lives than any others that could be named to raise the standard of giving in the Irish Presbyterian Church, proposed that instead

---

[1] The Rev. David Hamilton was born in 1805, near Ballynahinch, and received his education from before he was seven years old at Dr. Edgar's well-known academy there. In 1821 he entered the old Belfast College, and in 1827 was licensed by the Presbytery of Dromore. In 1829 he was ordained in Connor as assistant and successor to the venerable Rev. Henry Henry, one of the most faithful ministers in the Synod of Ulster. In 1840 he was called to Belfast to become the first minister of the newly-built church in York Street. Here he toiled with a zeal and devotion which are not yet forgotten, till a fever, caught in the discharge of pastoral duty, terminated his too brief career in January, 1860. See a memoir of him by the present writer.

of £5000, they should raise £25,000, promising that in case his suggestion was adopted he and his brother (the late Mr. Thomas Sinclair of Hopefield) would subscribe £1000.[1] The proposition was startling. But it was accepted, supported as it was by such an offer. Other large subscriptions were promised, small ones too. The Church took the matter up with wonderful heart. In one day £3700 was contributed by seventeen individuals in Belfast. Soon it was announced that the same town had promised more than a third of the whole amount proposed to be raised. In the country also 'the people had a mind to work,' and, in the sequel, nearly £35,000 were subscribed, to the astonishment of the General Assembly itself. This fund did more than any other effort which had ever been made to show the Irish Presbyterian Church wherein its great strength lay. Hitherto, when any enterprise was to be undertaken involving large expenditure, the mode of accomplishing it which most readily suggested itself had been an application to Government. In 1846 the Assembly had knocked at the door of a British Ministry for aid in this very business of erecting manses, and had been refused. Now it did the work itself, with the great gain not only of the rich offering, by which the people proved that they were to be trusted, but with the still greater gain of the learning of a lesson of self-help which after events,

---

[1] Mr. John Sinclair died in 1856, at the early age of forty-seven. The Presbyterian Church at Conlig was built almost entirely at his expense, and after his death the beautiful Sinclair Seamen's Church in Belfast was erected as a memorial of him. One of his sons, Mr. W. P. Sinclair, sat in the House of Commons as a representative of Antrim, his native county, in 1885, and in 1886 was elected Member of Parliament for the Falkirk Burghs. Mr. Thomas Sinclair died in London in 1867. It may safely be said that the Irish Presbyterian Church has never had a son whose name is more imperishably interwoven with her history. His givings to the cause of Christ were incessant, and his labours, as a Sabbath-school teacher and superintendent, as a ruling elder, on committees of the Church, and in many other spheres, were unwearied. Duncairn Church (with its manse and school-house) owes its origin to him, and much more than its origin. In his son and namesake the virtues of the father are well continued into a second generation.

coming in the near future, were destined to utilize. This fund was the means of raising ecclesiastical buildings over the country to the value of over £100,000.[1]

While the Church was thus firmly rooting herself in the land, a remarkable work of grace broke out. In 1859 its first signs appeared, and all through that year the most remarkable scenes were witnessed all over the province of Ulster. Beginning at a little prayer-meeting in the parish of Connor, it soon overspread that district, extended thence to Ballymena, Ahoghill, Belfast, into County Down, and away through Tyrone and Derry. The earnestness with regard to religion was intense. The churches were crowded, not only on the Sabbath, but in many cases every night during the week,—crowded with most earnest congregations, who literally hung upon the simplest preaching or exposition of the gospel, and could with difficulty be got to leave the place of meeting. Multitudes were deeply convicted of sin. While a meeting was proceeding, perhaps in the midst of a sermon, a piercing shriek would be heard, and immediately it would be found that some one had fallen down, 'stricken.' Soon cry after cry of agony would be heard ringing through the church, until in some cases several scores would have been carried out, and stretched in some adjoining room, or on the 'green' outside. Here the affected person would lie in a state of semi-unconsciousness, strangely convulsed, and

[1] Congregations were only helped when they were able to show that they themselves had made a proper effort. It may be mentioned here that a second Church and Manse Fund, which included also provisions for the erection of school-houses and for the extinction of congregational debts, was started in 1861, with the Rev. Dr. Edgar as convener, followed subsequently by the Rev. Lowry E. Berkeley, one of the ablest and most energetic ministers of the Church. To this fund over £20,000 were subscribed. Again, in 1875, a third fund was established through the influence of the Rev. Dr. Porter, Moderator for that year, which aimed at assisting congregations still unprovided with manses to obtain them through the help of the Glebe Loan Acts. Several thousands of pounds were given to it. One happy result of these repeated building schemes is that there are now only some 150 congregations in the whole Church unprovided with manses for their ministers.

evidently in deep agony. By and by, cries of distress for sin would be uttered in agonizing tones, prayers of peculiar fervency would burst forth, and often, as minister or elder or godly layman conversed and prayed beside the penitent, peace would come into the distracted soul, and the man or woman would go home rejoicing. These strange manifestations were not exhibited in every instance. With very many there were no wild cries, no prostrations, nothing but an ordinary work of grace, only intensely earnest and concentrated.[1] But, whatever the form which it took, the movement was attended with the most blessed results. No doubt evils were mixed up with it, as they will always be mixed up with all things that are good on earth. But that over the province there was an unwonted outpouring of the Holy Ghost, with the result that multitudes were deeply convinced of sin, multitudes converted, and that, wherever the movement appeared, a change came over the entire face of society, the lapse of years has only made clearer than it was at the time. Not a few who still live look back with gratitude to that year as the date of their spiritual birth, and many who are now in glory spoke of it to the last as the beginning of all their joys. We have had several times of refreshing since 1859, but none altogether like it.

Two societies, which have proved of signal advantage to the Church, date their origin from shortly after this period. The first of these is 'The Sabbath-School Society for Ireland in connection with the Presbyterian Church,'[2] which was organized in 1862 for the purpose of fostering Sabbath schools in connection with the General Assembly, and supplying them with books, periodicals, and other requisites, and which has had a most

[1] See *The Year of Grace, a History of the Ulster Revival of* 1859, by the Rev. Professor Gibson, D.D., and *The Ulster Revival and its Physiological Accidents*, by Rev. James M'Cosh, D.D.

[2] The Rev. William Johnston, D.D., Belfast, has the high honour of having originated this admirable society.

prosperous and useful career. It has now in connection with it over 1000 Sabbath schools, with nearly 10,000 teachers, and an average attendance of nearly 80,000 children. Its issue of books, catechisms, periodicals, etc., amounts to nearly 700,000 per annum. The other, which is even more popular—is 'The Presbyterian Orphan Society.' On the 22nd May, 1866, its inaugural meeting was held in Linen Hall Street Church, Belfast. The Rev. Dr. Johnston was appointed its first secretary, and to his indefatigable exertions its great success is largely due. The Society has usually on its roll every year nearly 3000 orphan or fatherless children, and enjoys an income of about £10,000 per annum from all sources. A third benevolent scheme, established in 1873, is 'The Society for the Orphans of Ministers,' whose name sufficiently indicates its scope. The Rev. Dr. Johnston is also its chief moving spirit. In a very quiet fashion it has done untold good since its establishment.

An event occurred in 1869 which many feared would inflict the severest blow upon the Irish Presbyterian Church which she had ever sustained. In that year the Irish Church Act was passed, disestablishing Episcopacy, and depriving the Presbyterian Church of the endowment which she had enjoyed for almost two centuries. This was a trial calculated to test to the utmost her spirit and strength. Fortunately, it was met in a manner which not only did honour to the Church, and saved her from dreaded disaster, but conferred upon her lasting advantages. The Act allowed all recipients of the *Regium Donum* either to continue to draw it during life, or to commute it for a lump sum to be paid at once, and it was permissible that this commutation might be effected by each individual minister in his own private interest, had the Church so decided. A special meeting of the General Assembly was called in January, 1870, to consider the critical position of affairs. It was a memorable meeting, and throughout the country was looked forward to with great anxiety. If the ministers chose to retain their endowments for life, or to commute them in their own interest (one or other of which courses many advised them to adopt on the ground that they could not afford to subject themselves and their families to the risks inseparable from any other line of action), a very serious loss would be sustained, and the Church of the future would be left to face financial difficulties such as she had never encountered, and such as in a poor country like Ireland it would be very hard for her to surmount. The clergy had the matter entirely in their own hands, and no one could have much blamed them—poor and almost entirely dependent on the *Regium Donum* as many of them were—had they hesitated to give up the sure income, on which they knew they could depend, for an entire uncertainty. The anxieties of the Church were, however, soon set at rest. With only five dissentient voices the ministers of the General Assembly resolved to subordinate all other considerations to the welfare of the Church, and to commute their 'Bounty' in her interest.[1] The Presbyterian clergy of Ireland thus cast into the treasury as a free-will offering a sum of £587,735, which remains as an endowment fund to the Church for all time, and yields an annual interest of somewhere about £25,000. This was certainly one of the noblest offerings ever laid upon the altar of God by the clergy of any body. Meanwhile a 'Lay Conference' had been held in Belfast in September, 1869, to which all the congregations had been requested to send representatives, that the laity might consider what was their duty in the solemn and critical circumstances which had arisen. This was probably the most notable gathering of Irish Presbyterian laymen ever

---

[1] The Rev. Richard Smyth, D.D., Derry, was moderator of the General Assembly during this eventful year, and rendered signal service to the Church, which was acknowledged by his re-election to office a second year. He was born near Dervock in 1826, ordained in 1855 at Westport, translated to First Derry in 1857, and appointed a professor in Magee College in 1865. In 1874 he was elected one of the members of Parliament for County Derry, but his career in the Legislature, though brilliant, was but brief, as he died in December, 1878, after a short illness, at the residence of Samuel Lawther, Esq., J.P., Belfast.

held. The Church was represented from Derry to Cork, and from Dublin to Sligo. Mr. John Lytle of Belfast was chairman, and among the delegates were such men as Mr. John Young of Galgorm Castle, Mr. (afterwards Sir) Thomas M'Clure of Belmont, Mr. (afterwards Sir) James P. Corry of Belfast, Mr. Wm. Kirk, M.P., of Keady, Mr. Thos. Sinclair of Belfast, Mr. Wm. Young of Fenaghy, and Mr. James Sharman Crawford of Crossgar. This meeting expressed its earnest desire that the clergy should commute in the interest of the Church, and urged the advisability of the immediate establishment of a Sustentation Fund, to supplement the interest derivable from the Commutation Fund to be thus provided, the gentlemen present pledging themselves to use their best efforts to raise a fund of at least £30,000 a year. A deputation from this Lay Conference appeared before the Assembly, and pressed these views upon it. The Sustentation Fund was thus established, and although, owing to various reasons, it has never yet realized all the wishes or expectations of its founders, it has steadily held on its way in a manner which half a century ago would have been pronounced impossible. Its receipts usually average nearly £25,000 per annum. The Commutation Fund yields about the same amount, making a total annual sum of about £50,000, as against £39,000, which was the amount of the *Regium Donum* in the year before the passing of the Irish Church Act. At the same time the stipends throughout the Church have steadily risen from £38,000 per annum, the figure at which they stood in 1870, to nearly £48,000 in 1886.[1] Too much gratitude cannot be felt for the manner in which the Church weathered this storm, which seemed at one time to menace her so alarmingly.

Just before disendowment, with all its attendant changes, fell upon the Church, Dr. Cooke, its trusted leader for half a century, quietly passed away. He died on 13th December, 1868, and was

[1] The Rev. T. Y. Killen, D.D., was for many years the indefatigable Convener of this Scheme. Alas! *abiit ad plures.*

honoured by the town of Belfast with a public funeral, the largest, and in many respects the most remarkable, ever seen on its streets. A fine bronze statue of him has since been erected in College Square.

Of late years the peace of the Church was somewhat disturbed by a controversy regarding the lawfulness of the use of instrumental music in public worship. This question first came before the General Assembly in 1868 in connection with the employment of a harmonium in Enniskillen Church, and at almost every subsequent meeting of the Supreme Court the subject was brought forward for eighteen years. Debate after debate took place, sometimes in circumstances of much excitement. Indeed, at one time so intense had the feeling on the subject become, that it was feared by some that it would ultimately rend the Church asunder. The press lent its aid to the platform for the discussion of the point at issue, both publications and debates evincing conspicuous ability. The leading men who employed voice or pen on the side of the lawfulness of an instrumental aid in worship were—the Rev. President Killen, D.D., Rev. Professor Wallace, Rev. Dr. Watts, Rev. Dr. Morell, Rev. John Macnaughtan,[1] Mr. Thomas Sinclair, J.P., Rev. Dr. Wilson (Cookstown), Rev. Robt. Ross; while against its use were such men as the Rev. Archibald Robinson, Rev. Dr. Petticrew, Rev. Dr. Brown, Rev. Dr. Corkey, Rev. Dr. Robb, Rev. Dr. Crawford, and Rev. George Magill. The controversy dragged its slow length along, until, at the Assembly of 1886, a settlement was happily arrived at, according to which it was agreed, that 'having regard to the peculiar circumstances of the country and the Church,' all discussion on the subject should cease for five years, a committee, consisting of men who considered the use

[1] Mr. Macnaughtan was one of the most eloquent preachers and ablest ecclesiastics of his day. He came to Rosemary Street, Belfast, from Paisley, where he was minister of the Free High Church, in 1849, and soon rose to occupy a very prominent position in the Church Courts. He died, greatly lamented, in 1884, after a ministry altogether extending to nearly fifty-five years.

of instrumental music allowable, being appointed to use their utmost influence meanwhile to induce all congregations using instruments to give them up. In case their efforts should prove unsuccessful, it was provided that at the end of three years the discussion on the subject might be re-opened. General thankfulness was felt that peace was at last proclaimed on this question, never, it is hoped, to be seriously disturbed again.

The same year which witnessed this happy solution of the instrumental music question was further distinguished by the renewal of intercourse between the Irish Presbyterian Church and the Church of Scotland, after an interval of forty-three years. That Church, the Free Church, and the United Presbyterian Church are now all in communion with the Irish Presbyterian Church, and she with them. Another less pleasant circumstance will cause 1886 to be long remembered. Mr. Gladstone's 'Government of Ireland Bill,' providing for the establishment of a separate Parliament for this country, was then introduced into the House of Commons, and caused widespread alarm among the loyal population. On the first announcement of the intention to propose such a measure, a special meeting of the General Assembly was called, at which resolutions were unanimously passed, deprecating 'in the strongest manner, as disastrous to the best interests of the country, a separate Parliament for Ireland, . . . or any legislation tending to imperil the Legislative Union between Great Britain and Ireland, or to interfere with the unity and the supremacy of the Imperial Parliament.' At the ordinary meeting of Assembly in the following June these resolutions were reaffirmed. The unanimity and earnestness with which all attempts to weaken the connection between this country and Great Britain, or to establish Home Rule in Ireland in any shape, were thus condemned in the General Assembly, are all the more noteworthy, as they were but the reflection of an almost equal unanimity in the membership of the Church. The defeat of Mr. Gladstone's Bill on the 7th June, 1886, was hailed with deep satisfaction.

CHAPTER XXI.

CONCLUSION.

WE have now briefly told the story of the Irish Presbyterian Church from her infant days of feebleness up to her present era of strength and stability. We have seen how faithfully, in the earlier times of her history, she maintained her testimony to the truth in the face of opposition and persecution, and how she throve in spite of all efforts to crush her; how despotic monarchs, and intolerant Parliaments, and bigoted prelates, in turn planted the iron heel of oppression on her neck, but how, though they wounded her sorely, they could neither destroy her nor turn her away from her fidelity to the truth; how her ministers were driven out of church and manse; how they were imprisoned or forced to fly beyond the seas from the fury of persecution; how they had to face hostile Lord Deputies, and Privy Councils, and Courts of High Commission; how at one time they were threatened, and held up to obloquy, and treated as the offscouring of the earth, and at another offered bribes and rewards if they would forsake their Church; but how, rising superior to all temptations, they could neither be concussed nor cajoled to forsake what they believed to be the truth; how, when, instead of opposition from without, the Church had to battle with insidious error within, the same stern and unflinching allegiance to the truth was maintained—how the battle for it was fought and the victory gained; how thus, like some snowy-winged barque which we see glancing white in the sunlight on a smooth summer sea, but which by and by is shrouded in fog under a leaden sky, which anon, when the air has cleared, cleaves her way merrily along again, her sails filled with a favouring breeze, but to-morrow, in sore distress, is tossed up and down like a plaything on the angry main, swept from stem to stern by furious seas, her sails torn to shreds by tempests, and her crew at their wits' end, till she seems a hopeless wreck, but which, when the gale has spent its force, refitted by willing hands, again sets forward on her voyage, nothing daunted by the perils through which she has had to cleave her way, and once more we behold her speeding on her way, with nought but an occasional gust of wind, or at times a hissing, white-crested billow, passing under her keel and for a little perturbing her course, to remind her of the perils through which she has passed — so the Presbyterian Church of Ireland, after facing the storms and dangers of centuries, now speeds on her way, with the light of heaven shining on her, and the peace of God keeping her, and we cry to her and say—

> 'In spite of rock and tempest's roar,
> In spite of false lights on the shore,
> Sail on, nor fear to breast the sea!
> Our hearts and hopes are all with thee—
> Our hearts, our hopes, our prayers, our tears,
> Our faith triumphant o'er our fears—
> Are all with thee—are all with thee!'

If the question be asked, What has Presbyterianism done for the country? there can be no difficulty in giving an answer. It has changed Ulster, where its chief seat has always been, from a waste, shaggy with forests and dangerous with wild beasts, into the garden of Ireland. Its manufactures it owes largely to its Presbyterianism. The spinning of flax and the weaving of linen were brought from Scotland by the early colonists,[1] and little more than half a century ago Andrew Mulholland, a Belfast Presbyterian millowner, by the introduction of the use of steam-power into these trades, laid the foundations of that world-renowned manufacture whose tall chimney-stalks rise into the air on all sides in Belfast. There is no denying that to its Presbyterianism

[1] *Montgomery MSS.*

Ulster largely owes its prosperity, which all strangers notice. Forty years ago, the German traveller, Kohl, tells us he seemed to himself to have entered a new world as he came from Leinster into Ulster, and to-day the difference is as conspicuous as ever. Ulster pays 46 per cent. of the entire Income-Tax paid in Ireland under Schedule D. It is a stranger to the chronic starvation which the 'hated Saxon' is periodically called upon to relieve in other parts of Ireland ; and all over the country, wherever you find Presbyterians, you find thrift and industry and peace. Irish workhouses contain a pauper population of 48,991 Roman Catholics, 4781 Episcopalians, but only 1995 Presbyterians are within their walls.[1] There is usually a garrison of nearly 30,000 troops in Ireland. Only 3000 of these are usually quartered in Ulster. The strength of the Royal Irish Constabulary is over 12,000 men. Of these, in order to preserve the peace and protect life and property, there are required in Cork 24 policemen for every 10,000 inhabitants ; in Kilkenny, 36 ; Westmeath, 45 ; Kerry, 32 ; Galway, 46 ; in Down, only 11 ; Antrim, 11 ; Armagh, 11 ; Derry, 11 ; and Tyrone, 12. These figures tell their own tale. If we turn to the statistics of crime, we find them pointing a similar moral. In Irish jails there were confined on 31st March 1885, 35,218 prisoners. Of these 29,766 were Romanists, 3690 Episcopalians, only 1762 Presbyterians. Along with all this, Presbyterianism has proved itself a most powerful moderating force in the social life of the country. It has been the advocate of popular rights, but not of communism ; of liberty, but never of licence. It has been the best friend both of landlord and tenant, for it has held the scales even between the two. It has firmly stood up for the rights of the sovereign, but it has as determinedly insisted on the rights of the subject.[2] The value of such an element in a state of society so

---

[1] These are the figures for 1885. According to the Census of 1881, the percentages of the pauperism of the country were as follows :—Romanism had 87·7 per cent.; Episcopacy, 8 ; Presbyterianism, 3·6.

[2] One evil of which the Irish Presbyterian Church has had loudly to com-

CONCLUSION.   191

strangely complicated as that which exists in Ireland, only those who have had experience of its good effects can properly estimate.

But the distinctively religious blessings which Ireland owes to it are still more noticeable. It has powerfully contributed to the maintenance of a pure Protestantism in Ireland. Of all the Churches of the Reformation, that of Scotland came out cleanest from Rome at the Reformation, and of all the branches of that Presbyterian family there is none which more conservatively clings to Bible truth, or has a sterner hatred of the errors of Romanism, than the Irish sister. Her influence has helped to spread a Protestant atmosphere all round. She has been one of the best strongholds of Evangelicalism in the land. A pure gospel sounds out from all her pulpits. Brice and Blair and their companions in the seventeenth century regarded it as their main business to lift up Christ among the people, and the same ruling thought was never more conspicuous than it is

plain is the unfair treatment which she receives in the matter of public appointments. Although religious equality is the theory in Ireland, the following statistics, taken from the excellent *Presbyterian Map of Ireland*, published in 1886, which the Church owes to the thoughtfulness and enterprise of the Rev. J. W. Whigham, Ballinasloe, Moderator of the General Assembly in 1885-86, show that it is far from being the practice :—

	Roman Catholics.	Episcopalians.	Presbyterians.
Irish Peerage,	13	174	..
Irish Privy Council,	9	36	..
Lieutenants of Counties,	2	29	1
Judges,	5	11	1
County Court Judges,	6	14	2
Resident Magistrates,	25	53	2
Inspectors-General of Constabulary,	1	4	..
County Inspectors of Constabulary,	9	30	..
District Inspectors of Constabulary,	37	188	5
Royal University Senators,	17	9	8
Intermediate Education Commissioners,	4	3	2
National Education Commissioners,	10	6	3
Do. Secretaries and Heads of Departments,	5	3	1
Board of Works, Commissioners, etc.,	3	18	..
Local Government Board, Members, Secretaries, etc.,	5	16	1
Superintendents of Lunatic Asylums,	5	19	..
Land Commissioners, Chief,	3	2	..
Land Commissioners, Assistant,	7	3	..

among their ecclesiastical successors in these closing years of the nineteenth century.

The Church was never more heartily united than at present. She has a life and a vigour about her which augur well for her future. The old dead days of dry pulpit routine and pew somnolence are all but extinct. There is a fervour in the prayers of the sanctuary, and a heartiness in its songs of praise, which are at once the evidences of life and a powerful means of further developing life. There are higher ideals of Christianity among us. An earnest evangelistic spirit yearns over the lost sheep, and exhausts every means which a sanctified Christian ingenuity can suggest to bring them into the fold. All over the Church the missionary spirit never rose so high as it has done within the last few years. The evangelization of the world is now seen to be the grand duty of the Bride of Christ. Altogether, the present condition of the Church may well inspire the deepest gratitude and the brightest hope. She has done much not unworthy of such a Church. But there are yet greater things in store for her, if, looking around with a large eye, and recognising the breadth and grandeur of the mission which lies at her door, she braces herself earnestly to her work in the strength of God. 'The isles shall wait for His law,' and among them it may confidently be said of Ireland, in a higher and holier meaning than the words of one of her own poets were intended to convey,—

> 'Though slavery's cloud o'er thy morning hath hung,
> The full noon of freedom shall beam round thee yet.'

INDEX.

ABERNETHY, Rev. John, 116.
Adair, Rev. Patrick, 102.
—— Rev. William, 102.
—— Sir Robert, 52.
Aghadoey, 76, 83, 121, 126, 156.
Ahoghill, 131, 181.
Aird, Rev. John, 61.
Allen, Rev. Robert, 178.
Alvey, Rev. Henry, 174.
Ambrose, Mr., 105.
America, 47, 51, 133.
Anaghlone, 166.
Anahilt, 151.
Anne, Queen, 111, 177 *note*.
Antiburghers, 127.
Antrim, 43, 44, 62, 80, 89, 113, 116, 139, 151.
—— Presbytery of, 109, 121.
Arian Controversy, 146.
Armagh, 102, 109, 120, 126, 128, 166.
Arrott of Markethill, 131.
'Articles of Religion,' 38.
Assembly, First General, in Scotland, 33.
—— First General, in Ireland, 164.
—— Glasgow, 35.
—— Westminster, 65.
Associate Presbytery, 124, 131.
—— Synod, 125.
Association, Southern, 177.
Aughmacart, 176.

BAIRD, Rev. John, 61.
Baker, Major, 90.
Bale, Bishop, 24.
Ballintoy, 60.
Ballybay, 126.
Ballybrittas, 176.
Ballycarry, 60, 76.
Ballyeaston, 102.
Ballykelly, 76, 126.
Ballymena, 31, 40, 62, 74, 76, 139, 181.
Ballymoney, 76, 126.
Ballynahinch, 140, 179 *note*.
Ballyrashane, 126.
Ballyroney, 126, 131.
Ballywalter, 40, 62.
Balteagh, 126.
Bangor, 18, 31, 40, 62, 76, 126.
Barber, Rev. Samuel, 142.
Belfast, 31, 49, 62, 70, 76, 102, 109, 111, 114.
—— Society, 116.
Belleek, 99.
Belturbet, 99.
Berkeley, Rev. L. E., 181 *note*.
Bigger, Rev. William, 107.
Birch, Rev. T. L., 143.
Black Oath, 53.
Black, Rev. Robert, D.D., 137 and *note*.
—— of Boardmills, 131.
Blair, Rev. Hugh, D.D., 40 *note*.
—— Rev. Robert, 39, 45, 46, 47, 62.
Blood's Plot, 76.
Boardmills, 126, 131.
Bovedy, 120.
Boyne, Battle of the, 103.
Boyse, Rev. Joseph, 175.
Bramhall, Bishop, 48, 52.
Brice, Rev. Edward, 36 and *note*, 49, 50.
Brigh, 76, 116.
Broughshane, 110, 152 *note*.

Brown, Rev. James, 146.
—— Rev. John, D.D., 146, 156 note.
—— Rev. N. M., D.D., 186.
—— Rev. Solomon, 146.
Bruce, Rev. Dr., 150.
Bryce, Rev. James, 144.
Bryson, Rev. James, 136.
Burghers, 127.
Burt, 82.

CAHANS, 128, 131.
Cairncastle, 62.
Calvert, Rev. Mr., 49.
Campbell, Mr. Henry, 172 note.
Carland, 76.
Carlile, Rev. James, D.D., 162 and note.
Carlingford, 77.
Carlow, 157.
Carnmoney, 76, 147.
Carr, Rev. G. W., 160.
Carrickfergus, 61, 102, 170.
Carrowdore, 173 note.
Castlereagh, 76.
Castlestuart, Lord, 48.
Charles I., 35, 55, 64, 69.
Charles II., 74.
Charnock, Stephen, 174.
Chichester, Sir Arthur, 30.
Choppin, Rev. R., 109 note.
Claneboy, Lord, 27.
Clarke, D. K., 167.
Clerk, Rev. M., 120.
Clonakilty, 173 note.
Clonmel, 176.
Clough, 152 note.
Cloughey, 172 note.
Cœlestius, 3.
Cole, Dr., 24.
Coleraine, 30, 89, 109, 127.
Colleges, Assembly's, 172.
—— Queen's, 171.
Columba, 15.
Columbanus, 19.
Colville, Rev. Alexander, 116.
Comber, 75, 84, 116.
Commonwealth, Times of the, 64.
Conlig, 180 note.
Connaught Presbytery, 178.
—— Schools, 178.
Connor, 76, 120, 179 note.
Cooke, Rev. Henry, D.D., LL.D., 148, 149, 152, 153, 154, 158, 185.
Cookstown, 107, 109, 153, 156, 157 note.

Cork, Congregation of, 176.
Corkey, Rev. Joseph, LL.D., 186.
Corry, Sir James P., Bart., 172, 185.
Coulter, Rev. John, D.D., 163, 166.
Covenant, National, 35.
—— Solemn League and, 66.
Covenanters, The, 131.
Cox, Rev. Samuel, 74.
Crawford, James S., M.P., 185.
—— Rev. J. D., D.D., 186.
Creggan, 173 note.
Cromwell in Ireland, 71.
—— his treatment of Presbyterianism, 73.
Crookes, Rev. William, 97.
Croskery, Rev. Thomas, D.D., 173 note.
Cullohill, 176.
Cunningham, Rev. Hugh, 61.
—— Rev. Robert, 40.
Curwin, Primate, 26.

DAVIS, Rev. Samuel, 82.
Denham, Rev. James, D.D., 170.
Derry, 30, 85, 109, 111, 137, 170, 173.
Dickson, Rev. William Steel, D.D., 142.
Dills, The, 146, 166.
Dobbin, Rev. H. J., D.D., 166.
Donacloney, 120.
Donaghadee, 31, 62.
Donegore, 48, 76, 116, 139, 149, 165.
Downpatrick, 113, 120.
Drogheda, 71.
Dromore, 56, 76, 88.
Drumachose, 131.
Drumlee, 158.
Drummond, Rev. Thomas, 77.
Dublin, 79, 110, 116, 147, 162, 174, 177.
Dunbar, Rev. George, 46.
Dunboe, 126, 146.
Dundalk, 71.
Duneane, 149.
Dungannon, 56, 76, 122, 137, 138.
Dunmurry, 120.

'EAGLE WING, The,' 50, 51.
Echlin, Bishop, 37, 45, 48.
Edenderry, 176.
Edgar, Rev. John, D.D., 127, 157, 160, 178, 181.
—— Rev. Samuel, D.D., 127, 148.
—— Rev. Samuel, Armagh, 128.
Education, National, 161.

INDEX.

Edward VI., 24.
Ejections, The, of 1661, 75.
Elder, Rev. James, 146, 164.
—— Rev. John, 121.
Elizabeth's reign, 25.
Emlyn, Rev. Thomas, 110
'Engagement, The,' 71.
Enniskillen, 56, 98.
Erskine, Rev. Ebenezer, 124.

FAMINE, Irish, 177.
Fannet, 77.
Ferguson, Dr. Victor, 121.
Ferrie, Professor, 154.
Fethard, 176.
Findlater, Mr. A. S., 172 *note*.
Finvoy, 146.
Fisher of Kinclaven, 124.
Fitzgerald, Lord Edward, 139.
Fleming, Rev. James, 112.
Forbes, Sir Arthur, 79, 80.
Foreign Mission, 168.
Franklin, Sir William, 102.
Fridolin, the Traveller, 19.
Fullarton, Sir James, 27.

GALLUS, 19.
Galway, 107.
Gamble, Rev. Henry, 172 *note*.
—— Mrs., 172 *note*.
Geddes, Janet, 35.
General Fund, 114.
George I., 115.
Gibson, Mr. James, Q.C., 125 *note*.
—— Mr. John, 125.
—— Rev. Professor, D.D., 172 *note*.
Gillebert, Cardinal, 19.
Gilnahirk, 143, 163.
Gladstone's Home Rule Bill, 187.
Glascar, 128, 164.
Glasgow, Rev. James, D.D., 168.
Glasslough, 114.
Glastry, 142.
Glendermot, 76, 85.
Glendy, Rev. John, 143.
Gordon, Rev. James, 85, 95.
Goudy, Rev. A. P., D.D., 146 *note*.
—— Rev. James, 146.
Gowan, Rev. Thomas, 80.
Grattan, Henry, 137.
Greer, Mr. S. M., Q.C., 146.
—— Rev. Thomas, 146.
Greyabbey, 142.

HALL, Rev. John, 146.
Halliday, Rev. Samuel, 118.

Hamilton, Rev. Archibald, 102.
—— Rev. David, 128, 169, 179.
—— Rev. George, 168.
—— Rev. James, 27, 40, 41, 49, 62.
—— Rev. John, 97.
—— Sir James, 27.
—— Sir James, of Belfast, 168 *note*.
—— Colonel Anthony, 100.
—— Lieutenant-General, 88.
Hampton, Rev. John, 82.
Hanna, Rev. Samuel, D.D., 146, 147, 164.
—— Rev. William, D.D., LL.D., 147 *note*.
Harrison, Rev. Joseph, 146.
Hart, Rev. John, 77.
Henderson, Rev. Alexander, 35.
—— Mr. Samuel, 125.
Henry II., 20.
Henry, Rev. Henry, 179 *note*.
—— Rev. P. S., D.D., 166.
Higinbotham, Rev. Robert, 127.
Hillsborough, 102, 105, 166.
Hincks, Archdeacon, 160.
Holywood, 40, 61.
Hopkins, Bishop Ezekiel, 86.
Horner, Rev. James, D.D., 146.
Howe, Rev. John, 80.
Hubbard, Rev. Mr., 39.
Huston, Rev. Clark, D.D., 170.
Hutcheson, Rev. John, 120.
—— Dr. Francis, 120, *note*.

INDEMNITY, Act of, 134.
Institution, Belfast Academical, 147, 170.
Instrumental Music Controversy, 186.
Iona, 16.
Iredell, Rev. Francis, 175.
'Irish Church Act,' 183.
Irish, Preaching in, 114.
Island Magee, 37, 60.

JAMES I., 32, 33.
James II., 84.
Johnston, Rev. John, D.D., 166.
—— Rev. William, D.D., 183.

KEADY, 142.
Kelburn, Rev. Sinclair, 142.
Kells, Synod of, 19.
Kelso, Rev. Robert, 99.
Kennedy, Rev. Charles, 146.
—— Rev. Gilbert, 120.
—— Rev. Thomas, 77.
Kerr, Rev. Alexander, 168.

Kilian, 19.
Killaig, 144.
Killala, 176.
Killead, 152.
Killen, Rev. T. Y., D.D., x. *note*, 185.
—— Rev. W. D., D.D., viii., 39, 165, 186.
Killinchy, 40, 76.
Killyleagh, 31, 58, 62, 110, 149.
Kilmore, 167.
Kilraughts, 126.
Kilrea, 60, 120, 142.
Kirk, William, M.P., 185.
Kirkpatrick, Rev. Jas., 114, 116, 120.
Knox, John, 33, 35.

LANGFORD, Sir Arthur, 176.
Larne, 40, 62, 76, 139, 166.
Laud, Archbishop, 35, 55.
Lay Conference, 184.
Leathes, Capt. Robert, 102.
Lecky, Rev. Mr., 76.
Leechman, Professor, 129.
Leland, Rev. John, 175.
Leslie, Bishop, 49, 69, 77.
Letterkenny, 76, 77.
Limavady, 150.
Limerick, 107, 176.
Lisburn, 56, 58, 89, 113, 126, 157.
Lisnaskea, 100.
Livingstone, Rev. John, 40, 41, 46, 47, 61.
—— Rev. William, 125.
Loughgall, 57.
Lundy, Governor, 87.
Lurgan, 112, 154, 165, 171.
Lylehill, 125.
Lynd, Rev. Matthew, 132.
Lytle, Mr. John, 185.

M'ALPINE, Rev. James, 110.
M'Bride, Rev. John, 106, 113, 114.
M'Clure, Sir Thomas, 185.
—— Rev. William, 166, 170.
M'Cracken, Rev. Mr., 113.
M'Dowell, Rev. Benjn., D.D., 147.
M'Ewen, Rev. W. D. H., 146.
M'Gregor, Rev. Mr., 83.
M'Kee, Rev. David, 166.
Mackenzie, Rev. John, 97.
Macnaughtan, Rev. John, 186.
Macosquin, 166.
Magee, Rev. William, 171.
—— Mrs., 171.
—— College, 172.

Maghera, 93, 143, 148.
Magherally, 76.
Magill, Rev. George, 186.
—— Rev. Robert, 151.
Makemie, Rev. Francis, 81, 132.
Makie, Rev. Josias, 82.
Malcom, Rev. John, 120.
Manse Fund, 179.
Markethill, 126, 131.
Marriage Controversy, 108, 135.
Marshall, Rev. James, 146.
Mary, Queen, 25.
Mastertown, Rev. Charles, 120 *note*.
Matthews, Rev. Lemuel, 105.
Mayn, Rev. Thomas, 131.
Melville, Andrew, 34.
Milton, John, 70.
Minterburn, 76.
Missionaries, Early Irish, 18.
Missions of Synod of Ulster, 168, 169, 170.
—— of Secession Synod, 169.
—— of General Assembly, 168, 169, 170.
Mitchelburn, Colonel, 90.
Moira, 126.
Molyneaux, Rev. H. W., D.D., 166.
Monaghan, 56, 109, 110, 131, 167.
Moneymore, 116.
Monro, Major-General, 60.
Montgomery, Rev. Henry, LL.D., 152, 155.
Morell, Rev. Charles L., D.D., 186.
Morgan, Rev. James, D.D., 157, 160, 168.
—— Rev. Thomas, 158.
Mount-Alexander, Earl of, 85.
Mountrath, 176.
Mulholland, Andrew, 189.
Multifarnham Abbey, 59.
Munster Presbytery, 177.
Murphy, Father, of Boolavogue, 140.
Murray, Adam, 89.
—— Rev. Thomas, 58.

NEVIN, Rev. Thomas, 120.
New Light, The, 116.
New Ross, 160.
Newry, 71, 150, 167.
Newtonbutler, 100.
Newtownards, 31, 56, 62, 142.
Nonjuring Controversy, The, 113.
Non-Subscribers, The, 119.

O'CONNOLLY, Owen, 56.
O'Donnell, Earl of Tyrconnel, 28.
O'Neill, Earl of Tyrone, 28.

O'Neill, Lord, 140.
—— Sir Phelim, 56, 59.
Oldstone, 42.
Omagh, 76.
Orphan Society, The, 182.
Orr, Rev. Thomas, 116.
Owen, Rev. John, 174.

' Pacific Act, The,' 117.
Paparo, Cardinal, 19.
Park, Rev. Robert, 154.
Patrick, Saint, 5.
Patton, Rev. Isaac, 125, 131, 152 note.
Peebles, Rev. Thomas, 61.
Penny, Rev. Joseph, 159.
Perth, Articles of, 34, 35.
Petticrew, Rev. Francis, D. Lit., 186.
Plantation of Ulster, The, 28, 29.
Plunket, Rev. Patrick, 114.
—— Lord, 114.
Portadown, 57.
Portaferry, 62, 142.
Portarlington, 176.
Porter, Rev. James, 142.
—— Rev. J. L., D.D., LL.D., 181.
—— Rev. William, 150.
Potitus, 5.
' Presbyterian Loyalty, Kirkpatrick's,' 114.
' Presbyterian Theological Faculty,' 173.
Presbyterianism, What it has done for Ireland, 189.
Presbytery, The First, 61.
' Presbytery, The Plea of,' 166.
' Pride's Purge,' 69.
Pringle, Rev. Francis, 143.

RAHUL, 176.
Ramelton, 76, 77, 81, 165, 185.
Randalstown, 116.
Raphoe, 76.
Rasharkin, 132.
Rathbreasail, Synod of, 19.
Rathfriland, 76, 113, 142.
Ray, 76, 126.
Rebellion of 1641, 56.
—— of 1798, 139.
Reformation in Ireland, 22.
' Regium Donum,' The, 80, 102, 109, 135, 144, 183.
Reid, Rev. Edward, 165.
—— Rev. J. Seaton, D.D., viii., 150, 165.
—— Rev. Thomas M., 131.

' Remonstrance, The,' 153.
Remonstrant Synod, The, 136.
Rentouls, The, 128.
' Representation, The,' 70.
Revival at Sixmilewater, 42.
—— of 1859, 181.
Rickamore, 125.
Ridge, Rev. John, 39, 44, 49.
Robb, Rev. J. G., D.D., 186.
Robinson, Rev. Archibald, 186.
Rogers, Rev. James, 164 note.
—— Rev. John, 164 note.
Rosemary Street Church, Belfast, 120.
Rosen, Marshal, 92.
Roseyards, 126.
Ross, Rev. Robert, 186.
Rostrevor, 158.
Rowat, Rev. John, 97.
Russel, Thomas, 139.

SABBATH SCHOOL SOCIETY, The, 182.
Saintfield, 76, 139, 143.
St. Johnston, 82.
' Sample of Jet - black Prelatic Calumny,' 114.
Schomberg, Duke, 102.
Scotia, 2.
Scott, Rev. John, 61.
Scullabogue, 141.
Seceders, The, 123, 130, 135.
Semple, Rev. William, 77.
Simpson, Rev. James, 61, 142.
Simson, Professor, 129.
Sinclair, Mr. John, 180.
—— Mr. Thomas, 167, 180.
—— Mr. Thomas, jun., 185, 186.
—— Mr. William P., 180.
Sixmilewater Awakening, The, 42.
Sligo, 176.
Smethurst, Rev. John, 149.
Smith, Mr. Samuel, 120.
Smyth, Rev. John, 142.
—— Rev. Richard, D.D., M.P., 184 note.
Solemn League and Covenant, The, 66.
Spenser, Edmund, 26.
Stevenson, Rev. W. F., D.D., 168 note.
Stewart of Drumachose, 131.
—— Rev. Andrew, 40, 48.
—— Rev. Robert, D.D., 151, 152.
—— Mr. Henry, 53.
Stone, Primate, 132.
Stonebridge, 109.

Strabane, 76, 146, 150, 168.
'Subscribers, The,' 119.
Summerhill, 113, 176.
Sustentation Fund, The, 185.
Swanston, John, 127.
Swift, Dean, 112, 121.

TAUGHBOYNE, 77.
Taylor, Bishop Jeremy, 75.
—— Rev. William, 116.
Temperance Reformation, The, 159.
Templepatrick, 40, 62, 114, 125, 142.
Tennent, Rev. William, 82.
Test Act, The, 110, 134.
Theological Committee, The, 153.
Thomson, Professor James, 128 *note*.
—— Sir William, 128 *note*.
—— Rev. John, 146, 147 *note*.
Tithes enjoyed by the Presbyterians, The, 38, 74.
Todd, Mr. William, 172 *note*.
Toleration Act, The, 115.
Tomkins, Alderman, 85.
Tone, Theobald Wolfe, 139.
Trail, Rev. William, 82.
Travers, Rev. Walter, 27, 174.
Trinity College, Dublin, 27.
Tullylish, 120, 166.
Tyrconnel, 84.

UNION OF THE SYNODS, The, 163.
Upton, Colonel, 120.

Ussher, Archbishop, 4, 27, 37, 46, 64.

VINEGAR HILL, 141.
Volunteers, The, 136.
Vow, 132.

WALKER, Rev. George, 90, 103.
Wallace, Rev. Professor, 186.
Waterford, 176.
Watts, Rev. Robert, D.D., 186.
Waugh, Rev. Dr., 147.
Weir, Rev. John, D.D., 167.
Welsh, Rev. Josias, 40, 46, 48.
Wentworth, 47, 55.
Westminster Confession of Faith, The, 38, 65.
Westport, 184.
Whigham, Rev. J. W., 191 *note*.
White, Rev. Adam, 77.
—— Rev. Fulk, 110.
—— Rev. Patrick, 153.
Whitehouse, 102, 108.
William III., 100.
Wilson, of Perth, 124.
—— Rev. H. B., D.D., 186.
—— Rev. Josias, 166.
—— Rev. Robert, D.D., 128, 165.
—— Mr. Charles, 172 *note*.
Wolves in Ireland, 31 *note*.

YOUNG, Right Hon. John, 185.
—— Mr. William, 185.

PUBLICATIONS OF
T. AND T. CLARK,
38 GEORGE STREET, EDINBURGH.

GRIMM'S LEXICON.

Just published, in demy 4to, price 36s.,

A GREEK-ENGLISH LEXICON OF THE NEW TESTAMENT,
BEING

GRIMM'S 'WILKE'S CLAVIS NOVI TESTAMENTI.'

Translated, Revised, and Enlarged

BY

JOSEPH HENRY THAYER, D.D.,

BUSSEY PROFESSOR OF NEW TESTAMENT CRITICISM AND INTERPRETATION IN THE DIVINITY SCHOOL OF HARVARD UNIVERSITY.

EXTRACT FROM PREFACE.

'TOWARDS the close of the year 1862, the "Arnoldische Buchhandlung" in Leipzig published the First Part of a Greek-Latin Lexicon of the New Testament, prepared upon the basis of the "Clavis Novi Testamenti Philologica" of C. G. Wilke (second edition, 2 vols. 1851), by Professor C. L. WILIBALD GRIMM of Jena. In his Prospectus Professor Grimm announced it as his purpose not only (in accordance with the improvements in classical lexicography embodied in the Paris edition of Stephen's Thesaurus and in the fifth edition of Passow's Dictionary edited by Rost and his coadjutors) to exhibit the historical growth of a word's significations and accordingly in selecting his vouchers for New Testament usage to show at what time and in what class of writers a given word became current, but also duly to notice the usage of the Septuagint and of the Old Testament Apocrypha, and especially to produce a Lexicon which should correspond to the present condition of textual criticism, of exegesis, and of biblical theology. He devoted more than seven years to his task. The successive Parts of his work received, as they appeared, the outspoken commendation of scholars diverging as widely in their views as Hupfeld and Hengstenberg; and since its completion in 1868 it has been generally acknowledged to be by far the best Lexicon of the New Testament extant.'

'I regard it as a work of the greatest importance. . . . It seems to me a work showing the most patient diligence, and the most carefully arranged collection of useful and helpful references.'—THE BISHOP OF GLOUCESTER AND BRISTOL.

'The use of Professor Grimm's book for years has convinced me that it is not only unquestionably the best among existing New Testament Lexicons, but that, apart from all comparisons, it is a work of the highest intrinsic merit, and one which is admirably adapted to initiate a learner into an acquaintance with the language of the New Testament. It ought to be regarded as one of the first and most necessary requisites for the study of the New Testament, and consequently for the study of theology in general.'—Professor EMIL SCHÜRER.

d

T. and T. Clark's Publications.

Just published, in demy 8vo, price 10s. 6d.,

THE JEWISH
AND
THE CHRISTIAN MESSIAH.

A STUDY IN THE EARLIEST HISTORY OF CHRISTIANITY.

By VINCENT HENRY STANTON, M.A.,

FELLOW, TUTOR, AND DIVINITY LECTURER OF TRINITY COLLEGE, CAMBRIDGE; LATE HULSEAN LECTURER.

'Mr. Stanton's book answers a real want, and will be indispensable to students of the origin of Christianity. We hope that Mr. Stanton will be able to continue his labours in that most obscure and most important period, of his competency to deal with which he has given such good proof in this book.'—*Guardian.*

'We welcome this book as a valuable addition to the literature of a most important subject. . . . The book is remarkable for the clearness of its style. Mr. Stanton is never obscure from beginning to end, and we think that no reader of average attainments will be able to put the book down without having learnt much from his lucid and scholarly exposition.'—*Ecclesiastical Gazette.*

Now ready, Second Division, in Three Vols., 8vo, price 10s. 6d. each,

HISTORY OF THE JEWISH PEOPLE IN THE TIME OF OUR LORD.

By Dr. EMIL SCHÜRER,

PROFESSOR OF THEOLOGY IN THE UNIVERSITY OF GIESSEN.

TRANSLATED FROM THE SECOND EDITION (REVISED THROUGHOUT, AND GREATLY ENLARGED) OF '*HISTORY OF THE NEW TESTAMENT TIME.*'

'The First Division, which will probably be in a single volume, is undergoing revision by the Author. (The Second Division is complete in itself.)

'Under Professor Schürer's guidance we are enabled to a large extent to construct a social and political framework for the Gospel History, and to set it in such a light as to see new evidences of the truthfulness of that history and of its contemporaneousness. . . . The length of our notice shows our estimate of the value of his work.'—*English Churchman.*

'Messrs. Clark have afresh earned the thanks of all students of the New Testament in England, by undertaking to present Schürer's masterly work in a form easily accessible to the English reader. . . . In every case the amount of research displayed is very great, truly German in its proportions, while the style of Professor Schürer is by no means cumbrous, after the manner of some of his countrymen. We have inadequately described a most valuable work, but we hope we have said enough to induce our readers who do not know this book to seek it out forthwith.'—*Methodist Recorder.*

T. and T. Clark's Publications.

LOTZE'S MICROCOSMUS.

Just published, Second Edition, in Two Vols., 8vo, price 36s.,

MICROCOSMUS:
CONCERNING MAN AND HIS RELATION TO THE WORLD.
By HERMANN LOTZE.

CONTENTS:—Book I. The Body. II. The Soul. III. Life. IV. Man. V. Mind. VI. The Microcosmic Order; or, The Course of Human Life. VII. History. VIII. Progress. IX. The Unity of Things.

'These are indeed two masterly volumes, vigorous in intellectual power, and translated with rare ability. . . . This work will doubtless find a place on the shelves of all the foremost thinkers and students of modern times.'—*Evangelical Magazine.*

'The English public have now before them the greatest philosophic work produced in Germany by the generation just past. The translation comes at an opportune time, for the circumstances of English thought, just at the present moment, are peculiarly those with which Lotze attempted to deal when he wrote his "Microcosmus," a quarter of a century ago. . . . Few philosophic books of the century are so attractive both in style and matter.'—*Athenæum.*

'Lotze is the ablest, the most brilliant, and most renowned of the German philosophers of to-day. . . . He has rendered invaluable and splendid service to Christian thinkers, and has given them a work which cannot fail to equip them for the sturdiest intellectual conflicts and to ensure their victory.'—*Baptist Magazine.*

In Two Vols., 8vo, price 21s.,

NATURE AND THE BIBLE:
LECTURES ON THE MOSAIC HISTORY OF CREATION IN ITS RELATION TO NATURAL SCIENCE.
By DR. FR. H. REUSCH.

REVISED AND CORRECTED BY THE AUTHOR.

Translated from the Fourth Edition

By KATHLEEN LYTTELTON.

'Other champions much more competent and learned than myself might have been placed in the field; I will only name one of the most recent, Dr. Reusch, author of "Nature and the Bible."'—The Right Hon. W. E. GLADSTONE.

'The work, we need hardly say, is of profound and perennial interest, and it can scarcely be too highly commended as, in many respects, a very successful attempt to settle one of the most perplexing questions of the day. It is impossible to read it without obtaining larger views of theology, and more accurate opinions respecting its relations to science, and no one will rise from its perusal without feeling a deep sense of gratitude to its author.'—*Scottish Review.*

T. and T. Clark's Publications.

CREMER'S LEXICON.

In demy 4to, Third Edition, **with Supplement**, price 38s.,

BIBLICO-THEOLOGICAL LEXICON
OF
NEW TESTAMENT GREEK.

BY

HERMANN CREMER, D.D.

Translated and Arranged from the latest German Edition

BY

WILLIAM URWICK, M.A.

The Supplement, which is included in the above, may be had separately, price 14s.

'It is not too much to say that the Supplement will greatly enhance the value of the original work; while of this we imagine it needless to add many words of commendation. It holds a deservedly high position in the estimation of all students of the Sacred tongues.'—*Literary Churchman.*

'We particularly call attention to this valuable work.'—*Clergyman's Magazine.*

'Dr. Cremer's work is highly and deservedly esteemed in Germany. It gives with care and thoroughness a complete history, as far as it goes, of each word and phrase that it deals with. ... Dr. Cremer's explanations are most lucidly set out.'—*Guardian.*

In Two Vols., crown 8vo, price 16s.,

THE APOSTOLIC
AND
POST-APOSTOLIC TIMES.

THEIR DIVERSITY AND UNITY IN LIFE AND DOCTRINE.

BY

GOTTHARD VICTOR LECHLER, D.D.

Translated from the Third Edition, thoroughly Revised and Re-Written,

BY

A. J. K. DAVIDSON.

'Scholars of all kinds will welcome this new edition of Dr. Lechler's famous work. It has for long been a standard authority upon the subject which it treats. ... The book has not only been "revised," but actually "re-written" from end to end.'—*Literary World.*

'In the work before us, Lechler works out this conception with great skill, and with ample historical and critical knowledge. He has had the advantage of all the discussions of these forty years, and he has made good use of them. The book is up to date; so thoroughly is this the case, that he has been able to make room for the results which have been won for the early history of Christianity by the discovery of the "Didachè," and of the discussions to which it has given occasion. Nor is it too much to say that Dr. Lechler has neglected nothing fitted to throw light on his great theme. The work is of the highest value.'—*Spectator.*

T. and T. Clark's Publications.

In demy 8vo, price 12s.,

AN INTRODUCTION TO THEOLOGY:
ITS PRINCIPLES, ITS BRANCHES, ITS RESULTS, AND ITS LITERATURE.

By ALFRED CAVE, B.A.,
PRINCIPAL, AND PROFESSOR OF THEOLOGY, OF HACKNEY COLLEGE, LONDON.

'We can most heartily recommend this work to students of every degree of attainment, and not only to those who will have the opportunity of utilizing its aid in the most sacred of the professions, but to all who desire to encourage and systematize their knowledge and clarify their views of Divine things.'—*Nonconformist and English Independent.*

In crown 8vo, price 4s. 6d.,

THE BIBLE
AN OUTGROWTH OF THEOCRATIC LIFE.

By D. W. SIMON,
PRINCIPAL OF THE CONGREGATIONAL COLLEGE, EDINBURGH.

'A suggestive and helpful essay towards the right understanding of Holy Scripture considered as a revelation. The book will repay perusal. It contains a great deal of learning as well as ingenuity, and the style is clear.'—*Guardian.*

In crown 8vo, price 3s. 6d.,

THE RELIGIOUS HISTORY OF ISRAEL.
A DISCUSSION OF THE CHIEF PROBLEMS IN OLD TESTAMENT HISTORY, AS OPPOSED TO THE DEVELOPMENT THEORISTS.

By Dr. FRIEDRICH EDUARD KÖNIG,
THE UNIVERSITY, LEIPZIG.

TRANSLATED BY REV. ALEXANDER J. CAMPBELL, M.A.

'An admirable little volume. . . . By sincere and earnest-minded students it will be cordially welcomed.'—*Freeman.*
'Every page of the book deserves study.'—*Church Bells.*

In crown 8vo, price 6s.,

NEW TESTAMENT TEACHING IN PASTORAL THEOLOGY.

By J. T. BECK, D.D.,
PROF. ORD. THEOL., TÜBINGEN.

EDITED BY PROFESSOR B. RIGGENBACH.

TRANSLATED BY REV. JAS. M'CLYMONT, B.D., AND REV. THOS. NICOL, B.D.

'The volume contains much which any thoughtful and earnest Christian minister will find helpful and suggestive to him for the wise and efficient discharge of his sacred functions.'—*Literary World.*

T. and T. Clark's Publications.

In demy 8vo, price 7s. 6d.,

LECTURES ON ST. PAUL'S EPISTLE TO THE PHILIPPIANS.

By JOHN HUTCHISON, D.D.

'This book has one great merit which separates it from the mass of commentaries and expository lectures—it is not only instructive, but it is also delightfully interesting. . . . The author's moral and spiritual tone is lofty, and these sermons are characterized by a sweet and sunny grace, which cannot but charm and make better those who read them.'—*Literary World.*

BY THE SAME AUTHOR.

In demy 8vo, price 9s.,

LECTURES ON PAUL'S EPISTLES TO THE THESSALONIANS.

'Certainly one of the ablest and best commentaries that we have ever read. The style is crisp and clear; and the scholarship is in no sense of a superficial or pretentious order.'—*Evangelical Magazine.*

In demy 8vo, price 9s.,

OUTLINES OF THE HISTORY OF CHRISTIAN DOCTRINE.

By Rev. T. G. CRIPPEN.

'The essence of a whole library is included in Mr. Crippen's "History of Christian Doctrine." . . . It is a scholarly work, and must have entailed an incalculable amount of research and discrimination.'—*Clergyman's Magazine.*

Just published, in crown 8vo, price 2s. 6d.,

THE WORK OF THE HOLY SPIRIT IN MAN.

Discourses,

By Pastor G. TOPHEL,

GENEVA.

'An admirable book on a subject of the deepest importance. We do not remember any work on this theme that is more impressive, or seems more fitted for general usefulness.'—*British Messenger.*

In crown 8vo, price 4s. 6d.,

THE CHRIST.

By ERNEST NAVILLE.

'They are masterly productions.'—*Methodist Recorder.*

'We look upon these lectures as a valuable contribution to Christology; and to young ministers and others interested in the grand and exhaustive subject, they will be found to be highly stimulating and helpful.'—*Literary World.*

BY THE SAME AUTHOR.

In crown 8vo, price 4s. 6d.,

THE PROBLEM OF EVIL.

TRANSLATED FROM THE FRENCH.

'The subject is dealt with by M. Naville in a truly philosophic manner, and at the same time with a brilliancy of illustration that seizes and enchains the attention, and with a simplicity of style that places the subject within the reach of all.'—*London Quarterly Review.*

BY THE SAME AUTHOR.

In crown 8vo, price 5s.,

MODERN PHYSICS.

HISTORICAL AND PHILOSOPHICAL STUDIES.

In crown 8vo, price 5s.,

MESSIANIC PROPHECY:

ITS ORIGIN, HISTORICAL CHARACTER, AND RELATION TO NEW TESTAMENT FULFILMENT.

FROM THE GERMAN OF DR. EDWARD RIEHM.

'Original and suggestive, and deserving careful consideration.'—*Literary Churchman.*

'Its intrinsic excellence makes it a valuable contribution to our Biblical literature.'—*British and Foreign Evangelical Review.*

In demy 8vo, price 10s. 6d.,

THE BIBLE DOCTRINE OF MAN.

(SEVENTH SERIES OF CUNNINGHAM LECTURES.)

By JOHN LAIDLAW, D.D.,

PROFESSOR OF SYSTEMATIC THEOLOGY, NEW COLLEGE, EDINBURGH.

'An important and valuable contribution to the discussion of the anthropology of the sacred writings; perhaps the most considerable that has appeared in our own language.'—*Literary Churchman.*

T. and T. Clark's Publications.

In crown 8vo, price 6s.,

OLD AND NEW THEOLOGY:
A CONSTRUCTIVE CRITIQUE.

By Rev. J. B. HEARD, M.A.

'We can promise all real students of Holy Scripture who have found their way out of some of the worst of the scholastic byelanes and ruts, and are striving to reach the broad and firm high road that leads to the Eternal City, a real treat from the perusal of these pages. Progressive theologians, who desire to find "the old in the new, and the new in the old," will be deeply grateful to Mr. Heard for this courageous and able work.'—*Christian World.*

'Among the many excellent theological works, whether English or German, published by Messrs. Clark, there are few that deserve more careful study than this book. . . . It cannot fail to charm by its grace of style, and to supply food for solid thought.'—*Dublin Express.*

BY THE SAME AUTHOR.

Fifth Edition, in crown 8vo, price 6s.,

THE TRIPARTITE NATURE OF MAN:
SPIRIT, SOUL, AND BODY.

Applied to Illustrate and Explain the Doctrines of Original Sin, the New Birth, the Disembodied State, and the Spiritual Body.

'The author has got a striking and consistent theory. Whether agreeing or disagreeing with that theory, it is a book which any student of the Bible may read with pleasure.'—*Guardian.*

'An elaborate, ingenious, and very able book.'—*London Quarterly Review.*

In demy 8vo, price 9s.,

THE DOCTRINE OF THE HOLY SPIRIT.

(The Ninth Series of the Cunningham Lectures.)

By GEORGE SMEATON, D.D.,
Professor of Exegetical Theology, New College, Edinburgh.

'The theological student will be benefited by a careful perusal of this survey, and that not for the moment, but through all his future life.'—*Watchman.*

'Very cordially do we commend these able and timely lectures to the notice of our readers. Every theological student should master them.'—*Baptist Magazine.*

'It is a pleasure to meet with a work like this. . . . Our brief account, we trust, will induce the desire to study this work.'—*Dickinson's Theological Quarterly.*

T. and T. Clark's Publications.

HISTORY OF THE CHRISTIAN CHURCH.
By PHILIP SCHAFF, D.D., LL.D.

A New Edition thoroughly Revised and Enlarged.

Now Ready,

APOSTOLIC CHRISTIANITY, A.D. 1-100. In Two Vols. ex. demy 8vo, price 21s.

ANTE-NICENE CHRISTIANITY, A.D. 100-311. In Two Vols. ex. demy 8vo, price 21s.

NICENE AND POST-NICENE CHRISTIANITY, A.D. 311-600. In Two Vols. ex. demy 8vo, price 21s.

MEDIÆVAL CHRISTIANITY, A.D. 590-1073. In Two Vols. ex. 8vo, price 21s.

'For a genuine healthy Christian criticism, which boldly faces difficulties, and examines them with equal candour and learning, we commend this work to all who are interested in investigating the early growth of the Christian Church.'—*Church Quarterly Review.*

'These volumes cannot fail to prove welcome to all students.'—*Freeman.*

'No student, and indeed no critic, can with fairness overlook a work like the present, written with such evident candour, and, at the same time, with so thorough a knowledge of the sources of early Christian history.'—*Scotsman.*

In Three Volumes, demy 8vo, price 12s. each,

A HISTORY OF THE COUNCILS OF THE CHURCH.
FROM THE ORIGINAL DOCUMENTS.

TRANSLATED FROM THE GERMAN OF
C. J. HEFELE, D.D., BISHOP OF ROTTENBURG.

VOL. I. (*Second Edition*) TO A.D. 325.
By Rev. PREBENDARY CLARK.

VOL. II. A.D. 326 TO 429.
By H. N. OXENHAM, M.A.

VOL. III. A.D. 429 TO THE CLOSE OF THE COUNCIL OF CHALCEDON.

'This careful translation of Hefele's Councils.'—Dr. PUSEY.

'A thorough and fair compendium, put in a most accessible and intelligent form.'—*Guardian.*

'A work of profound erudition, and written in a most candid spirit. The book will be a standard work on the subject.'—*Spectator.*

'The most learned historian of the Councils.'—*Père Gratry.*

'We cordially commend Hefele's Councils to the English student.'—*John Bull.*

T. and T. Clark's Publications.

In Twenty-four handsome 8vo Volumes, Subscription price £6, 6s.,

ANTE-NICENE CHRISTIAN LIBRARY.

A COLLECTION OF ALL THE WORKS OF THE FATHERS OF THE CHRISTIAN CHURCH PRIOR TO THE COUNCIL OF NICÆA.

EDITED BY THE
REV. ALEXANDER ROBERTS, D.D., AND JAMES DONALDSON, LL.D.

CONTENTS:—Apostolic Fathers, one vol.; Justin Martyr, Athenagoras, one vol.; Tatian, Theophilus, The Clementine Recognitions, one vol.; Clement of Alexandria, two vols.; Irenæus and Hippolytus, three vols.; Tertullian against Marcion; Cyprian, two vols.; Origen, two vols.; Tertullian, three vols.; Methodius, etc., one vol.; Apocryphal Gospels, Acts, and Revelations, one vol.; Clementine Homilies, Apostolical Constitutions, one vol.; Arnobius, one vol.; Dionysius, Gregory Thaumaturgus, Syrian Fragments, one vol.; Lactantius, two vols.; Early Liturgies and Remaining Fragments, one vol.

Any Volume may be had separately, price 10s. 6d.,—with the exception of ORIGEN. Vol. II., 12s.; *and the* EARLY LITURGIES, 9s.

In Fifteen Volumes, demy 8vo, Subscription price £3, 19s.,

THE WORKS OF ST. AUGUSTINE.

EDITED BY MARCUS DODS, D.D.

CONTENTS:—The 'City of God,' two vols.; Writings in connection with the Donatist Controversy, one vol.; The Anti-Pelagian Writings, three vols.; 'Letters,' two vols.; Treatises against Faustus the Manichæan, one vol.; The Harmony of the Evangelists, and the Sermon on the Mount, one vol.; On the Trinity, one vol.; Commentary on John, two vols.; On Christian Doctrine, Enchiridion, On Catechizing, and On Faith and the Creed, one vol.; 'Confessions,' with Copious Notes by Rev. J. G. PILKINGTON.

Any Work may be had separately, price 10s. 6d. per Volume.

SELECTION FROM ANTE-NICENE LIBRARY AND ST. AUGUSTINE'S WORKS.

THE Ante-Nicene Library being now completed in 24 Volumes, and the St. Augustine Series being also complete in 15 Volumes, Messrs. CLARK offer a Selection of 12 Volumes from both of those series at the *Subscription price* of THREE GUINEAS (or a larger number at same proportion).

T. and T. Clark's Publications.

CHEAP RE-ISSUE OF
STIER'S WORDS OF THE LORD JESUS.

To meet a very general desire that this now well-known Work should be brought more within the reach of all classes, both Clergy and Laity, Messrs. CLARK are now issuing, for a limited period, the *Eight* Volumes, handsomely bound in *Four*, at the *Subscription Price* of

TWO GUINEAS.

'The whole work is a treasury of thoughtful exposition. Its measure of practical and spiritual application, with exegetical criticism, commends it to the use of those whose duty it is to preach as well as to understand the Gospel of Christ.'—*Guardian.*

BY THE SAME AUTHOR.
THE WORDS OF THE RISEN SAVIOUR, AND COMMENTARY ON THE EPISTLE OF ST. JAMES.
8vo, 10s. 6d.

THE WORDS OF THE APOSTLES EXPOUNDED.
8vo, 10s. 6d.

New and Cheap Edition, in Four Vols., demy 8vo, *Subscription Price* 28s.,

THE LIFE OF THE LORD JESUS CHRIST:

A Complete Critical Examination of the Origin, Contents, and Connection of the Gospels. Translated from the German of J. P. LANGE, D.D., Professor of Divinity in the University of Bonn. Edited, with additional Notes, by MARCUS DODS, D.D.

'We have great pleasure in recommending this work to our readers. We are convinced of its value and enormous range.'—*Irish Ecclesiastical Gazette.*

BENGEL'S GNOMON—CHEAP EDITION.
GNOMON OF THE NEW TESTAMENT.

By JOHN ALBERT BENGEL. Now first translated into English. With Original Notes, Explanatory and Illustrative. Edited by the Rev. ANDREW R. FAUSSET, M.A. *Five* Volume Edition bound in *Three* Volumes at the *Subscription Price* of

TWENTY-FOUR SHILLINGS.

The Five Volume Edition may still be had at the Subscription Price of £1, 11s. 6d.

'Bengel stands out still *facile princeps* among all who have laboured, or who as yet labour, in that important field. He is unrivalled in felicitous brevity, combined with what seldom accompanies that excellence, namely, perspicuity. Terse, weighty, and suggestive, he often, as a modern writer observes, "condenses more matter into a line than can be extracted from pages of other writers."'—*Spurgeon's Commenting and Commentaries.*

PROFESSOR GODET'S WORKS.

Just published, in Two Volumes, demy 8vo, price 21s.,

COMMENTARY ON ST. PAUL'S FIRST EPISTLE TO THE CORINTHIANS.

By F. GODET, D.D.,
PROFESSOR OF THEOLOGY, NEUCHATEL.

'A perfect masterpiece of theological toil and thought. . . . Scholarly, evangelical, exhaustive, and able.'—*Evangelical Review.*

'To say a word in praise of any of Professor Godet's productions is almost like "gilding refined gold." All who are familiar with his commentaries know how full they are of rich suggestion. . . . This volume fully sustains the high reputation Godet has made for himself as a Biblical scholar, and devout expositor of the will of God. Every page is radiant with light, and gives forth heat as well.'—*Methodist New Connexion Magazine.*

In Three Volumes, 8vo, price 31s. 6d.,

A COMMENTARY ON THE GOSPEL OF ST. JOHN.

'This work forms one of the battle-fields of modern inquiry, and is itself so rich in spiritual truth, that it is impossible to examine it too closely; and we welcome this treatise from the pen of Dr. Godet. We have no more competent exegete; and this new volume shows all the learning and vivacity for which the author is distinguished.'—*Freeman.*

In Two Volumes, 8vo, price 21s.,

A COMMENTARY ON THE GOSPEL OF ST. LUKE.

'Marked by clearness and good sense, it will be found to possess value and interest as one of the most recent and copious works specially designed to illustrate this Gospel.'—*Guardian.*

In Two Volumes, 8vo, price 21s.,

A COMMENTARY ON ST. PAUL'S EPISTLE TO THE ROMANS.

'We prefer this commentary to any other we have seen on the subject. . . . We have great pleasure in recommending it as not only rendering invaluable aid in the critical study of the text, but affording practical and deeply suggestive assistance in the exposition of the doctrine.'—*British and Foreign Evangelical Review.*

In crown 8vo, Second Edition, price 6s.,

DEFENCE OF THE CHRISTIAN FAITH.

TRANSLATED BY THE HON. AND REV. CANON LYTTELTON, M.A., RECTOR OF HAGLEY.

'There is trenchant argument and resistless logic in these lectures; but withal, there is cultured imagination and felicitous eloquence, which carry home the appeals to the heart as well as the head.'—*Sword and Trowel.*

www.ingramcontent.com/pod-product-compliance
Lightning Source LLC
Chambersburg PA
CBHW021829230426
43669CB00008B/909